The Way to Perfect Horsemanship

UDO BÜRGER

THE WAY
TO PERFECT
HORSEMANSHIP

Translated by Nicole Bartle

TRAFALGAR SQUARE
North Pomfret, Vermont

This paperback edition published in the United States of America in 2012
Trafalgar Square Books
North Pomfret, Vermont 05053
www.horseandriderbooks.com

Trafalgar Square Classic Series edition 1998

ISBN: 978-1-57076-551-3

Library of Congress Control Number: 98-85575

First published in Germany as *Vollendete Reitkunst* by Paul Parey, Berlin and Hamburg, in 1959. Reprinted 1966, 1972, 1975. Fifth, revised edition published in Germany in 1982.

Printed in the United States of Amerca

Foreword

This is one of the very few books published this century to have become recognised as a classic of equestrian literature and both translator and publisher are to be thanked for the contribution they make to the development and the expansion of educated riding by making the book available in English.

The author gives a true meaning to that much abused phrase, the art of riding by giving the reader a detailed account of the science and the psychology of equitation. He thus introduces us to equestrian creativity, to the point where mere craft ceases and art begins.

Although the book was first published in 1959 it succeeds in recreating for us the equestrian scene of pre-war years when educated riding was the prerogative of the privileged few who devoted their lives to the study of the art and, perhaps with some justification, regarded the rest as dilettante who were to be frowned upon. This attitude may perplex the modern reader who has grown up in our more democratic age, one in which riding has become a mass activity. It is worth reminding ourselves though that in rendering us this account the author not only gives us an historical picture of the times but also gives us some insight into the fact that in those days both dressage and High-School reached such heights as have not been emulated since.

His comments on the deterioration of dressage from the time it began to be treated as a sport as opposed to an art are as valid today as when first written and what he has to say about the appeal of dressage competition to the general public is of the greatest relevance to present day conditions.

The greatness of this book lies in the author's ability to reduce sublime concepts and aspirations to a level of coherence which provokes and stimulates both intellect and imagination. The book is a true *rara avis*—a source of deep inspiration.

Daniel Pevsner, F.B.H.S.

Contents

List of Illustrations

Preface to the Fifth German Edition

Udo Bürger once casually remarked that in order to understand horses, one ought to become a horse and behave like a horse. The pronouncement characterises the man. He was involved with horses from an early age, and even in his latter years became fretful if unable to spend some time every day in the company of a horse. His intense empathy was certainly based to a considerable extent on his remarkable veterinary knowledge. Renowned for the forthrightness of his diagnosis, he could be blunt when incensed by callous disregard of the horse's nature. On the other hand, he would be tolerant and patient when his advice was sought by clients who were sincere in their desire for guidance.

His book remains immensely valuable for all genuine horsemen, and will only disappoint readers who hope to find recipes for quick results. It is a stimulating, thought-provoking work, that arouses the courage to experiment and broaden knowledge and experience. Some may not find it sufficiently modern, since the author strongly disparages the use of gadgets which may produce spectacular success but lead to quick ruination of the horse. His objective was to inspire greater regard for the nature of the animal: how can a horse enjoy its work, if its rider does not understand its personality.

In producing this latter edition, great pains have been taken to ensure the continued appeal of the book by using more up-to-date illustrations. It is slightly abridged but essentially unchanged, and remains a compendium of a life with horses, as relevant to horsemanship today as when it was first published.

Gerhard Kapitzke
1982

Translator's Note

Udo Bürger was one of Germany's most esteemed equine veterinary surgeons, an accomplished and complete horseman, a learned and observant animal psychologist, a highly respected judge of horseflesh and horsemanship. He died in 1980, aged 66.

His book stands out in the vast literature devoted to the subject of horsemanship because for the first time we are given a clear insight into the psychological make-up of the horse, its muscular system and mechanics of movement. Instead of offering the reader a method of training based on tradition, it provides him with an understanding of the basic principles of training and a rational explanation of the effects of the aids. Horse trainers in all disciplines, teachers of equitation, dressage judges and all riders who have genuine sympathy for horses cannot afford to neglect studying this work. Fortunately, unlike so many other learned treatises, this one is as enjoyable to read as it is informative.

Nicole Bartle

Glossary of Terms

The vocabulary of horsemanship contains words or terms that are not defined in ordinary dictionaries and the Germans especially have expressive ways of describing concepts or actions for which there are no exact English equivalents. The following short glossary may help the reader. I have also included short notes about some of the masters mentioned by the author.

ARRET OR ARREST   A simultaneous jolt with hand and spur (at the girth) to cause a horse to flex its haunches.

FLUIDITY   The German term *Durchlässig* literally means porous. The author describes the concept very clearly. Since something that is fluid consists of particles that move freely among themselves, so as to give way before the slightest pressure, I feel that fluidity is the nearest equivalent to *Durchlassigkeit*. The French talk of lightness.

IPSILATERAL   Belonging to or occurring on the same side of the body.

INSTERBURGER   A yank with one rein, up against the corners of the mouth, to punish a horse that locks its jaws. The French call this a *remonte de dents*, that is, a lifting up of the teeth. *Insterburger* is a derogatory word; it is dialect for offal merchant.

PARADE   A co-ordinated action of hands, seat and legs to get a horse to flex its haunches and collect itself. However, contrary to the *arret*, it is not an absolutely simultaneous use of leg and hand. The word belongs to the classical language of dressage. It has no place in utilitarian equitation, where the rule is always legs without hands, hands without legs. A *parade* is too tricky for the average rider and can teach a horse disobedience to hands and legs.

FELIX BURCHNER   A remarkable horseman and teacher who continued to obtain remarkable results after the amputation of one of his legs.

RIDINGER   German painter and engraver whose collection of engravings depicting the schooling of horse and rider was published in 1760.

STENSBECK   (1857–1937) German trainer of circus and dressage horses.

Introduction

Riding is one of the most enjoyable of human activities. For some it is pleasant recreation, for others it has become a fiercely competitive sport and for yet others it is an art worthy of serious study. It is always a shame when it ceases to be pleasurable and, after all, what matters most is our love of the horse. If we know how to treat them fairly, horses reward us with their trust and obedience. And to be fair to them, we must first learn to recognise the limits of our knowledge and competence. If we are prepared to study in depth the art of equitation, we may perhaps eventually transcend the limits of mere competence, but even if this is beyond our ability, sporting spirit should make us want to undertand our horses better. Instead of behaving like autocratic dilettantes, we should take the trouble to learn the rules of the game and teach them to the other creature in terms which he can understand. We must know the *How* and the *Why* for knowledge always precedes ability. We all tend to believe that we know more than we actually do. It is a bad fault and more common in riders than in other mortals.

Horsemanship is a science, with ancient laws based on certain elementary principles. In a scientific spirit, I have researched the anatomical, physiological and psychological factors which explain how the rider influences the balance, movement and behaviour of the horse, though this book is also the result of experience and of daily contact with the animal. I have tried to explain what one should feel and do on horseback and how, eventually, one feels as if one were part of the horse, completely united with him in all his movements.

The philosophy of medicine, the study of the general principles of health and disease, is the foundation of the art of healing. The art of riding must also be based on a philosophy, and this is what this book is about. It is a primary and a supplementary treatise which, I hope, will help the rider to think of riding as something worthy of study rather than just a mechanical skill. For all serious students of the art, the way is full of difficulties, disappointments and setbacks, which only knowledge and thought will help them to overcome. Books cannot teach us to ride, we all need to be guided by a master of the craft, but to progress beyond technical competence and to benefit from experience, we also need the ability to appraise ourselves and become conscious of our sensations and doings.

Horses are too strong to enable us to control them by strength of arms and legs. Nevertheless, to become a good horseman one needs to be bold, agile and relaxed. These qualities are not physical attributes; they are psychological ones. If we do not understand the mind of the horse, we run the risk of alienating its good will or, on the other hand, of letting it discover that our ascendancy is illusory. Riding is not a game either for the timid or for the ruffian.

Udo Bürger
1959

Horsemanship

Should horsemanship be called an art? It could be argued of course that perfect workmanship is art and that anybody who develops a talent into a skill and becomes highly proficient in the practise of his particular skill can be called an artist. In this sense there would be many different forms of art, but not everybody would agree that all skill is art. If, for example, there is an art in administering business or affairs of state, those who practice it might not concede that horsemanship is also an art and most riders would be offended to hear cookery compared in difficulty with the art of horsemanship. Craft is perhaps a better word. It satisfies the need to find a precise term for a general concept while it is sufficiently vague to avoid offending anybody. Thoughtful riders, however, would contend that craft evokes the idea of routine, a more or less mechanical and repetitive performance of certain actions, while art is creative. There is a difference between a good artifact and a work of art and good craftsmen are more usual than artists. Even gymnasts deserve to be called artists when they give us the enchanting spectacle of fantastic feats of strength and agility performed with harmony of movement and apparent ease, but ugly acrobatics which aim only at producing astonishment can certainly not be called artistic.

If horsemanship can be called an art, it is rather a unique one, in the sense that it combines the pictorial element of sculpture (it is the modelling of a living animal) with the musical elements of dancing: rhythm and beat.

Every form of art has its own special tools and particular laws but sculpture and music conform to the same aesthetics: proportion, rhythm, harmony, beauty. Horsemanship is an art only when it conforms to these criteria. When it is routine, that is a more or less automatic repetition of certain movements without aesthetic quality, it is a sport. There must be no confusion. As a work of art, the horse is an idealised image, a stylised representation, though never a distortion of nature, and is therefore a human creation. On the other hand, the sport of horsemanship consists in the skill of according the movements of the human body with the natural movements of the horse, in order to utilise these movements for a special purpose. As an artist, the rider wants to shape, even transform, his living raw material, while the sportsman does not seek to transform: he must develop his ability to feel the natural movement of the horse and to develop for his particular purpose the natural quality of the movement. There is a point where art and craft merge into one another because all artists must be good craftsmen. However a good craftsman will never become an artist if he remains content with routine improvement of skill and never pauses for deeper thought. Many talented craftsmen might have been artists if they had meditated on the subject of art.

The first thing that a rider must learn, if he aims to become an artist, is the art of relaxation. This means detachment, serenity, enjoyment of work for the sake of beauty, unconcern with success or failure, praise or criticism. In this sense—power of total concentration of the mind on the senses—the relaxed rider can become the central pivot of the movement of the horse, an integral part of the horse, and all his reactions will be so immediate that they will elude the eye of the most observant spectator. Total harmony of movement between the two bodies is the essence of the art. But the first thing the rider must learn is complete mastery of technique and it is only after years of application that he will discover that he has developed not only the ability to follow effortlessly every movement, but also to feel every impulse of the horse flow through his whole being. Towards this end he must learn to meditate whenever he is given the opportunity to relax, to loosen excessive mental or physical tension. No valuable work can be produced without thought. The rider who has learnt to observe himself will suddenly discover that he has completed without conscious effort the picture which he had visualised as the ideal and that riding has become his whole being instead of a matter of legs, reins, seat and spurs.

Relaxation, in the sense of total concentration of the mind on the senses, which is the teaching of Zen-Buddhism, is more essential to the art of riding than to any other art.

Furthermore, riding is an art which has to fascinate and entirely satisfy those who sincerely dedicate themselves to it, for, while other works of art can survive to be admired by future generations, the horse so lovingly fashioned by the rider must age and die, so that nothing is left of this creation except memories and tales.

Artistic talent is in the blood. It is something entirely personal to each artist which can never belong to anybody else and cannot be transmitted. It is talent which makes a work unique. However, inborn talent alone is not sufficient to create a work of art and all artists have to continue forever developing their sensibility and perfecting their technique. Nevertheless, it is creative talent which distinguishes a work of art from a well-made artifact and marks it with the indelible signature of the artist.

The art of riding really belongs to a bygone age. Like hunting, riding was once the privilege of persons of noble blood. The modern shooting of game needs little skill and there is no reason for wanting to learn traditional skills which cannot be practised in a world that has no need of them. Similarly, as the horse has had his day as an indispensable means of transport for hunting, for war or long distance travelling, nobody nowadays is obliged to learn to ride. In years gone by, it was as difficult to hide a poor seat on horseback as it is today to conceal inability to swim or to ride a bicycle. Because of this general involvement with riding, a few talented horsemen could perfect their technique and become artists. Nowadays, they are even more rare and few people still exist who can appreciate truly artistic riding. Furthermore, it is an art which can never be learnt in a short time: one can learn to copy, but learning to create is very difficult. All would-be artists have to start at the bottom and work their way to the top. Nobody can begin somewhere along the way and hope to continue to progress along a path which has already been discovered and smoothed by someone else. Nobody can get himself a perfectly made dressage or show-jumping horse in the hope of being recognised as an artist unless he is prepared to work. A rider who does not recognise the necessity of educating himself will destroy within a short time the work of art created by a master. Of course, he can learn much with a well-schooled horse, and he may well be recognised at some time as a master of the art. However, to be ready for this good fortune, he can never afford to relent in his search for knowledge and sensibility.

Amongst the followers of the art of riding, we recognise: true amateurs who practise it for pleasure; serious students, who recognise its difficulty and are determined to work; professionals, for whom it is bread and butter and sometimes an irksome necessity; really creative artists who get the raw material and transform it into a perfectly finished work of art.

There are also good copyists who can reproduce the work created by an artist but cannot form anything—and there are many of these. There are connoisseurs, who can recognise art but cannot practise it.

Finally, there is a vast number of self-satisfied dilettantes, full of conceit and totally devoid of understanding.

Like all other arts, the art of horsemanship must respect certain laws, and any breaking of those laws should hurt like a discord in a musical harmony.

The first three laws state that:

1 The natural movement must never be distorted.

2 The beat must always remain distinct and regular.

3 Proper balance must be established and continuously perfected.

The fourth law states that a saddle-horse must have a conventional outline or posture. This gives the rider the ability to control the horse and to use him for general riding or specialised purposes, but this posture must be the result of obedience to the first three laws.

The fifth law applies to the use of the rider's own forces—his aids. The law states that they should never contradict the natural movement of the horse. Riding is not a contest of strength, and the much superior force of the horse can only be controlled by the relatively small force of the rider if the latter can feel the natural movement, and knows how to utilise it to promote speed or how to slow it down, or direct it. He must be able to feel and control, at every moment, not only the main movement, which is the determinant element of control, but also must recognise the sources of power and agility of the horse, namely the neck which should be arched like a bow in front of his seat, the swing of the back, and the engagement, flexion and extension of the powerful hindlimbs. These three main parts of the horse—neck, trunk and hindlimbs—are capable of independent reflex actions, which can be synchronised provided that their freedom of movement is not impaired. If only one of these parts is prevented from functioning freely, the whole mechanism of movement is disturbed and the horse is said to be disunited. His poise is impaired, so that he stiffens and resists the rider's controlling actions.

The rider must also learn to economise his own force. He exhausts himself uselessly when he squeezes with all the strength of his legs to produce impulsion and at the same time pulls with all the strength of his arms to slow the horse down.

The sixth law states that no horse should ever be trained to specialise until he has completed his basic education. Before he can be taught anything, a horse must learn to trust, understand and obey his trainer; he can never be comfortable to ride until he has acquired an efficient technique of movement at all gaits; his strength must be developed by exercise before he can be made to move on small circles or forced to displace himself sideways. Whether we intend to use him eventually as an ordinary hack, as a hunter or in any kind of competition, he will never progress if his elementary education has been neglected.

It should never be forgotten that the elementary schooling of the horse must consist of the education of his intelligence as well as the training of his body. Specialisation for dressage as a distinct sport, or for the other sports, forms part of the secondary education of the horse, and must never start before his elementary education is complete.

The final law says that the aids must always be adapted to the degree of understanding and physical strength of the horse. They must therefore vary in intensity, and in form, and will have to be used separately or in combination, according to progress. Eventually, the aids should become indications rather than commands. Educating the horse to obey the aids is a gradual and continuous process of awakening his understanding and developing his intelligence. It is therefore important to realise that the aids are not mechanical actions which automatically produce results; they are just human actions which the horse must learn to interpret; they are commands which he must be taught to obey, even at the cost of some inconvenience to himself. These commands should never be harsher than is necessary to make our intentions perfectly clear. It is not affectation that makes us prefer sensitive aids. Tactfulness, or the ability to feel and sympathetically to influence movement, is the quality that creates unity of mind and purpose between rider and horse.

It seems that the only sort of riding which can be called truly artistic is the High-School, practised nowadays in Europe only at two academies; the Spanish School of Vienna and the Cadre Noir of Saumur. Watching a display of the Lipizzaner stallions is like seeing an old print by Ridinger springing to life. The horses show the same high degree of collection, the same elevation in the airs above the ground, and the riders have all the elegance of true representatives of the classical art. The fascinating displays of the Spanish School are probably the only true examples of the ancient art in existence today and some people consider that the airs above the ground are the best example, perhaps the only example, of the classical art of riding.

The reprises of the Cadre Noir of Saumur are not as majestic, but the impression of lightness which they give is enchanting. The horses are not as powerful as the Lipizzaner and their movements are less elevated, but they appear to dance light-heartedly in harmony with a swinging music. The drill is perfect, but the special charm of the display is the gracefulness of the horses. It is when we try to get our own horse to do the same thing that we discover how difficult it is to perform a *Pas d'Ecole* (High-School walk) of 100 steps to the minute. For this, the rider must be effectively united with the horse, for it cannot be done just with hands and legs. It shows that the essence of the art of riding is the complete merging of horse and rider into one body, so light that it seems to have wings attached to its feet.

This complete blending of the rider's movements with the movements of the horse is what we should want to see when we watch a dressage display. The best way to train the eyes and the other senses to recognise this harmony between two living beings, is to observe people dancing. Some dancers haul their partner around the room, count aloud the beat of the music or fail altogether to discover the rhythm, while others move with lightness and ease, each partner appearing to be animated by the same rhythm felt by the other. It takes only a quick glance to recognise a perfect partnership. The impression of harmony is much more important than the intricacy of the steps and figures which can be learnt at a dancing class. Harmony is the quality which we must learn to recognise also when we watch a dressage display and should want to show when we give a display. It is too frequently ignored in the sport of dressage, because it cannot be precisely measured in marks.

One might believe that the laws of the art of classical riding are not relevant to show-jumping. However aesthetic laws are invariable and should apply to all artistic riding. We should want to see the same harmony between horse and rider in show-jumping as in dressage and, in fact, aesthetically pleasing performances are neither more nor less frequent in one arena than in the other. However, artistic merit counts for even less in show-jumping, where success is often due to luck despite crude technique.

The true art of the High-School should never be confused with its parody which is often seen in bad circus riding. Some charlatans would have us believe that the swaying, shuffling, hovering steps of a horse restrained by tight side-reins are airs of the High-School. It is equally sad to see some show-jumping riders become so intoxicated by their fortuitous successes with a bold horse that they think that they can continue to flout with impunity all the basic laws of the art and restrict the horse with all sorts of so-called auxiliary reins.

The art of riding must always remain based on well-established principles. The essential basic requirements listed above are equally applicable to hacking, to competitive sport and to the High-School.

THE SPORT

All strong and healthy men have always derived enjoyment from activity, physical exertion and tests of courage. Sport is an activity which should not only give pleasure, but which should also give the body an outlet for its surplus energy. The essence of sport is physical exertion and the fact that it is also fun is just an additional benefit. Although sport must be fun, it also involves a lot of hard work. What makes it enjoyable is that the exertions are not imposed by economic necessity, by the need to earn one's bread by the sweat of one's brow. What seems strange is that stricter ethics prevail in sport than in the world of business. Sportsmen subscribe to a code of honour, fairness, comradeship, equal chances for all and generosity in victory and in defeat.

Show-jumping has opened up for the sport of riding a larger field than it has ever enjoyed since the Age of Chivalry. The idea of sport is inseparable from the notion of contest and pure love of the art of horsemanship cannot be called a sport. This was already true in the times when knights jousted on heavily armour-plated horses and then as nowadays the outcome of a contest depended more on the agility of the horse than on the skill of the contestants. The grounds for this single combat of man against man no longer exist, but in the sport of horsemanship, in our time as then, the horse matters more than the rider. It is only in racing, however, that the fight to the finish, nose to nose, provides all the excitement of single combat. All other equestrian sports involve the rider in a solitary performance and despite the rider's activity and influence on the result, the horse is still the dominant partner.

Some extraordinary performances in show-jumping and not a few victories are the result of fear and strength. They are the heroic deeds of naturally talented riders, who are entitled to enjoy their laurels and to be applauded by their parents and their friends. The pluck or even recklessness of some riders, frequently children, going at breakneck speed around a course of formidable obstacles has always delighted audiences. These riders make us gasp with astonishment, because it is extraordinary that anybody should be able to force a horse to perform unnatural stunts, but if we think of horsemanship as an art, as total harmony between rider and horse, as something which gives aesthetic pleasure, that kind of show-jumping cannot be called artistic. Fortunately, we are also given sometimes the pleasing sight of a perfectly united pair, flying easily over formidable obstacles. Experience and cool thinking are sometimes rewarded, so perhaps there is also a Muse of show-jumping. Successful and talented young riders in this sphere could also become artists, but in show-jumping the stimulation of competition will usually prevent them from giving much thought to art. The popular appeal of this sport has turned it into a mixture of genuine art and mere circus acrobatics.

The situation in dressage is not as different as one might think. It is difficult to understand why dressage has become a sport. I believed for a long time that dressage had something to do with the art of the High-School and that success was measured by the same criteria. At all levels, dressage tests were supposed to show that the rider had educated his horse to be perfectly obedient to the most discreet aids and to be always light and attentive to the intentions of his rider.

The standards by which dressage tests should be judged ought not to differ from those of the High-School and can be summed up as purity of movement. Constant improvement of the gaits is the whole object of dressage training, but, in the sport of dressage, it is common to find that horses who do not measure up to this standard are preferred by the judges to horses who have correct gaits but have committed a trifling fault in the prescribed movements of the test. An important criterium of a horse's gaits, which makes it easy to judge whether he is using his back correctly and not just moving his legs, is the seat: the rider must be comfortable at all gaits. Far too little importance is attached in modern dressage tests to seat and position, although they reveal so much. Good marks are given to horses whose gaits are basically wrong: they may have executed an accurate test, but their walk can only be called a weary march, their trot obliges the rider to grip in order to prevent himself being tossed, their piaffe is executed on one spot, but with insufficient flexion of haunches and lowering of the croup—the rider himself imitating the movement to unload the horse's stiffened or sagging back—and their passage is a sort of floating action without elevation of the forehand.

However, in the sport of dressage, one test must quickly succeed another and, if the judges took enough time to note everything, spectators would lose patience. Judging has therefore been simplified. Furthermore, if the same criteria were applied to the sport as to the art, new participants would be discouraged by the difficulties and the time it takes to educate a horse up to such exacting standards. It may therefore be necessary to take into first account the accurate performance of the prescribed movements of the test, even if the rider has to hold his horse firmly, at all times, between hands and legs in order to ensure instant obedience. In the sport, accuracy matters more than grace and elegance, while if dressage tests were judged by the same artistic standards as the High-School, the first consideration would be the purity of the gaits. Points would be deducted for any failing in this respect, and gross irregularity would result in elimination, even if the movements had been executed accurately.

As dressage has become a sport, dressage competitions are trials of strength and skill, and a world champion must eventually be found. Only craftsmanship has to be judged. It cannot be denied that it takes a lot of skill and experience to get the feel of a horse and of his response to the aids in a short time, especially when he has been schooled, as is so often the case, by a person other than the rider. Considerable presence of mind and complete mastery of the infinitely various effects of legs, seat and reins are needed to realise the limits of what can be achieved and the difficulties to avoid in order to show something acceptable. The rider is obliged to compromise, which amounts to sacrificing some of the principles to the necessity of accomplishing a set task without provoking resistances. The artist must bow to the rules of the sport. It is the necessity of compromise that explains why dressage championships are so disappointing from an artistic point of view. The winner has to be selected on the merits of technical competence and competitive experience and, if he fails, on a particular horse, to present a picture of perfect harmony, it does not necessarily signify that he will never become a real artist. We must face the fact that although some of the performances in the sport are aesthetically disappointing, it is from the ranks of sportsmen that artists will emerge. If it were not for the sake of sport, few riders would practise dressage and the art would perish. Sport is the launching platform of art, although for many, dressage will remain just a sport, like rowing or athletics, which they will give up once their body has ceased to clamour for exertion and their spirit for competition; art, after all, is of no practical use. Fortunately, other riders may discover within themselves an artistic vocation which they will be able to satisfy after they have lost interest in competing. Even in the days when the art of dressage was better understood, there were never many young riders with enough artistic talent as well as sporting spirit to enable them to practise both art and sport. This is another reason why so few genuine artists can be seen in dressage arenas.

Art is pleasurable activity which only involves appreciation of beauty and happiness in selflessly pursuing an ideal. Sport is a test of strength and courage in which ambition and the desire for applause play a major part. Nevertheless, the sport of dressage could more closely resemble the art if more importance were attached by judges to rhythm, form and style than to exact execution of prescribed movements. However, sport has become nowadays something so serious that rules must be devised for every kind of physical activity; even the graceful and gentle game of badminton has become a sport that is precisely regulated. Consequently, if dressage is a sport, fighting spirit, records, championships, rosettes and prize money must be considered as in all sports. Even amateurs are concerned about the financial return of competitions; this is understandable, for the price of horses that perform well in major competitions has risen to astronomical heights, and rightly so since they are products of craftsmanship and craftsmanship ought to be properly rewarded. Nevertheless, the fun of competing does not entitle all and sundry, regardless of experience and skill, to perform in public. Spectators pay to witness a display of grace; they should not be cheated. In all other sports, matches between players for the selection of members of a team are private affairs, and only the best performers are seen in public. Why should such sensible restrictions not apply in the sport of dressage riding? If it is a convincing argument that the sport of dressage will never arouse sufficient interest unless it is opened to the widest number of participants, the point can also be made that it will appeal to the uninitiated only if it offers them a pleasing spectacle. In show-jumping, any kind of coercion which might offend spectators, either in or outside the ring, incurs elimination. In dressage, similarly, spectators should not see the toils and pains that go with the preparation of a successful performance. We owe this to the public.

Complete harmony between horse and rider can be said to exist when the trot is so comfortable that rising is for the rider an unnecessary expenditure of energy; when the reins can be safely surrendered completely at the gallop; when the horse can be ridden confidently either between hands and legs or without reins, with the sole aids of seat and legs. Complete harmony is the whole essence of the art of dressage and it is unfortunate that it cannot be better rewarded in dressage competitions. In dressage, as in show-jumping, the winner is not necessarily the best rider. Judges must never cease to defend the general principles of the art and are bound to enforce respect of these principles when they are obviously infringed, but they also have to accept that dressage has become a sport. They can, however, rejoice at the fact that it can be a nursery for artists. There are no Raphaels or Rembrandts alive, yet the art of painting continues to survive. We should keep our eyes open, to discover riders with real talent who may be using the sport to show their artistic quality; they can be seen only in competitions and if they devoted themselves in solitude to the art, they would never be recognised, followed and imitated

Three-day eventing is king of the competitive riding sports, a tremendous test of stamina and courage for both horse and rider. It does not appeal to specialists or acrobats because it is not possible to get to the top quickly in this sport by virtue of possessing a horse naturally endowed with tremendous jumping ability or spectacular movement. The gaps in the basic education of the horse would be revealed in one of the three parts of the competition. This form of competition was first called "The Military": a most innappropriate name. It would have been very unsoldierly to gallop at great speed over a course of big obstacles or to jump into water. Only fire and smoke, or an enemy on one's heels would justify this behaviour. A soldier would never have been allowed to endanger the life and soundness of his horse by galloping for pleasure over difficult country. In three-day eventing, the roads and tracks, steeplechase and cross-country are a tough test of stamina, while the dressage and show-jumping phases reveal the temperament of the horse. Although an insufficiently schooled horse can win the speed and endurance test, his shortcomings will show up in the dressage and show-jumping. These events can be an excellent opportunity for selecting suitable stock for breeding good saddle-horses and a mare who has performed honourably in a three-day event without coming to harm ought to be retired for breeding. Three-day eventing is for the stout-hearted. Only very fit, very well-schooled horses, only tough, intrepid riders can hope to be in the running at the end. All the same, the decisive factor in eventing, as in racing, is speed and there are quite a number of not particularly good horses or remarkable riders who can complete the cross-country and steeplechase without incurring time penalties.

Keeping a horse is an expensive luxury and it is only sport that will continue to support the breeding of good horses and encourage people to learn to ride; the art of dressage would not have ensured the survival of the horse. All horse lovers should therefore be grateful to sportsmen who take up riding and prefer to satisfy their competitive spirit on horseback rather than behind the wheel of a motorised machine. In contrast with all other sports, the sport of riding involves two living beings, and it is not always the athletes endowed by nature with merely strong and supple bodies who win. Strength and agility are invaluable assets, but in riding, feeling, skill and, above all, intelligence will always be the most important factors of success in sport, just as they are the most important qualities for an artist. The determination to win, which in all sports drives the athlete to fight on until he has exhausted every ounce of his own energy, is not sufficient in the sport of riding. Success depends also on the strength of the horse himself and furthermore on his co-operation, which cannot be secured just by force. He will never be a completely reliable partner unless experience has taught him that he need never fear punishment in failure, and will always be rewarded in success by a friendly pat on the neck. When a horse has been eduated to become a good partner, he never deliberately lets his rider down. He should be forgiven if he occasionally makes a mistake and it is to him first that his rider must show a sporting spirit.

RACE-RIDING

Racing is the sport of the thoroughbred horse. It measures not only his speed and stamina, but also his inherited constitution and willing-ness to expend every ounce of his strength. The tough programme of training to which thoroughbreds are subjected is a means of selecting for breeding purposes only those horses likely to transmit soundness, courage, stamina and intelligence to the progeny. Selection is the real sense and object of the classical races, but they also provide entertainment for the gambler. The official handicapper decrees what weights have to be carried by various horses, according to his judgment of their merits, in order to equalise their chances. The unreliability of the handicapping system provides the betting public with an inexhaustible source of excitement and the money collected from betting is infused back into the racing and breeding industry. Without a constant influx of young thoroughbreds the whole horse breeding industry of a nation would perish.

Very few riders can participate actively in racing because so few can remain sufficiently light in weight. In the other equestrian sports, the majority of competitors are amateurs riding their own horses, but race-horse trainers and jockeys are a well-organised fraternity of professionals. The race-horse must earn his oats and, if possible, a profit for his owner. If he never wins, he is a worthless animal, not entitled to the love of his owner. Racing is a tough game and very often just a business venture. On the other hand, steeplechase or point-to-point has always been a sport for amateurs who enjoy the excitement of a fight girth to girth and the thrills of throwing their heart over a big fence without fear or thought for safety. Even in racing, the artist is conspicuous. He has his horse on the aids from start to finish and he remains in control of the speed. Instead of resigning himself to the disadvantage of the handicap and the luck of the game, he considers most carefully the influence of the extra weight. The heavier the load, the better it must be balanced over the horse's centre of gravity, neither too high nor too far forward, where it would burden the forehand. If the rider's weight is too far forward, the horse has to struggle to remain balanced and must either lean on the rider's hands or fight to free himself from the bit. His overloaded forelegs become quickly fatigued. There is an art in feeling how to influence the balance of the horse through the position of rider's centre of gravity and knowing how, in the race to the finish, to dispose the weight in such a manner that the gallop can gain in scope instead of becoming a succession of hurried, shortened, flat strides. The lighter the horse, the more he can be hindered by a faulty distribution of the rider's weight.

A jockey must be able to recognise at all moments the muscular tension, the state of balance and the reserves of energy of his horse, to distinguish between unwillingness and inability, to judge the moment to start the race to the finish and, while preserving his feeling for strength, speed and stride, he must also watch the opposition—and all this happens in a matter of seconds. Nothing can develop the sense of balance better than racing and, provided that the rider is not too heavy, galloping on a racing saddle is excellent for the purpose of strengthening the muscles which are particularly stressed in the forward seat.

As regards the horse, the required qualities are calmness and independent judgement, agility and a good sense of balance. These qualities cannot be imparted by even the best dressage methods, for human reactions will never be sufficiently quick to help the horse in difficult situations. The well-schooled dressage horse and the successful show-jumper will always be poor substitutes for a horse naturally gifted with these qualities—if the necessities of our daily life have prevented us from giving them the experience of using their own intelligence in the way nature intended; they always remain much too dependent on our aids. Unfortunately, hunting over big natural obstacles, which is an excellent way of giving horses the necessary experience, is a sport that can be enjoyed in very few countries nowadays.

RIDING FOR RECREATION

It is wonderful to enjoy riding for the pleasure of observing nature, for enjoyment of life, to explore field and forest and for the pleasure of being with a horse; to ride in happiness or in sorrow; to ride beside the woman one loves; to ride in sunshine or rain, at the crack of dawn or in the darkness of night. The pleasure of using a horse for transport and getting out in the fresh air is a privilege denied to so many men nowadays. Riding has the magical power of keeping young all those men who can continue to be delighted by the power and stamina of a horse galloping over fields and soaring over hedges and ditches, who love to hear him whinny with pleasure when they go to saddle and bridle him, and to see him come eagerly to call.

It is rarely necessary nowadays to have to ride for the purpose of carrying out business or professional obligations. It is often glibly said that dressage is not an end in itself but only a means to an end, but what is the end, may one ask? We cannot play at being cowboys

Riding out to hounds.

Riding in open country *(above)* improves the muscular condition of young horses. *(Below)* Horse and rider relaxed and in perfect harmony. Riding energetically forward out of previous collection, the rider in excellent equilibrium gives the horse freedom to extend itself over the obstacle. Jürgen Webers on Aboukir.

whirling a lassoo, nor go hunting with a falcon on our wrist, nor chase wild beasts over distant horizons. There is really no practical reason for riding and the type of horse most riders prefer nowadays is, in any case, unsuitable for all those purposes. Horsemen have to concentrate far too much on control to have the time to do anything else. Nearly all our modern horses are the instruments of sport. We seem unable to rediscover the pleasure of riding to explore the countryside without worrying about competing, although it is such an excellent way of acquiring confidence, skill and good reactions. Long distance riding also teaches us to understand ourselves and our horses. As a form of competition, it was introduced once only between the two world wars (the 100 km race in the region of Verdun, in France, in 1932). The reason why it did not catch on was that some ignorant competitors flogged their horses to death. Furthermore, the craze for motoring was then at its height and such an expenditure of energy seemed pointless; but was show-jumping. less pointless?

Training for long distance riding necessitates long training for fitness, thoughtful planning and considerable self-discipline. The rider must be able to look after his horse himself and all these things are very good if we want the spirit of horsemanship to survive.

BOGUS HORSEMANSHIP

A mysterious reason drives some people to want to learn to ride although they have never had any contact with a horse in their life. The beginner usually finds the experience enjoyable and after he has overcome his initial nervousness and can contemplate his image in the mirror of the manege with some pride and satisfaction, he can go out in the world, look down on other mortals and contemplate the countryside from a greater height. But the pleasure of hacking on a docile animal soon palls, so he decides to buy his own horse to do all the clever things which he sees other riders doing. This is the beginning of dissatisfaction. He is no longer a complete tyro, but he is neither sufficiently patient nor self-disciplined to want to learn the basic principles. He watches the experts and listens to them, picking up fragments of knowledge here and there. We must pity the poor horse as the rider tries to apply these fragments of knowledge and veers between timidity and violence. These are not the sins of cruelty, but of ignorance. The rider loves his horse, but he has started a battle of wills. He practises assiduously every day all the so-called schooling figures of the manege and dismounts every time feeling thoroughly depressed and dissatisfied with his plagued and obstinate horse. The only way of rediscovering the pleasure of riding would be for him to recognise the limits of his talent and his aims, and to start again from the beginning in order to find out the meaning of harmony between horse and rider. Unfortunately, nature who has so cleverly designed the human body, has also given pride to the human spirit in order to protect the ego against the painful recognition of its shortcomings. This is why the ranks of the unteachable are never depleted. They include experienced riders who remain unaware of their lack of ability and knowledge and go from teacher to teacher without ever thinking of examining themselves as critically as they examine others.

IMPROVING PERFORMANCE

"Of all the things I have created, man and horse are dearest to me." Thus said the Lord to Adam. (Arab saying.)

Any person with a normally developed sense of balance can sit on a horse and will call himself a rider as soon as he has acquired enough confidence. Many people also dance and enjoy themselves although they have never felt the exhilarating pleasure of being in harmony with their partner. Riding and dancing fulfil a need for movement and entertainment, which is a good enough raison d'etre. Of course, the woman should be attractive and the horse must be sound and obedient. Many will continue into old age to enjoy their fun without feeling any ambition to perform any better or to succeed in competition. Horsemanship is not a complicated skill in the mind of those who fail to understand its complexity, but riders who have studied it seriously for years may regret the passing of that time in their life when they imagined that they could ride. I am reminded of my school days and of a balmy evening in May when I was riding my brown gelding Hans. As we sailed over a big ditch, I had a glimpse of two startled faces quickly drawing apart and one of these faces belonged to my formidable professor of German, of nature study and of sport. I could not make out at the time whether he was studying nature or sport on that particular occasion, but soon after this incident he scolded me in class for spending more time on learning to ride than on my studies. What upset me was that he said *learning*. I could jump over hedges and ditches, I often went hunting, and he called that learning. My pride was deeply wounded at the time, but it occurred to me, many years later, that he was a very astute man. Are they remarks of this kind that have brought other riders to their senses and made them resolve to learn, or is it the desire to emulate an admired rider, or the experience of riding a well-schooled horse? It is difficult to realise at the beginning how slow and arduous progress is going to be, how little one knows, how much there is to learn. The most offensive riders are those who soon believe in their own perfection. They never stop explaining how they work their horse and spend hours in the manege nagging him into shape, practising with painful earnestness all the manege figures and endlessly going over a variety of obstacles with more pluck than sense. If the horse is obliging, they are delighted, but if things go wrong, he is accused of bad temper, laziness, stubbornness and other vices. It is as easy to deceive oneself as it is difficult to deceive others and self-deception prevents one from accepting well-meant and profitable advice.

A little knowledge is more dangerous than no knowledge at all, because those who know only a little rarely realise the extent of their ignorance. Yet consciousness of his inadequacy is essential to anyone who sincerely wants to improve himself. We may confidently let a beginner ride a well-schooled horse, knowing that he will not try to interfere, but put a conceited, half-educated rider on the same horse and he will immediately start nagging to produce an outline which he fancies, thereby provoking all sorts of resistances, even rearing.

Schooling a horse must be constructive work, but it should remain a pleasure. Sincere students of equitation forget too easily that they should be aiming at creating a perfect partnership with their horse instead of trying to tame him.

At the beginning, it is the horse who educates the rider. An intelligent person will acknowledge for a long time that he is a beginner and will want to ride as many different horses as possible—and not only the better-schooled ones—because the first thing he must learn is to feel; to feel not only whether a horse is comfortable, but also to feel every movement of his body and limbs. In private lessons (class lessons can only be drilling), the rider's education will have to go through the following stages:

1 He must gain confidence and learn balance at all gaits.
2 He must learn to feel the movements of the horse.

3 He must apply what he has learnt on a number of horses.

4 He can start learning to school a horse.

5 He should be able to educate horses to move in good balance and form and to re-school badly educated horses.

Anybody who thinks that he can miss one of these stages or believes that he is ready to start nearer the top, will fail to achieve satisfactory progress.

It is not possible for every rider to receive such a complete education and it is very natural that a young rider should wish to school his own horse. However, though most riders have heard in riding lessons, or read in books, that the education of the horse has to be progressive, they often fail to understand that their own education should be just as progressive. If they have had a few fortunate wins in competition, understandably they will have gained so much confidence in their ability that they cannot understand why their horse does not improve. The horse cannot say anything and other riders will keep quiet, knowing that well-meant advice is not usually well received.

Although the horse cannot speak, he does tell his rider all that needs to be said, and the rider would understand this language if he had had, to start with, enough patience to learn to feel and analyse all the sensations which he receives through the reins and the movements of the horse's back. Though the principles and effects of the aids are fairly easy to understand, their complete mastery requires a feeling for movement, balance and rhythm which can only be acquired by hard work and perseverance.

Well-schooled horses and experienced riding masters, listening to good riders and watching them are all very useful, but only providing that one is able to recognise one's own shortcomings.

The first quality that a student must acquire is, therefore, attentiveness, he should not expect only the horse to have to be attentive. The second most important quality is self-awareness. Though we can learn a lot from a good teacher, we cannot expect him to see what we feel. Knowing what he has to do, the pupil must learn to discipline and educate himself. Neither can he expect his horse to become better balanced at all gaits and over obstacles if he, himself, does not try to develop his own sense of balance. He must understand that the aids are not mechanical in their effect but can be effective only if they are used at the right moment of the movement. The aids are the rider's tools and, as in all crafts, skill in the use of

tools can only be acquired by frequent practice and the at
recognise and correct mistakes. When a horse does not obey t
one should not curse him. It is the rider who should ap
because it is nearly always his own fault. He must learn to feel
immediately when he has acted incorrectly, and educate himself to
avoid repeating the same mistakes. Nobody has the right to control
another living creature unless he can control himself. It obviously
follows that riders must learn to remain relaxed and even-tempered
and that nobody who is easily swayed by fear, impatience or anger,
has any right to be called a horseman.

While riders who yearn for admiration or prizes are always subject
to pleasant or unpleasant emotions, those who ride in order to learn
to ride will develop their strength of character through frequent
practise and better understanding of the horse. It should be realised
that more self-control, equanimity and generosity are needed in the
sport of riding than in any other sport, because it is the only one in
which success does not depend entirely on human effort. Therefore,
weak personalities, who need to win to placate their ego, will never
improve by riding frequently in competition. They should get themselves a kind horse, not necessarily an old plodder, and, instead of
persecuting him with unreasonable demands, let him enjoy—and
enjoy themselves—the pleasure of galloping over fields and jumping
ditches and hedges.

If a rider believes that his vocation is to school horses, his first duty
must be to educate himself, no matter how old he may be. It is never
too late to learn to be fair to the horse, and one does not need to be a
particularly strong and versatile athlete to become a good rider.
Riding does not develop big, bulky muscles. However, riders must
have firm, elastic muscles, constantly under conscious control, quick
to contract and to relax to a precise degree. Soft bodies who do not
carry themselves properly in the course of the ordinary occupations
of life, who have weak backs and lifeless hands, will never be able to
control a horse. Horses hate to be bullied but they do not respect the
weak. Anybody who has to hold his hands on his hips or in his
pockets to help him hold his body up will have to practise dis-
mounted exercises to acquire a firm seat on horseback. Hand- and
elbow-stands, practised every day for a period of ten minutes are
incomparable gymnastic exercises for the seat. Perseverance is
needed; in all skills, it is the secret of success. *Perseverance . . . not*
persistency. Perseverance means courage and patience; persistence is

stubbornness and stupefies the rider and the horse. Perseverance goes with flexibility, readiness to try a new method, a different approach when others have failed, and to abandon it when circumstances require, although the same principles continue to be followed. Flexibility is, besides absence of rigidity, ability to feel the movement and the precise degree of emphasis necessary in the use of the aids; it is promptness in opposing a resistance and even greater promptness in yielding. Flexibility makes the work of schooling much more interesting for the rider and for the horse.

Riding must always remain a pleasure, rather than a duty that has to be performed every day, at set hours, for a definite length of time. For many competitive riders it has become, unfortunately, this sort of routine, because they lack sufficient leisure or space to ride anywhere else than in an enclosed area. It amounts to making a virtue out of necessity. They are depriving themselves of the happiness of enjoying nature in the company of a trusted horse. However, competition seems to be the only thing that matters for so many young riders, who cannot know that the sport of show-jumping is a modern and inferior substitute for military campaigning. As soon as they feel sufficiently secure, can grip with their knees and stand in the stirrups, they must jump and, for them, horses are no more than jumping machines which have to be worked in an enclosed space and the work is an unavoidable necessity. Genuine horsemen, on the other hand, enjoy the work because it is absorbing and satisfying, because it is good to feel that they have disciplined themselves and achieved some progress. For them, the quiet atmosphere of the manege is essential for serious work.

All riders should beware of giving unsolicited advice to all and sundry, besides wives, children or girlfriends. Anybody who likes to play at being a professor should remember that others will judge him by the way his own horse behaves. It is also very unwise to criticise other riders because they employ a professional to prepare their horses for competitions. Everybody has the right to spend his own money as he wishes and, besides this, riding a horse schooled by someone else in a competition is not so easy. Let us always guard our tongue. Riders are more sensitive to criticism of their riding ability than to accusations of dishonesty and we can lose a friend for ever by making fun of his riding ability. Self-criticism should give anybody more than enough to think about.

This susceptibility is quite normal. Shooting game, breeding horses and riding, which were once the exclusive privilege of persons of noble blood, can be nowadays the hobbies or obsessions of anybody who can pay for them. If he has made enough money in business, or become famous as a politician, modern man can take up shooting, even if he has never used a gun in his life. Breeding horses, on the other hand, needs not only money but also a lot of knowledge and patience. Only genuine interest or crazy profligacy can explain why anyone should want to start such a hazardous enterprise. As for riding, if the horse were as easy to manage as a gun, we would see more people take it up in their middle-age. It is normal that men who have worked hard in order to be able to aspire to the accomplishments of the aristocracy should not want to be derided. Every rider wants to be told that he is a good rider, and preachers who destroy cherished illusions are never popular.

Riders who are interested in riding, but not in learning to care for the horse, will never get to understand him completely. Association with horses since childhood is, in this respect, an invaluable advantage.

Although no rider who has not at some time in his life gained experience in racing, jumping and dressage can be called a complete horseman—one should always be modest—no rivalry should ever exist between horsemen, because all that matters is the love of the horse. It is this love that we serve when we learn to discipline ourselves. The principal educational value of riding is that it teaches self-knowledge and self-control.

UNDERSTANDING HORSES

The Lord said to man: "Besides thee, the horse is the most noble of my creations. Remember that I have endowed him, as thee, with a heart, a brain, nerves, flesh and blood." (Arab saying.)

Heart, brain, nerves, flesh, blood, the order is important. First, we must get the horse to trust us. Once we have gained his trust, we can start developing his intelligence and understanding: to this purpose, we use his natural reflexes and once he understands our aids we can improve his movement and build his form (outline). Then, having freed him from suspicion and apprehension and taught him to understand our aids, we develop his strength and suppleness.

As for blood, what we mean is not the fluid which carries nutrients to all the parts of the body, but rather that mysterious sap which makes certain horses exceptionally courageous, powerful and generous to the extent of self-sacrifice.

Like men, though easier to understand because they are incapable of dissimulation, horses are individuals that can vary in many respects. They vary in their *character*. Character and temperament are not completely synonymous words. When we talk of a horse's character, we are really referring to his disposition towards humans. In a considerable measure, this is the result of his experience of men and can be altered by new experience; a kindly disposed horse can become bad-tempered when he comes into the wrong hands, and vice-versa. Generally, stallions and mares are more sensitive than geldings. However some undesirable traits are inherited and it is known that certain vices run in the blood of some families (biting, kicking, jibbing, shying, fighting the bit and suspicion of man). Such vices are very difficult to correct and their cure should be attempted only by experienced professionals. Furthermore, the cure is rarely permanent, and a vice usually appears again when the horse goes to a new owner. Exceptional love is required because even necessary punishment must be inspired by love. However, good qualities also are passed on, such as kindness, attentiveness, honesty, stamina, enjoyment of jumping and aptitude for the High-School.

On the other hand, *temperament* applies to the sum total of characteristics that are the result of the body's physical, nervous and mental organisation. Historically, temperament was believed to be determined by the relative proportions of body fluids: the four cardinal humours—blood, phlegm, choler and melancholy. Horses are not as complex as man and usually are described as temperamental or phlegmatic. We can however go further and a temperamental horse could be described as sanguinous or choleric, while phlegmatic horses can be anything from dull to apathetic. Quite logically, in the mind of our ancestors, the humours determined behaviour and according to their combination would make a horse alert, lively, or fiery, or violent or crazy. Temperament has to be vented and it is in movement that it finds an outlet. Temperament can be cooled by wise heads and tactful hands, but for a really "hot" horse, there is no better cure than long hours of work. Phlegmatic horses can be dull to the point of stupidity, with varying degrees in between. The choice of a horse must be largely determined by temperament and, generally, temperamental horses are for cool, experienced, sympathetic riders who will make them trusting, willing and attentive, while being able to exploit their keenness. Phlegmatic horses are less worrying for beginners who can learn to make them more willing, attentive and active. The impulsion of a ridden horse, his desire to go forward, can appear to spectators as a manifestation of his temperament, when it is often the result of the stimulating, or calming, influence of the rider. It is only by riding the horse that we can accurately assess his temperament. Also, in certain circumstances, the desire to go forward may be the result of the rider's influence or of excitement. It can be noticed in hunting that a horse who has been fighting to get ahead of the field will often gallop calmly behind the other horses after he has got rid of his rider.

Horses vary in *intelligence*. We are generally inclined to grant more intelligence to finely-bred horses. They are certainly more impressionable, quicker to oblige or to get upset, more attentive to their surroundings and therefore less inclined to shy and, usually, they are less suspicious of man. However, intelligence is not necessarily linked to blood and amongst well-bred horses there are talented, attentive, mentally acute individuals, but also dull, dim-witted and fractious animals. A horse's intelligence shows up in his visual expression and, in the same way as men are attracted to women because of the charm of their countenance as much as by the harmony of their bodily proportions, a horse must appeal to us because of the kindness and intelligence of his facial expression and not only by reason of his conformation.

Determined by temperament and intelligence, attentiveness is an essential quality and, if it is not natural to a horse, it is the first thing that he must learn. We should realise, however, that a young horse is not capable of concentrating his attention on his trainer for longer periods of time than 15 to 20 minutes, after which time he becomes distracted by his surroundings. A trainer who ignores this fact loses his patience and compromises success. The education of horses is based on their capacity to remember frequently repeated impressions, and memory depends on attentiveness. We should also realise that memory, which gives horses such a remarkable sense of direction, causes them to shy at objects which have frightened them in the past and to resist human actions which are associated in their mind with painful or frightening treatment.

The faces of dogs are also expressive and we can learn much about horses by observing the facial expressions of dogs: dachshunds, boxers, hounds have an alert expression; Great Danes, St. Bernards have an expression of stoic equanimity. The faces of stallions and mares are very expressive, and in the selection of a brood mare we should want to recognise a look of motherliness. An experienced horseman can recognise a mare from a gelding by the look of the face, but even a fairly new horse owner can learn to know very quickly the mood of his horse by watching the expression of the eyes and the play of the ears. Once he has learnt to notice the play of the ears when he goes to greet his horse in the stable, he will be able to interpret his horse's mood from the saddle by knowing which movements of the ears denote contentment, attention, apprehension or annoyance. In work on the lunge, the trainer should observe both the eyes and ears which tell him how the horse is reacting to his influences. By developing his powers of observation, he learns to anticipate and control the horse's reactions and to recognise the awakening of understanding. The ears are the mirrors of the horse's soul, but like a dog he also speaks to us with his tail, a very revealing indicator of his mood. Eyes, ears and tail are all important elements of the vocabulary of the horse and we must learn to understand his language.

Whether intelligence is innate or not, it is certain that the horse's *understanding* develops through his association with man. This is true of other animals. A dog kept perpetually chained to a kennel will always remain as dense as a pig held in a sty, while the dog that goes wherever his master goes and lives with his family soon gets to understand human conversation and is easy to train. A horse can learn with pleasure only from an understanding, consistent master, who does not try to destroy all the animal's enjoyment of life nor restrict his natural movement. Such a master convinces the horse that man is his friend.

Like humans, horses also can suffer from *nerves*, and not only when their nervous system becomes damaged by trauma. It is understandable that young horses should be nervous and apprehensive, but when a mature horse will not allow himself to be bridled, or becomes agitated under the saddle, he is showing that he has lost his trust in man. Race-horses that breakout in the box and tremble when they hear the noises of a race-course, and will not stand still at the start of a race, are suffering from nervous strain. A horse that breaks out after a ruthless nagging and refuses his food is showing disturbance of the sympathetic nervous system. Consistently successful show-jumpers sometimes start rushing and refusing once they change hands, especially if they are manhandled by a bad rider.

When a horse has steady nerves, we accept this as perfectly normal. It may not occur to us that a calm horse is a credit to his rider. Therefore, if a calm horse starts becoming nervous and fractious when he comes into our care, we must search our conscience. Nervousness can be caused by rough handling, bad riding, the wrong kind of exercise, mistakes in the use of the aids, and, especially, inconsequence. Calmness is the result of trust and understanding.

It is by observing many different horses that one learns to recognise good *conformation* and there are enough horse-shows to enable all riders to develop their discernment. However, only experts, who understand the process of development of bone and muscle, can look at an untrained horse and imagine what he will look like after training. Furthermore, experienced horsemen can recognise, by the degree of development of certain muscles and their activity during movement, the extent and quality of training and schooling a particular horse has received. Horses are sometimes shown incompetently, but if the right groups of muscles are well-developed, the experienced horseman knows that it should not be too difficult to restore the picture to its previous form. Conversely, a poor development of the same important muscular groups denotes bad training or shows that the horse is incapable, for some reason, of moving properly; on the other hand, if a horse has a fairly good outline, but bad gaits, it is usually because his training has been hasty and his movement has been restricted. Nobody, however, regardless of experience, can accurately predict the picture that a growing horse will present at maturity. Every breeder knows that the mature horse will have more or less the same body shape as he was born with, but yearlings, two-year olds and three-year olds alter in appearance, in proportions, from one month to the next, because they grow alternately at the withers, at the croup, in length and in depth of chest. The art of the breeder is the ability to recognise the right time to sell the young animal, and the purchaser of a beautiful three-year old may eventually find himself in possession of a leggy Rosinante or a roly-poly. Not only horses, but also dogs, cats and humans may have to curse for the rest of their life the generosity of those who fed them in their youth and were so charmed by their child-like grace.

Regarding *condition*, except in racing circles, taste and knowledge are at variance. Trainers of race-horses understand the science of getting a horse fit, and they dread fatness. In showing, show-jumping and dressage circles, horses are seen so well-covered that they come near to being gross. The handicapping effect of over-weight, even in minor competitions, does not appear to be realised, so I think that it is helpful to consider some figures. A race-horse in full training carries between 4 and 5 kg, of belly and back fat. The average, well-fed, saddle-horse of hunting type carries 25 kg of belly and back fat and, on top of this, a sheet of fat approximately two fingers thick over the ribs and weighing approximately as much as 10 kg. A draught-horse carries 35 to 50 kg of belly fat and upwards of 30 kg of back and rib fat. Would an athletics coach accept for training athletes who presented themselves to him in such a gross condition? Fat is positively harmful; it imposes an excessive strain on tendons, ligaments and joints, it makes movement arduous and causes horses to be sluggish and fractious. Yet many fond owners who dread the effect of a heavy rider on their cherished horse, happily load the animal with so much fat on its own body that it greatly exceeds the weight of the rider.

As for talent, speed and jumping ability cannot be assessed without a trial. Conformation is not sufficiently revealing. The horse must be seen to gallop and jump, with or without a rider. As regards jumping, the height of the obstacle matters less than the jumping style of the horse. If he just lifts his forelegs, keeping the knees bent, it is with the elbows that he can make a fault and hit the obstacle. If, on the other hand, he lifts his hooves to the height of the shoulder joint and extends his knees, so that the breast is the lowest point at the height of the trajectory, we can assume that the horse has a great future as a show-jumper. He should also, however, be careful to avoid hitting the obstacle with his hindfeet, showing us that he has the determination and intelligence to jump clear. A demonstration of natural talent and willingness must be insisted upon whenever we are considering the purchase of a young horse for the purpose of producing a show-jumper of exceptional quality.

However, it is usually by chance that a horse with exceptional talent, either for dressage or for show-jumping is discovered and many a famous rider has made a name for himself with one exceptional horse and has been forgotten after parting with him. Discovering talented horses is an exceptionally difficult art.

Although experienced judges are seldom mistaken, they cannot measure a horse's stamina merely by examining him; they must ride him. Stamina is vigour of constitution, staying power, quick recovery from stress, resistance to disease. These qualities are "in the blood". We can gain limited information on this score by examining the horse's pedigree. Even so, we should remember that modern horses live in an artificial environment where natural selection, which in the wild ensured that only horses of exceptional stamina survived, no longer operates. Nothing can replace a sufficiently stressful test under saddle.

It is frequently on the basis of conformation, gaits and soundness that horses are purchased. Temperament and intelligence are at least as important however, if not more so. A horse that learns quickly can be forgiven minor faults of conformation and will always be preferred by a trainer to a more dull, though more beautiful one. There are many good horses, but the perfect horse is as rare as a perfect marriage and the essential thing in all partnerships is sympathy. It is not enough for a horse to be good-looking: he should immediately make us feel that we cannot wait to ride him. We always dance better with a person we love, and ride better on a horse that inspires us with sympathy. If he has set his heart on buying a particular horse, a rider without expertise must first of all be sure that he finds him comfortable and that he can control him. All other things, age, colour, handsomeness and gaits, are of secondary importance to that. So many good-looking young horses are bought at blood-stock sales and will be schooled by a professional while the owner waits despondently, often in vain, for the time when he will be able to ride the horse himself. Pride of ownership and desire to show one's horsemanship are understandable vanities, but it is often wiser to learn to love a kind hack and always more enjoyable to be able to ride every day with pleasure and peace of mind, than to remain a wistful spectator.

Although horses vary in so many respects, there is an invariable rule that applies to all: before he can be made to specialise either for eventing, show-jumping or dressage, every horse must be educated to become a good hack, in the sense that he must learn to allow himself to be used for transport, must be familiarised with all the sights of the countryside, taught to behave sensibly on the road, and to go wherever we wish at the pace we desire.

The argument that we do sometimes see a crazy horse fly over formidable obstacles, or that a confirmed shyer can win a dressage competition providing that death-like quiet reigns while he is in the arena, is totally irrelevant. Attentiveness to the rider, obedience, unconstrained regularity of the gaits and imperturbability are all essential requirements which must be satisfied before any horse should be put to specialised training.

The bodies of all horses are composed of a heart, a brain, nerves, flesh and blood, but only the saddle-horse, in the past, was thought of as being divided into two parts, a "forehand" and a "hindhand". Nowadays the words are unthinkingly used to describe the exterior of all horses, even draught-horses. However, the old masters of the classical art of riding understood withers, shoulders, forelegs, neck and head as being *in front of the hand*; loins, croup and hindlegs being *behind the hand* (hand and seat being synonymous in this case). Later, when riding became a popular pastime, less understanding horsemen started using these terms to describe the forelegs or the hindquarters.

Forehand and hindhand are not two separate, detachable, unalterable parts, with a throne in between, where we sit to command both ends like some kind of a more or less amiable despot. In reality, we sit on the back of the horse and control the forelegs with our hands and reins by utilising the *bow in front of the hand*; a bow which has one end at the withers and shoulders of the horse, extends over his neck and poll, and is fixed at the other end to his mouth and to the bit, which is connected to our hand by the reins. We must impart to this bow a permanent but flexible form, which the horse must learn to maintain of his own accord, because it is this form which allows us to use the part before the hand to control the part behind the hand. The power comes from behind and we must adjust the output of the motor to achieve the desired compromise between the propulsive force of the hindleg and the shock-absorbing capacity of the joints. To make the horse obedient and suitable for our purpose, we must be able to control speed, beat and length of stride. The parts behind the hand must also be formed like a well-strung bow, firmly braced and yet elastic. We give the desired degree of elasticity by commanding the contractions of the muscles of this bow. We can do this to a certain extent with the sole aids of our seat and legs, but for total control of speed, that is beat and length of stride, and obviously of direction, we have to establish the set form of the bow before the hand.

An essential element of the control of the bow in front of the hand is equal obedience on both reins. However, the expression "on the right rein" or "on the left rein" is an example of careless usage. The horse must not go on one rein, and when we ride a large circle to the right, the tension on both reins must remain equally light. If we feel the horse stretching the left rein more than the right, we change direction and ride a fraction of a small circle to the left, and to make him yield to the tension of the left rein and come up to our right hand. The correct expression is "to the right", "to the left", and "to hand" when the horse yields correctly to both hands.

All that has been said concerning the arching of the bows in front and behind the hand applies also to lateral inflexion which is obedience to the lateral aids. The muscles of both sides must be equally elastic, equally contractible and equally stretchable, relaxed but taut. Lateral suppleness is also an essential element of the posture which we must establish. A horse that refuses to inflex his body in obedience to the aids can resist and evade all our commands. We should not, however, forget that muscles become more elastic as they become stronger: they allow themselves to be stretched to a greater extent and can then contract more effectively. To develop a horse's suppleness, we must first develop his strength. If we attempt to force the horse to carry himself elegantly by constraining him with severe hands or contraptions, we spoil his movement and impose on him a painful effort. The sign of a well-schooled horse is a good posture which he maintains of his own accord.

2 Fundamental Principles

"Win thy horse's heart first, then speaketh to his brain; thou willst then be able to exploit his strength." (Arab proverb.)

A different order of priorities is unthinkable. A horse is an individual and not just another creature. Before we can gain his affection and then develop his understanding and composure, we will have to discover that he has moods and can be aloof, exuberant, timid, impertinent, obstinate. He cannot express these moods by wagging his tail or even by snorting, but in our presence, alongside him or on his back, he will either tense up because he distrusts us or relax because he does not fear us.

The behaviour of all horses is conditioned by their first contact with humans. Even very young foals can be educated and we can give them a first lesson in submissiveness by tying them up at the manger when we give them their feed. All foals should be taught to go to the manger at certain times every day, and will then learn to enjoy finding themselves tied-up as much as they enjoy their oats. This is the first lesson in docility, the basis of future relations between man and horse. In the case of a particularly timid youngster, a short length of rope, about 20 cm long, should hang from the head-stall so that we need not frighten him by seizing him by the nose to catch him. Daily tying-up will foster trust. At this stage, however, handling should be limited to leading the foal and teaching him to have his feet picked up. A handler who is not very experienced must avoid encouraging too much friendliness. The playfulness of a foal quickly turns into impertinence and the understandable human reflex of self-defence then provokes either anger and aggression, or fear and flight. Only a few minutes each day should be spent amongst young foals out at grass and it is a good thing always to have a walking stick, not ever to strike, but to ward off or firmly push away a youngster who becomes too inquisitive.

Education proper usually starts when the horse is fully grown and already reasonably well-acquainted with man. Education is a science, based on well-proved principles of psychology which every trainer must know. One of the most important of these principles is consistency. The only way to avoid setbacks is to adhere to a consistent system, even with a horse that has already been ridden. Gaps in a horse's education will always have to be repaired at some time or another. As no two horses are alike, a set procedure, guaranteed to succeed in all cases, cannot be described, but only a very experienced animal psychologist can afford short-cuts.

Worrying the horse with demands that he is not ready to understand shows remarkable ignorance and thoughtlessness. It is a mistake that will always have to be dearly paid for, and somebody's foolishness is always the cause of a horse's reaction of fear or anger to his trainer's orders: the horse may have been chased about while on the lunge by a loud-mouthed, whip-brandishing brute, or he may have been roughly and prematurely ridden. Unless the horse's understanding has been properly developed, he will never be willingly submissive. In a battle of wills, man is always the loser because he is fighting a combination of strength, cunning and stubbornness much greater than his own.

The extraordinary successes of some famous animal tamers were based on another important principle—that when it refuses to obey, the animal must automatically punish itself. In the case of horses especially, it is essential that they should grasp instantaneously the connection of cause and consequence, and essential, therefore, that our reactions be immediate, correct and consistent. Forgiveness, repentance, endearments and rewards for good behaviour are purely human notions which all animals are incapable of conceiving. A stream of insults will make no more impression on a horse's feelings than the hum of a bumble-bee. But a strong, well-fitting head-stall, a length of chain, a ring firmly fixed to a wall will soon convince him of the uselessness of struggling against a superior force.

Punishment must be convincing. A dog that has developed the habit of straining at his leash and dragging his master off his feet, can be cured providing that the master has the heart to give the leash such a hefty tug that it turns the dog over whenever he tries to pull away. The habit can usually be cured in ten minutes at most: choke-collars or prick-studded collars are useless, amateurish contraptions, akin to the innumerable and often cruel devices invented to control horses. There is also an indirect method of punishment, much more sophisticated: for example, to teach a dog that he should not greet his master by leaping at him, we tread on one of his hind paws, while at the same time patting him affectionately on the head. The dog will be thoroughly disconcerted, while his eyes will show how he hates to disappoint the object of his enthusiastic affection.

These simple examples were used only to illustrate the general philosophy of all animal training, which is that the animal must inflict pain on itself, at the very moment when it does something wrong, and that the punishment must be unexpected and sufficiently severe to make a lasting impression. A calm and educated horseman will inflict punishment commensurate with the degree of resistance to his orders, but the punishment must stop at the very first sign of obedience. This is sufficient reward, and anything more, even a pat on the neck, distracts the animal's attention. In the case of horses, the feeding of tit-bits makes them disrespectful, tiresome and importunate. The horse must not only learn to trust us, he must also learn to respect us. There is no harm in feeding delicacies when we go to greet him in his box, but it is better to place them in the manger than to present them from the hand. Patting the horse affectionately on the neck when we first greet him or when we leave him is a sign of friendliness which horses soon learn to understand. It must in any case be remembered that half-measures succeed only in producing irritation and disobedience, which is why a horse pulls harder when a rider tries to slow him down by pulling steadily on the reins.

When we speak to our horse, it should always be in a quiet and sensible manner, as we would to a young child learning to talk. Tongue-clicking, hand-clapping, whip-cracking, shoo-ing are only unpleasant sounds which should be used for chasing away unwelcome creatures. When they no longer impress, we must resort to louder abuse. Besides being unnecessary, these vocal exercises are irritating to other trainers who may be using the manege at the same time.

The next thing which I teach the horse is to stand perfectly still at my command, and to walk calmly at my side without constraint, attentive only to me. For this purpose, I always use a plain snaffle, a pair of reins of normal length and a whip. The horse must learn to walk forward calmly and without hesitation when I order him to do so, reinforcing my command with a tap of the whip if necessary. The horse must then continue to walk calmly beside me, on an easy rein, without dropping backward nor trying to get ahead of me, and when I say "Whoa", he must come to a halt. At first, I will allow him to walk on for another step or two, then I will give a little tug on the reins, and repeat these little tugs until he stands, but loosen the reins as soon as he obeys. The proper parade is too difficult for him to understand at this stage and would cause him to pull, and I want him to understand that pulling will never be tolerated. If he is disobedient, I act severely. It is absolutely essential to prevent the horse from finding out at this stage that he can pull, because I do not want him to lean on my hand when I start riding him. Therefore, I lead him on a slack rein. This is the modest beginning of self-carriage. Eventually, he must halt as soon as I do, showing me how attentive he is to all my actions. I do not want to distract his attention and the only reward I give him is the immediate slackening of the reins. At my very quietly given command "Walk", we both move on again. The same lesson is repeated day after day, until obedience is completely confirmed.

As soon as possible, instead of walking at his head, I take my place at the horse's left shoulder or even a little further back. I now pass the right rein over the neck to my right hand, continue to use the whip, if necessary, to urge the horse forward, and the little tug on the reins, to stop him, followed by an immediate slackening, but my actions become more and more imperceptible to anybody except the horse. In the course of time, these aids will become a proper parade, synchronised with the movements of the limbs. Once the transitions to the walk and the halt are perfect and I feel that I could control the horse with a thread of silk, I will—if possible—repeat all this work at the trot.

To forestall any objection to the use of the word "tug", I must explain that I do not mean a sharp downward jolt which would cause the bit to bruise the bars of the mouth. This would destroy the horse's confidence in me and make him bit-shy. It is in reality just a sudden immobilising of my hand as I cease to go forward. Later, as I have explained, the right rein to my right hand is passed over the horse's neck, and therefore moves the bit up towards the corner of the mouth. And so the tug is a passive action, not to be confused with the sock in the mouth which so scandalises spectators, but nevertheless has a much less detrimental effect than steady pulling.

In the mind of riders guilty of doing so, pulling should have the mechanical effect of braking, but as far as the horse is concerned, it has the opposite effect. It teaches him to pull in the opposite direction, just as when he is in harness he learns to throw his mass into the collar in order to drag the plough. Pulling makes the horse's mouth insensitive. The vice of boring on the bit or of leaning on the hands is always caused by a pulling hand, whereas the independent hand that suddenly fixes itself is an unmistakable command which the horse soon learns to respect.

Once the horse has learnt to understand it and has become promptly obedient, this restraining aid can be refined. It may be easy to accept the superiority of this method, but it will require much practise to apply it to perfection. However, the time can be most usefully employed because it gives us also an opportunity to let the young horse discover the world in our company and, while we provide him with entertainment, we also develop his trust. On these walks, we let him graze a little and allow him to pause to contemplate his surroundings peacefully. However, by inexorably imposing immobility between hand and whip, we firmly check any display of freshness, such as rushing ahead, shying, or rearing. Indiscipline must be nipped in the bud. When we say "Whoa", the horse must stop; he must not dare displace even one foot. Within a matter of days, he will have learnt to obey the whip and the word, a proper parade. He will be "to the hand", as docile as a dog trained to walk at heel. Teaching him to change direction at the slightest indication will then be very easy, though at first some horses hesitate to go forward and others hurry.

During this work in hand, we can also teach the horse to step backwards, to move straight and regularly. We can even start to correct onesidedness. We should never attempt to back him until he has become perfectly calm, completely attentive and sensible when we lead him from the ground.

The same method can be used to prepare a young horse for sale, except that in this case we will need an assistant because to show his action, the horse must trot, and it would be unreasonable to expect him to remain, of his own accord, at the same constant distance from our hand. However, we avoid exciting the horse, to make him move extravagantly, by means of flailing arms, loud clapping, cracking of the whip and stamping on the ground. These only show ignorance and are all obnoxious practices which will only give a tyro a misleading picture of a mettlesome horse, end by teaching the horse to fear any noise coming behind him, and to panic, later on, whenever he hears a sound as insignificant, for example, as the rattle of wheels of a harmless doll's pram.

It is not with the intention of being invidious that I have described a method of leading different from the usual one with the reins adjusted to a contact, separated by the forefinger of the right hand. It is only that I consider that this latter practice is acceptable only in the case of trained horses, well-accustomed to being ridden and inspected on familiar ground, under experienced and alert supervision, as, for example, in the cavalry. My aim is to educate the horse, and not just to accustom him to being led, so I want him to remain always between the aids (in this case, whip and reins) and, therefore, my place must be close to his shoulder or even further back. This method helps the trainer to start acquiring the art, which he will have to develop from the saddle, of checking and yielding without altering the horse's head and neck carriage, of reining back without losing contact with the mouth. We can also learn to observe the action of the hindlimbs and to forestall the turning aside of the hindquarters—or even of one hindfoot—by placing the shoulders in front of the hindlimbs. We learn to understand the significance of straightness. This method has the additional advantages of calming nervous, impetuous horses and of gymnastically working the hindquarters before schooling can be done from the saddle. It requires considerable feel, because side-reins are not used, but the penny alway drops quicker if we set our target high and tackle difficulties from the beginning; a crooked position due to a faulty placing of head and neck is more difficult to correct from the ground without the help of leg aids, so incompetent handling of the reins is clearly revealed by this work in hand.

The horse must always move ahead of the trainer. This principle applies equally to lungeing. One should never start lungeing until the horse trusts completely the trainer who has taught him to be led. An assistant is not needed, he would only be a nuisance. We start at the walk, placing ourselves slightly behind the girth, so that we can maintain steady forward movement and have the horse always between hand (lunge) and whip. At first the lunge is held rather short, but it can soon be paid out, although we must remain close enough to the horse to be able to touch him with the whip if he becomes insufficiently active. However, if our previous preparation has been thorough, the horse will never put up resistance. Battling with an upset horse on the lunge is bungling amateurishness, while lungeing merely to dispel freshness before being able to get onto the horse's back shows complete misunderstanding of the purpose of this work: it amounts to an abdication of authority on our part; it is bewildering for the horse, if he has previously been taught to concentrate all his attention on his trainer; it encourages excitability, instead of calmness, obedience and understanding. It amounts to mechanising the horse instead of educating him. "Lungeing," Steinbrecht wrote, "should not be mechanical exercising, but a mental exercise in concentration of body and mind." One wonders how a cavalry squadron could have been lined up and moved forwards if even a small number of horses had to be allowed a few capers on the lunge to dispel their exuberance.

Our next step will be teaching the horse to remain attentive to us at the halt for as long as we choose. I start by standing in front of him, the reins hanging loosely, and I look him in the eyes. If he moves at all, be it only by one step, I will give a little tug on the reins and say "Stand". If his attention wanders and he starts looking around, I will vibrate the bit gently and say "No", just to restore mental contact. Soon, I will be able to pick up the whip, coil up the lunge and walk away, apparently forgetting his presence, and if I have said "Stand", he will not attempt to follow me, but will continue to watch me expectantly. As I say "Come", at first I draw a little on the lunge, but eventually he will come of his own accord, at my command. This sort of free-schooling can make a horse so gentle, obedient and attentive that he can be left to stand unattended, or be trusted to follow me anywhere without having to be held.

A horse that has been properly trained to be mounted and ridden will remain perfectly still when the rider says "Stand" as he puts his foot in the stirrup. When I stand by his left shoulder, ready to mount, I expect the horse to concentrate his attention only on me and I want his eyes to express friendliness and anticipation of pleasure. I prefer to give the first mounting lesson in the box, and if the procedure that I describe is followed, the rider will be able to chuckle quietly to himself when he sees other riders plagued with a rough and disobedient horse who refuses to stand still to be mounted. People who do not mind having their feet trodden on and who allow themselves to be pushed about, ought to stick to cattle droving. When we decide to mount and ride a horse for the first time, it is essential to avoid any sort of trouble, and the time and precautions devoted to the first occasion are always amply rewarded. Nobody with whom the horse is unfamiliar (however experienced) should be allowed to be present. The horse must know the sound and smell of all concerned. He must sniff the rider, recognise him and allow him to put his arms around his neck. Nothing should ever go wrong, if everything happens without fuss in the familiar box. The young attendant is slowly lifted onto the horse's back while oats are offered in the manger. The same procedure is repeated daily, until the horse remains completely unconcerned, continuing to eat the carrots or grass placed on the floor. At this stage, and still in the box, a saddle is placed on his back and the girth is adjusted gradually, eventually by the rider himself. Once the horse is absolutely calm in the box, with the rider astride, he can be tied-up outside the box, at the place where he usually stands to be groomed, but never for longer than half-an-hour at a time. Eventually, he will stand calmly, unrestrained, totally unworried by the presence of a rider on his back and will start walking with the reassuring presence of the trainer at his side. Difficulties are unlikely to occur after this, and the horse is now ready to be ridden, either alone or with a suitable lead-horse. This method has worked, even in the case of horses that have had to be educated all over again; nothing more is needed than love and patience. Even if one has to remain content for a fortnight with just standing or walking, it will not be wasted time. A horse that has been taught to be mounted in the manner described will remain calm, trusting and attentive, and will never take advantage of his freedom.

Tenseness and irregular gaits are avoided in the same manner. We start by wandering around the stables, pausing frequently to observe the surroundings, like an estate manager inspecting his land. To avoid difficulties later, at the faster gaits, we ought to stay at the walk for a long time, and be very progressive in our demands, being attentive to the movements of respiration which must remain calm and regular. Before starting to trot, we will revise at the walk all the lessons which the horse has learnt in the work on the ground.

Sins of the past, which have upset a horse, can be redeemed by the same method, of frequently letting him stand perfectly still, completely unrestrained. My old master Oskar Stensbeck used to re-educate head-strong horses by riding into the manege, coming to a halt, and letting the horse quietly "chew" the bit from his hand; he would then light a cigar and read his newspaper until the cigar had burnt out. During all this time, he would never let the horse move from the same spot. Then he would quietly dismount and have the horse led back to his box. This "meditating exercise" for the horse, alternated with periods of walking with the reins adjusted to a contact, was one of our favourite lessons, the benefits of which were felt for the rest of their life by horse and rider. One wonders why such sensible methods appear to have been forgotten; they should be common knowledge. Two weeks devoted to teaching a horse to stand still on a loose rein, without allowing him to move by a single step, is not only an excellent way of calming agitated horses; it is also a very good cure for horses that have become pullers and are heavy on the hand, because it teaches them to balance the rider's weight by using their own forces. Those who object that this method would take up too much time, ought to give up riding.

Regarding the voice, its use as an educational aid is controversial. It is true that, if we school horses just for the purpose of preparing them for dressage competitions, we should be cautious about giving spoken commands, because they can give a horse the habit of anticipating the indications of hands, legs and seat and of executing transitions abruptly and prematurely. However, for general leisure riding and for cross-country, or when the rider is weak, it is extremely useful to be able to warn a horse of a change of speed by the use of certain words of command that he has learnt to obey. But we can compromise. The horse that I allow my guests to ride is very attentive to the indications of my hands and legs when I ride him myself in complete silence; he feels that I mean business. On the other hand, when he feels that he is being used to transport an inexperienced rider on a nature trek, he will occasionally pluck a twig from a bush, or even stop to graze, but he remains attentive to my voice. His walk becomes active again when he hears me say "Walk"; he trots as soon as he hears the sound "Trrr-ot"; he composes himself in readiness for the canter when he hears the word "Canter . . .", but he only strikes off when he hears me mutter "Now". A long drawn out "Whoa . . ." brings him back from the canter to the trot in three strides as smoothly as would well-executed half-parades, and from trot to the walk, without the rider having to do anything. My guests have never realised that I was talking to the horse; they would think that I was giving *them* a warning. Experienced riders would use their aids correctly and would expect the horse to be properly schooled; less experienced riders would be thrilled at obtaining a response to their aids and would praise the horse for his perfect obedience. Even with race-horses, sound can be useful. If during training, a hissing sound is co-ordinated with the whip to give the signal for the all-out gallop, it can then be used effectively in the final stage of a race. Conversely, however, I have found that quite loud chatting and singing have a soothing effect on both nervous horses and nervous riders.

Though it is generally accepted that bad riding habits produce horses with bad manners, it is easily forgotten that a horse will lose the good manners imparted in his early training if any lapses are overlooked. For example, whenever we mount, we must strictly discipline ourselves never to allow the horse to move, while we arrange our reins leisurely, and to let him walk on only in obedience to the pressure of our legs. Unless we insist on this, every time we mount, the horse will soon lose the habit of standing perfectly still. Bad riding manners will very quickly spoil the most carefully educated horse.

Cowboys, who are not taught our ingenious combinations of aids, manage even so to produce useful, attentive and perfectly obedient horses by riding with both reins in one hand, so that the other hand is free to wield the gun or the lassoo. I know that I will scandalise many of my readers by suggesting that their ways could be imitated, and I admit that they are atrocious when they are applied by unskilled and undisciplined riders, or in anger, or if the horse has not been educated to understand them. Nevertheless, they are logical. It is natural for an unspoilt, sound horse, to want to go forward and lift his feet high enough to avoid stumbling when his movement is not restricted by the reins, and to change his gait to a faster one when he feels the measured, though firm, pressure of the spurs on his sides. It is natural that he should invariably obey the restraining hand when the restraint is always in the form of careful, even energetic parades for the sole purpose of changing the gait, so that he will come back to the halt from a gallop in only a few strides. Even the abrupt and vigorous *Insterburger* is not in any way a senseless and vicious wrenching with the reins. It is an energetic bracing of the loin against the movement, which can vary in its force, and be just a small jolt; the horse quickly learns to obey this aid promptly in order to avoid the dreaded pressure on his back. The technique can be so perfected that the use of the spurs and the parades becomes inconspicuous, and the transitions beautifully smooth. The secret of this method's effectiveness lies in the fact that the horse is never annoyed by being compressed between hands and legs. In all methods of riding, the major sin is constant urging with the legs combined with simultaneous restraint by the reins. Riding is not as easy as driving a motorised vehicle: there is no smoke and no smell of burning to warn us that we are pressing on the accelerator and have forgotten to release the hand brake. Experimenting with the cowboy's method of riding with loose reins held in one hand would teach us how willingly horses obey the impulses of our legs if we stop trying meanwhile to put the brakes on with our hands; how willingly they come back to our hand when we stop urging them on with unconsciously tapping legs, or with tightly gripping legs. It would also teach us to use our aids with just sufficient determination to obtain exactly the desired result, and not more. To us, the method appears crude, because it is so different from the one which we know, but anybody who is prepared to experiment will never suffer again the consequences of holding on to the front while stimulating the rear. Getting the horse to collect himself is not done by restricting his movement and holding him tightly between legs and hands. Although the expression "breaking-in" is frowned upon nowadays, and we prefer to speak of "educating", taming and educating may have sometimes to go hand in hand; horses can misbehave in a thousand different ways, from stubbornly bucking on the spot to bolting, for reasons which can be fear, misunderstanding, clumsiness or plain cussedness. However, resistance can nearly always be nipped in the bud by intelligent, psychologically sound educational methods, without having to resort to coercive measures. The use of a lead-horse to act as a school-master is one example of a psychologically sound educational aid.

In the training of animals, we must always have sympathy and we will often have to rack our brain to understand their reactions. It is, in any case, fatal ever to act in anger. Whenever a conflict arises, it is essential that the outcome is in our favour and it is precisely for this reason that we must employ convincing means of control which the animal is capable of understanding at his actual stage of education. It is never by design that a horse refuses to obey his rider; he is incapable of scheming. Therefore, whenever he behaves in an objectionable manner, we must first find out the reason for his misbehaviour and this is not always obvious. Having discovered it, we must then carefully consider the appropriate counter-measures and carry them out with determination. If the thought sometimes occurs that it is our mistake which has caused the horse's rebellion, and if we can recognise our mistake and avoid repeating it, it will be apparent that we are gaining greater understanding and sympathy, the essential qualities of good riders and good trainers.

ELEMENTARY TRAINING

In the reporting of competitive events, it is frequently said that the success of the winning partnership is the result of the perfect harmony existing between the rider and the horse. Now harmony is not merely a mechanical adjustment of the movements of the rider to the movements of the horse. It is also harmony of wills, a psychological bond between the rider and the horse. The psychical attributes of horses are an endless subject of discussion: can they be said to have a soul, intelligence or just instincts? The arguments are only of theoretical interests. Every rider knows that all horses have a will of their own and that their powers of understanding vary considerably. The process of educating the horse can be based on three premises:

1 A horse can set his will against all the demands of men, as a result of unpleasant experience.
2 Given patience, his wilfulness can be broken and he can be compelled to obey.
3 Horses can be persuaded, by a gradual development of their understanding, to put all their strength, agility and intelligence, joyfully and trustingly, at the disposal of their riders for the common achievement of special performances; this is the ideal.

The learning capacity of all horses depends on their powers of perception and understanding; alert, watchful horses will obviously learn more easily than dull horses. However, in all cases, horses can learn to behave as we would wish them to behave by repeated experience of certain situations in which they eventually recognise an invariable pattern of sights and sounds. As teachers, our task is to provide them, in a consistent manner with such a pattern of impressions from which they will eventually learn to recognise the relationship between cause and effect. Obviously, the teacher himself must understand this relationship and be able to present the animal with clearly distinguishable impressions. He must have a deep knowledge of the science of horsemanship and he must be sympathetic. He must have a carefully considered plan of progressively increasing demands, of daily repetition of previous lessons, paying special attention to the horse's weaker points. Satisfactory progress will never be achieved by repeating the schooling figures of the manege while continuing to allow the horse to move in faulty posture and with irregular gaits.

There exist, however, two entirely different views on education. On one side we have the traditionalists, who believe in firm discipline; on the other side we have the exponents of learning by play, a method which has been so successful in the education of small children in kindergartens.

The first method is well-known and applies to the young horse as well as to the experienced and advanced horse: he must be taught to obey the aids, and must be disciplined and corrected every time he is inattentive or disobedient. For example, if he changes lead at the canter, out of fatigue or awkwardness, he must be checked immediately and made to canter again on the prescribed lead; it is firmly impressed upon him that changing lead is wrong and therefore forbidden, although at a later stage in his education he will be required to do precisely that.

The second method rejects pedantry, but it must be admitted that it is only suitable for particularly talented horses, who will need very little gymnastic work to become perfectly straight and to acquire an ideal outline. According to this method, the rider accepts what the horse presents him with; he does not demand, he does not forbid and he does not adhere to a systematic plan of schooling, providing that the gaits are correct and continue to remain correct. If the horse takes a certain position in preparation for a particular movement, the rider will adjust his own position accordingly to create in the mind of the horse an association between the impressions of the aids and the movement required. Thus, if the horse changes lead at the canter, the rider emphatically changes his own position in accord with the new position of the horse. If the horse canters false (counter-canter) on the circle, the rider will go with the movement, adjusting his seat and other aids to the position of the horse. After a short time, the horse will respond to the rider's change of position by a change of his own position, or of his gait. He will have learnt to understand the connection between the canter on one lead and a change of lead. The rider will even accept a tense and hovering trot, providing that it is a manifestation of abounding energy and high spirits, though he will aim at transforming the exaggeratedly exalted gait into a correct, smooth and elastic, trot. The bouncing action will eventually become a true, elegant passage, but in the meantime the horse's spirits will not have been completely dampened by strict prohibition of the movement at the beginning of schooling. The secret lies in steering the horse so adroitly that he discovers himself, almost accidently, how to transform his showy but over-tense action into a conveniently correct movement. The ability of the rider to recognise correct movement by feel is obviously essential; there is, for example, no point in insisting on a lower, more extended outline at the beginning of training, if the horse is already sufficiently strong and well-balanced to move straight and freely with a rider on his back and if the rider can sit easily to the movement. Why destroy at the beginning the verve which we will want the horse to show later? It is a retrograde step. If the rider feels perfectly comfortable at the sitting trot, it is a sure sign that the young horse is strong enough to be allowed a natural elevation of the forehand; he is, thanks to his natural constitution, in a class above the one which his rider was aiming for. It would be pointless to try to change his outline; all that remains to be done is to develop an even better poise.

By now, I hope that my readers will have realised that there are two objects to aim for in the education of the horse. The first is fulfilment of the prime requisites of a good saddle-horse: free forward movement, relaxation, style, carriage, balance, purity of the gaits; the second is performance at all levels of dressage or in the other equestrian sports. Satisfaction of the primary requirements must always be taken into consideration in the marking of dressage tests. The purpose of schooling, of the daily gymnastics to which we submit the horse, is fulfilment of the prime requisites; the accurate execution of the prescribed movements of the various tests should be of secondary importance. The movements are designed, firstly to show the results of schooling at various stages in the horse's education and, secondly to help rider and horse to acquire a sense of rhythm. The accurate execution of turns, circles, voltes, serpentines and movement on two-tracks is of little value if carriage and regularity suffer in the performance. Dressage riding is a dull and graceless pursuit when it does not primarily aim at satisfying the basic principles of good horsemanship.

Sympathy towards the horse is a first essential if we wish to preserve his enjoyment of life and his personality. Not all riders, unfortunately, possess this quality. It does not occur to these riders that nature designed the horse to move swiftly over great expanses of land and they become ill at ease whenever the horse shows exhilaration at feeling the turf under his hooves. For these riders, dressage is an object in itself. Fearing loss of control, they bridle the horse in tightly and never allow him to take an interest in his surroundings.

They never trust him to take care of himself and to adopt a natural position suitable to the requirements of self-preservation; their ideal is a dreary, subservient dressage robot. Yet horses, like humans, must learn by experience to recognise unevenness of the ground, to judge the height of obstacles and the point of take-off for a jump, to decide on the speed of the approach to an obstacle, to jump calmly from the walk, the trot or the gallop. They must learn to beware of overgrown ditches and of hedges that sometimes conceal a ditch on the landing side, and therefore always to jump these obstacles boldly to be sure of clearing them well. If all riders allowed their horses to be guided by instinct and to develop their intelligence by increasing their experience progressively, instead of trying to turn them into senseless jumping machines, we would not see so many rushing horses, jumping maniacs that get out of control as soon as an obstacle appears before them. They are like foolish dogs who can find no other pleasure in life than fetching and carrying the little pebbles which we throw for them. Nowadays, unfortunately, there remain so few open spaces where we can give our horses the opportunity to use initiative. Nevertheless, there can be no sadder fate for a young horse than to fall into the hands of someone who will nag him unmercifully towards a quick sale. While his former playmates are getting stronger and enjoying life out-of-doors with a confident, understanding rider, the less fortunate youngster is let out of his box only minutes each day. Not even given time to loosen up muscles stiffened by long hours of confinement, he is then made to go round the square of the manege, the corners of which frustrate any possibility of learning to move straight with the weight of a rider on his back or of extending himself to relax his sore muscles. If he is sometimes let loose, it is still within the confines of the walls of the dreary manege, and his violent antics on those rare occasions ought to strike us as a desperate protest against the violence done to his nature. His work is as dull and stupefying as the dreary toil of a gin-horse. Because he never gets a chance to gallop, his muscles cannot develop and his joints wear out prematurely; he loses any natural impulsion he may have had and either becomes emaciated or grossly fat, according to his temperament. When, at last, the time comes to ride him outside, the consequences of this unnatural upbringing are disastrous and either the rider or the inexperienced horse, intoxicated by this first taste of freedom, will come to grief.

A rider who has no time or no inclination to take a young horse hunting should at least let someone else who enjoys it, do so. It is out-of-doors that a horse must be trained in the early stages of his education, so that he learns to enjoy work while gaining strength and experience. We cannot expect a horse to be calm, to have impulsion and to perform brilliantly in competitions, unless he has previously been given sufficient opportunity to notice and recognise the sights and sounds of the world outside his home surroundings; all his senses must be given time to adjust to strange impressions and, towards this end, it is essential that, at the beginning of his training, he is allowed freedom of forward movement and an unconstricted head and neck carriage. He will have to learn to obey the quiet but firm commands of his rider to go forward, even when his eyes order his limbs to stop moving; but until he has become accustomed to this sort of experience, it is normal for a young horse to be startled at the sight, for example, of a flock of sheep on the roadside and, ignoring his rider for a moment, come suddenly to a standstill. It is only out-of-doors that a horse can learn by experience while also learning to remain attentive to his rider, to obey the aids, to maintain regular gaits and forget his fears.

The training of all horses must consist of three equally important elements: education, exercise and dressage gymnastics. As training procedures have been described in numerous books, I do not intend to do so again, but will merely compare each of these elements with the others and attempt to explain why difficulties and setbacks are unavoidable unless equal attention is devoted to each one of these parts. If the rider wants to establish permanently mutual trust between himself and his horse, he will have to consider things other than his own influence; he will have to learn to distinguish between unwillingness and inability, and to select the most appropriate methods of teaching or correcting behaviour. For example, insufficient impulsion can be due to several factors: muscular weakness, abnormal co-ordination or movements, or untamed will, due to hidden reserves of strength which only show up in particular and awkward situations. A dangerous refusal to go forward can happen at any gait, and the rider must first be able to recognise its cause. If our aim is to produce a useful, sensible and reliable horse, we must never concentrate more on one of the elements of training than on the others. Neither rider nor horse should ever be allowed to become bored by dogged repetition of a monotonous programme which will dull the senses and, besides this, the horse must learn to recognise man as a friend who makes life interesting; the relatively short period of time which he spends out of his box each day should be made enjoyable, so that he will always look forward to it with pleasure. As strolling out-of-doors is a natural thing for all animals reared outside, we must take advantage of this and ride outside as much as possible, preferably over rough and hilly ground which will compel the horse to look after himself. Providing we adopt a light seat which does not disturb him, a healthy horse easily accommodates himself to our weight, and his gaits will remain regular. Jogging, hurried or hesitant steps are always caused by restraining hands and we must, therefore, confine our influences to the occasional and discerning use of our legs or whip to maintain regular gaits, or of our hands only when we wish to change from one gait to a slower one, or when we want to come to a halt. We may sometimes have to act energetically, but we must always yield as soon as the horse submits; pulling and all other resistances to the hands will then never occur. Furthermore, frequently halting to let a young novice graze, helps him to stretch the muscles of his back and relax the muscles of his jaws.

A horse must never be ridden on taut reins until his obedience to the impulsive aids has become unquestionable, and, once a tension of reins is permissible it must always remain sufficiently easy to preserve complete freedom of movement and absolute regularity of the gaits. The rider who thinks that he can let a horse feel a tension of the reins must be very sensitive to straightness and equilibrium: the tension should never produce an increase or decrease of speed, it should never spoil the forward movement and if the rider cannot feel a change in the regularity of the movement, he will let the horse get away with resistance. In the early stages of training, at any rate, exercise is more important than gymnastic schooling, as the latter is understood in dressage, though obviously the horse must be controllable so that he can be ridden anywhere, through streams, across ditches, over small obstacles; at the beginning, it is useful to let him follow a lead, but as soon as possible he must go alone.

As soon as the horse understands the simple controls of legs without hands, and hands without legs, he must go for long rides across country. The gradual building up of muscles will make future dressage work much easier; most of the difficulties of dressage are due to weakness of the muscles of the back and the hindquarters. Long, easy gallops are especially good, favourable as they are to the development of body and mind, and because the gallop is, next to

Riding up and down hills strengthens muscles, tendons and ligaments.

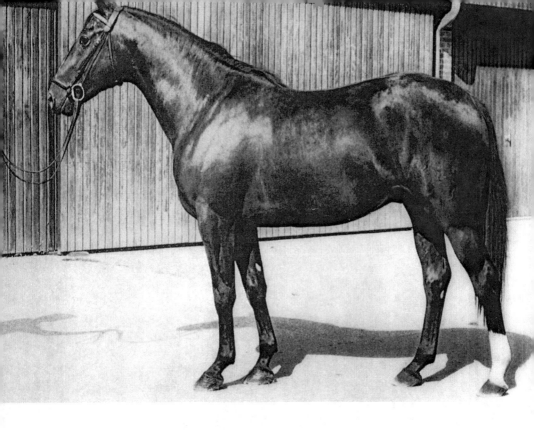

Young horses are frequently shown *(above)* in excessively gross condition. *(Below)* A properly-conditioned horse, well muscled-up and fit for work.

the walk, the natural gait of the horse. I do not mean a fast gallop; the aim is to settle the horse and to sharpen his perceptions, certainly not to excite him. Long, calm galloping is especially beneficial to young thoroughbreds before they go into training for racing; it teaches them that they must not run away under saddle but must accept the rider's orders.

Another advantage of uneven terrain is that it strengthens tendons and ligaments. Like humans who are used only to the smooth pavement of cities and easily sprain an ankle when they have to run on a rutted stretch of ground, horses also quickly damage themselves on the first occasion of a gallop out-of-doors if they have always worked on the smooth surface of the manege. In youth, the lameness which results from a strain of muscle, tendon or ligament is not, usually, long lasting and recovery is nearly always complete; later on in life, a horse that has not been rationally exercised in his youth easily injures his tendons and joints with little chance of perfect healing.

Regarding character, horses with a lot of natural impulsion have an energetic temperament and are strong-minded. They must be taught perfect obedience. For a good rider, obedience means quick response to his aids and he knows that this will come as a result of education; on the other hand, it is when they ride very well-schooled, sensitive and energetic horses that weak riders feel helpless; their aids are confusing and exasperate the horse. As good horses cannot always be ridden by good riders, it is necessary to accustom them from an early age to being ridden out-of-doors so that they learn to be sensible and to use their own intelligence. Some people believe that horses need the tension of the reins if they are not to stumble; I would answer them by saying that a system of training which leads to such unreliability must be wrong. A horse should be calm, sure-footed and energetic on a loose rein as well as on a taut one. He must always obey the impulsive aid calmly, not by running away. If there is an obstacle in his way, he must recognise it from a sufficient distance, judge its size carefully, and increase his speed just enough to be able to clear it. On steep downhill slopes or stiff uphill climbs, he must learn to look after himself and should never want to rely on the reins.

Many riders confuse "cannot" with "will not". For example, when a young horse that has learnt to jump on the lunge is ridden, and stops at an obstacle which we know that he can jump with ease, it would be wrong to punish him, be it only by making him rein-back. This would increase his fear and upset him. If the horse is obedient to the legs, he will jump on a second approach if he has been shown the obstacle and been allowed to smell it; he may have to be given a lead with another horse. If, on the other hand, obedience to the legs is not confirmed, it is better to give up the attempt to make him jump than to start a long argument which will lay the ground for a worse form of disobedience, running-out. The hunting field is always the best first school for jumping. Turning round after an obstacle to jump it in reverse direction is nonsensical; the horse must first learn that, if he has to jump, it is in order to be able to proceed, straight ahead, and training over a winding course of obstacles in preparation for show-jumping must never start before a horse has learnt to jump confidently on straight lines in open country. As for jumping over a pole and into water, this is contrary to the common sense of man and beast and this sort of obstacle is included in competitons for the sole purpose of testing unquestioning obedience. When teaching a young horse to jump out-of-doors, it is very good practice to dismount sometimes immediately after passing over an obstacle so as to let him have a taste of grass. Horses that are not yet very calm and clever can thus be taught to stand still and graze if a rider dismounts unintentionally. Permission to graze with the bridle on but the noseband unbuckled is a well-proven method of creating a solid bond of friendship between horse and rider.

Open disobedience, however, must always be punished instan-taneously and the rider's will must always prevail. For example, if a horse kicks out at the whip and refuses to move onward, he must be punished with several strokes of the whip—rein tension abandoned —until he consents to go forward; even if he rushes forward, he must then be rewarded immediately, for this is in accord with the law of cause and effect which horses quickly learn to understand. When a horse runs out before an obstacle, he cannot be too sharply checked, turned around and firmly urged on again. Contrary to stopping, which is due to uncertainty or faint-heartedness, running out is flagrant disobedience and must always be punished.

Habitual shying is a very unpleasant vice. A young horse who trusts his rider will seldom shy; when he sees an unknown object, he usually stops to have a good look at it. In the case of the young horse, still learning that everything strange is not necessarily dangerous, the rider must remain patient and passive and communicate his own confidence to the horse by speaking in a soothing manner; the young horse must be allowed as much time as he needs to convince himself of the inoffensiveness of the new object. However, if he turns about and tries to run away, he must be immediately stopped, not punished, but made to walk back to the same place until he has realised that there is no danger and has regained his confidence. This sort of procedure will teach him to respect the rider's commands, whilst also allowing him to notice the sights and sounds which he will normally encounter on his way. He must learn to heed from far away any movement or object not normally part of the country scene. The acute senses of horses have warned many patrol riders in wartime of a danger which their human eyes or ears were unable to dectect early enough. Human impatience and punishment are usually responsible for habitual shying, a vice against which neither soothing words nor familiarisation with every possible cause of fear are of any avail; the confirmed shyer will always startle at the sight of every object which he has not seen before; if he is already perfectly obedient to the aids, it may be possible to control him by putting him in a counter-shoulder-in position before coming level with an object that might frighten him, providing that his respect for the rider is greater than his fear of the unknown and that he knows that he will suffer pain if he dares to disobey. All the same, riding an habitual shyer is as relaxing as sitting on a keg of dynamite.

There cannot be many riders still alive who know the pleasure of riding at night, and perhaps only men who can remember night patrols in wartime will be able to understand what I mean. The night is always friendly to animals and she can also be friendly to those men for whom she holds no fears. In the dark of night, an impatient rider will learn to love his horse better, because he has to rely on the horse's better night vision. Nothing can be more soothing than riding an experienced campaign horse in darkness, and if the night has such an effect on the rider, she can become our ally in the training of horses; the most restless horse will become amenable when darkness forces him to be careful; he will lower his head and relax his back muscles; he will obey our leg aids without running away; he doesn't shy, for fear of jumping into a ditch or running into a solid obstacle; he becomes more alert and cautious and also more sure-footed, more active and, therefore, less liable to stumble. So many impressions will be striking his senses that he will forget his usual resistances, will gladly accept his riders guidance and will learn much more from a few lessons in the dark than from a long course of instruction during the day.

Meanwhile, his rider will also be learning. If one rides at the canter alongside a ditch in the twilight of evening, one will discover that the horse's tendency to veer towards the side of his normal inflexion (nearly always towards the right) must be continually corrected; one gets to understand balance, because if the horse goes on the forehand, one feels as if one was sliding down a hill. Cantering along a bridle-path in the dusk, in the woods, forces one to look up instead of constantly watching the horse's head, because it is only by the dim light showing through the branches overhead that one can find one's way; however, it is in pitch darkness, when one cannot see the horse at all, that one is effectively compelled to sit straight. There are so many advantages to riding in the dark that all riders should try it; the night will present them with many things that they can only obtain by force or stratagem from a wayward horse in daylight.

Horses must learn to economise effort, and this they will never do unless they are frequently made to exert themselves to the point of fatigue while they are young. If they are allowed to gallop very occasionally, for short periods of time, over short distances, they quickly and vainly use up all their energy in the first flush of excitement. On the contrary, if they are made to gallop regularly over the same ground, after a few kilometres at the trot, they learn to gallop calmly in long, rounded strides and, even more importantly, they learn a good breathing technique. This is the way to get them fit and to teach them to husband their strength for the last decisive effort at full speed. Long hunts are a very good school for future race-horses; the frequent checks will teach them how silly it is to pull in order to keep up with the field if the other horses are so frequently stopping, galloping and stopping again; fatigue will teach them to behave sensibly. Fatigue is also the easiest and most rational cure for calming highly-strung horses; if they are ridden at the walk three times a day, each time, if possible, for two hours, they soon calm down and start sighing with weariness. However, when stolid horses pull, it is because they haven't the energy to carry themselves properly under the weight of the rider and find it easier to go on the forehand; then the rider must sit heavily instead of riding in a light, forward seat as is usual in the early stages of training.

We must remember that riding in a manege or an outdoor enclosed arena is merely a means to an end. It has become the usual thing because of excessive emphasis on dressage and insufficient leisure. Yet, education and physical exercise are as important as dressage and, for this reason, one should ride out-of-doors as often as possible. If our aim is to produce a sensible, obedient and hardy horse, we cannot neglect any of the three aspects of training.

RELAXATION

What does the word "relaxed" mean when it is applied to human movements?

If we watch children doing gymnastics, we cannot fail to notice how much they vary in agility; they may all be doing the same exercises, but some are strikingly nimble and graceful, others are clumsy and ungainly. The graceful ones are relaxed, the clumsy ones are tense. Those who are relaxed can use their limbs easily and effectively, but the tense ones are awkward. Awkwardness is not innate; it is the result of lack of suitable exercise, aggravated by timidity and lack of self-confidence. Persons who are awkward in their movements, are also usually too shy to raise their voice; this is why experienced athletic coaches start loosening-up exercises by getting the whole class to shout in unison, so that the awkward ones can forget their inhibitions. A considerable degree of ability to relax is obviously very important for the difficult art of gymnastics (and I do not mean those exercises which have degenerated into ugly acrobatics), but relaxation is also obviously present or absent in the far less complicated movements of walking and running. Good development of strength and agility is not possible if the body is tense; relaxation is essential for muscular control, for good reflexes, for good breathing technique, for any kind of activity. However, the body cannot relax unless the mind is also relaxed.

Horses also, even when they are at liberty outdoors, show different ability to relax and if they are startled, we notice that some of them gallop with beautifully co-ordinated movements and others with tense backs and a choppy action. We cannot predict from this observation how they will behave under saddle because this will depend as much on their temperament as on their physical aptitudes; initial experience of men and early training days are determinant factors; an unintelligent and impatient trainer will aggravate the physical and mental tensions which all horses feel at the beginning, while a good trainer eases these tensions because he knows how to get the horse to trust him and accept his weight in the saddle. Like humans, horses remain rigid in their bodies while they remain anxious and suspicious; we cannot expect them to be able to trot or canter or gallop while they still feel insecure with a rider on their back at the halt or the walk. They should first be allowed to "meditate", as I have already explained, first in familiar surroundings and later in leisurely walks full of interest for them. These meditating exercises for the horse make great demands of patience on the rider and are just as wholesome for him as for the horse—frequently even more necessary.

Relaxed use of muscles, of groups of muscles or of the whole body is not inherent and cannot be learnt quickly just in a few lessons at the beginning of training; it is an ability which comes with practise and habit; it is the final result of education, exercise and gymnastic schooling; it is an ability which once acquired is never forgotten, but can continue to be perfected.

The loosening-up exercises which we should do at the beginning of every lesson are necessary to warm-up, to limber-up joints stiffened by long hours of standing; they can do no more than restore the degree of relaxation of which the horse is already capable. Loosening-up is not the same thing as working in a relaxed manner. Looseness and relaxation are often confused.

There are various methods of loosening joints, some better suited to certain horses or riders depending on their preference or aptitudes. I have known riders of perfectly poised horses start with a few steps of piaffe as soon as they ride out of the stable; others choose to trot or to canter on loose reins, others prefer a long period of exercise at the walk and some limber up over cavalletti and small jumps. It all depends on the temperament and the physical condition of the horse and on the rider's feeling; he must know the degree of skill that the horse has already achieved and must be able to recognise how soon serious gymnastic work can start. When the horse moves freely and calmly, when he neither hurries nor holds back, then he has loosened-up.

There are no hard and fast rules, there is no typical method for loosening-up. I once lived in an hotel at the same time as an acrobat who would limber-up as soon as he got out of bed by performing several somersaults around his room. I, personally, would be quite content to reach a less spectacular degree of suppleness by just hopping. The aptitudes of horse and man are variable; the will to loosen-up is what matters and, providing the will exists, long sessions are unnecessary. The perfectly poised horse is already relaxed when he comes out of his box and loosens up after only a few strides.

Tenseness, tension, stiffness, relaxation, looseness, slackness, as they affect the mechanisms of posture and movement, are much used words which need to be better understood and I will explain these concepts later *(Chapter 5)*. At present, I will merely affirm that horsemen ought to have a sound knowledge of the functional anatomy of muscles and ought to make the effort to gain this knowledge instead of using a jargon which they do not understand.

To produce movement, muscles can alternately shorten and lengthen to their maximum possible extent; they then produce optimum range of movement. All muscles can also be maintained in a shortened, contracted state, not only when shortening to the utmost possible limit but also when they shorten to a reduced length. If they remain in this contracted state, they start aching, become fatigued and lose their power. We can demonstrate this fact when we use our biceps muscle to carry a heavy bucket of water with a flexed elbow; not only the biceps muscle itself soon starts aching, but also all the other muscles which must co-operate in the action. Muscles are under tension in this state of sustained contraction, but an excessive, therefore harmful tension. It is hypertension that is undesirable. Therefore, what we mean when we say that the horse must not be tense, is that he must not be hypertense. We certainly do not want absence of tension, which is slackness. Tension is needed for locomotion, but a passive tension of unresisting muscles; in this state, they are controllable, reliable, effective organs; when they are thus stretched, they are like elastic bands, always ready to shorten quickly to produce a desirable form, and the more they have allowed themselves to be stretched, the more powerful can their contraction be. It is the elastic tension of muscles, easily maintained through force of habit, which gives the sporting horse a posture, or carriage, in which all groups of muscles are constantly returning to their normal length; it allows optimum scope of movement, imparts liveliness, beauty and harmony to the gaits with minimum effort.

Hypertension is a condition in which muscles are held in a shortened state; it is fatiguing and impairs the activity of other groups of muscles. However, in certain conditions, some groups of muscles must be contracted, for example, when a horse lands after clearing an obstacle, he must strongly contract his forearm muscles to resist gravity and immediately relax them sufficiently to dampen the shock of impact. So this is an opposite event, a relaxation of the tightness of a contracted muscle, but only within limits, in contrast to the active shortening of a muscle from its maximum stretching, for the purpose of movement. When we jump off a wall, we keep our knees slightly bent and contract our thigh muscles but they must be ready to relax to allow the deep flexion of the knees which softens landing. We see the same sort of event in the Levades and other airs above the ground performed by High-School horses. It must be noted, however, that this sort of tension is only possible for a matter of seconds; if it is sustained any longer, it produces cramp.

We must clearly understand the two different functions of muscles: production of movement and gravity resistance; and if we understand the difference between fast contraction of a stretched muscle, and relaxation of tension of a contracted muscle, we will also be able to understand how, by elastically bracing the top of the horse's neck (the bow in front of the hand), we also brace elastically the loins (the bow behind the hand) and thus engage the hocks.

Now I come to the sort of looseness of muscles which is slackness and produces disunity. Admittedly, the muscles are also lengthened, but this sort of stretching is not at all the same as the tautness of a relaxed muscle. Slack muscles have lost normal, healthy tonus, either temporarily because of laziness or fatigue, or permanently as a result of debility. In the first case, they are unready to contract, in the latter case, they are unable to do so. In both cases, we have a disunited horse, with shambling movements.

All that has been said about muscles and groups of muscles, applies to the complete musculature of the body. Unyielding contraction of either the flexor groups of muscles, or of the extensors, impairs the activity of the opposing groups, prevents natural movement, causes stiffness and an ungainly attitude. In contrast, the relaxed horse can be elastically bent like a bow, at all paces but especially at the gallop, and his paces can be extended or collected while always remaining lively. A horse galloping in a state of relaxed tension appears to fly over the ground.

Smooth, alternation of shortening and stretching of strong, elastic muscles gives good body control, quickness, reflexes, cleverness in all situations. In the absence of muscular tension there can be no animation; conversely, if there is no animation, there can be no tension and no possibility of varying the scope of movement. It is the elastic muscular tension of the horse which must present us with the elastic tension of reins and, in turn, it is the latter which enables us to play with the muscles of the neck, of the poll and the mouth as if they were the strings of a firm bow.

We will examine later the functions of the principal groups of muscles of the horse and realise that there are two kinds of muscles:

1 Mainly fleshy, very elastic muscles for the production of movement.
2 Mainly tendinous muscles, in which the fleshy tissue is considerably interspersed with fibrous tissue; they are the anti-gravity muscles.

The function of the first is dynamic, the function of the latter is static.

The tendinous muscles act as braces, leaving the fleshy muscles free to serve the purpose of locomotion. The co-ordinated action of tendinous muscles helps the horse to maintain his balance under the weight of a rider and allows the muscles of locomotion to function freely. It is only when muscles can function in their normal capacity that intelligent training will develop their strength, volume and elasticity.

In order to progress in his training, the horse must learn to carry himself effortlessly in good posture; to this end, he will need daily exercise, just like the fingers of a pianist. It is, however, essential that the rider himself learns to acquire a firm, relaxed posture. A slack or a stiff rider has on the horse the effect of a foreign body, impairing balance and hampering movement. A faulty posture of the rider prevents the horse from relaxing and destroys his muscular co-ordination.

Humans show the same varying degrees of muscular tension as horses: slack, rounded backs; rigid backs; firm, erect, relaxed backs; rigidly bent elbows, unyielding hands; stiffly straightened elbows, heavy hands; hands correctly held in front of the body keeping contact with the horse's mouth with elastic arm muscles always ready to yield, shoulder blades blending into the back as a result of overall poise, but not stiffly; gripping legs; slack, thumping legs; or, correctly, legs that effortlessly maintain contact with the horse's sides and are thus able to feel the movements of the trunk and the hindlimbs.

The rider can accord his movements with the movements of the horse only if he holds himself firmly and easily upright; conversely, a young horse will not be able to relax the muscles of his back nor properly to trust the bit unless the rider carries himself well, without stiffness or slackness, and carries his hands in front of his body, steadily, but always ready to yield. A stiff rider, his face contorted by effort, his jaws so tightly clenched that their muscles ache, who cannot play with his stirrups and the muscles of his legs, is useless, despite his efforts to maintain a correctly upright position.

With the horse, the outward signs of the beginning of relaxation are rhythmical, pure and free gaits, relaxed oscillations of the straightly carried tail, contented snorting showing calm respiratory movements, relaxed tension of the muscles of the top of the neck, relaxed "chewing" of the bit, smooth movements of the back which cushion the rider instead of jolting him. The overall impression is one of calmness and contentment; the movements are fluent and elegant.

Hypertension, in contrast, shows up in stiffness of the neck, continuously flicking ears, choppy gaits with uneven steps and a tail which either lashes furiously or is held continuously to one side or is clamped between the buttocks. The worst manifestations of hypertension are jogging and pacing but there are other signs, such as a dead pull on one rein, a crooked tail carriage, grinding or regular clacking of teeth, tongue over the bit, and, in the case of male horses, a ceaseless wind-sucking noise of the sheath.

Relaxation is essential when horse and rider have to negotiate uneven terrain and difficult obstacles. Only relaxed muscular co-ordination leaves all the other senses free to concentrate and gives those quick, precise, unconscious reactions at the sudden appearance of unsuspected hazards, which enable rider and horse to avert a fall, or to escape injury if a fall cannot be avoided. How many times have we seen a horse save himself from a fall after jumping by reaching out, in the nick of time, with a foreleg, or seen him take a tumble innocuously while his equally relaxed rider rolls safely away as the horse falls down; how many times also, have we seen horse and rider prematurely brace themselves against danger so that the horse, restricted by the reins, lands on his chin and breaks his neck and the rider, arms outstretched, lands on his face and shoulder and breaks his collar-bone? Cross-country riding despite any amount of experience will always remain a dangerous sport for nervous riders and nervous horses who cannot relax. The ability to relax is equally indispensable to the sport of racing. Trainers of race-horses know that it is the ability to relax which protects horses against breakdown of tendons and other injuries; there is no doubt that most accidents are caused by the strain of endeavour in the crucial moments of a race rather than by fatigue.

The ability to relax is partly inborn, but also a matter of practise. Rider and horse will have to work all their life at perfecting this ability, to the same extent as they will have to work at improving their style and their sense of balance. However, even after they have acquired this ability and learnt to apply it in all situations, they can lose it through lack of practise or as a result of painful experience; also because of anxiousness due to pain in some part of the body or limbs, stage-fright in public performance, or because of normal apprehensions and cautiousness which come with age.

After all said and done, good performance always depends on relaxation; it is a basic requirement for specialisation in all branches of competitive riding.

BALANCE

The purpose of all the gymnastic dressage exercises is the achievement of perfect balance. This is the beginning, the means and the end of the training of horse and rider, whether the final object is artistic equitation or sport. In this chapter, I will not discuss the position of the rider when mounted on the horse, but try to explain how the horse first learns to balance his own mass and then learns to balance the weight of a rider. It is obviously not enough to discuss and understand the theory of balance; we must educate ourselves to acquire a good sense of balance, with our feet on the ground, before we get into a saddle.

Very few humans are naturally endowed with a good sense of balance; they must achieve it by educating themselves. It is most entertaining to observe how other people walk and easy to criticise certain postures which may, at some time, have struck us as graceful and elegant. However, having amused ourselves at the expense of others, we must then examine our own posture and gait. Our self-esteem may suffer a shock the first time we attempt to do some gymnastic exercises and try to stand on a length of rail or on a gymnastic beam, but we will discover instinctively that we can use two methods to stay in balance.

First of all we use our outstretched arms as an aid to stay balanced; later we will discover that a better method is to bend the knees and lower our centre of gravity; the more we lower our centre of gravity, the better we place it over the forward bent knee, the better we will be able to walk, and then to stand securely on the narrow rail. This lowering of the centre of gravity by bending the knees is what all beginners learn in their first ski-ing lesson. An even more difficult test of lateral balance comes when we close our eyes, or take them off the rail to look around.

Once we have learnt to control our lateral balance by slightly flexing our knees, the next disappointment comes when we attempt to turn round or to stand obliquely across the rail; we then discover that perfect longitudinal balance, that is backward and forward, is even more difficult to achieve; a good exercise consists in laying a number of parallel rails on the ground, approximately 50 cm apart and then trying to step from rail to rail, like a bird hopping from one branch to another, or to stand on one leg for as long as possible. This exercise makes us discover, even better than the previous one, that we can use two systems to control balance: extrinsic and intrinsic. We can either gesticulate more or less frantically with arms and legs (extrinsic controls), or we can use our abdominal, back, and shoulder muscles to keep a median position, in which our centre of gravity rotates around a small area of support (intrinsic control). If we devoted ten minutes daily to the above exercises, we would be rewarded with the most acute sense of balance and astonishingly improved agility; they are surprisingly difficult exercises, which demand firm back and abdominal muscles and preclude fatness in these regions.

We may feel rather ridiculous when we start applying our newly acquired technique to the ordinary action of walking; some might think that we were playing at being a Red Indian stalking his prey; but the underlying principle is that the weight of the body must be entirely supported and balanced on the leg in advance, slightly bent at the knee. In this newly discovered equilibrium, we no longer stagger from one leg on to the other, we stop swaying and our walk will have greatly gained in elasticity. After a certain amount of training, walking will have become a really enjoyable sport. These experiments on our own body will begin to convince us that dressage gymnastics can effectively improve a horse's skill and sporting performance.

Of course, comparisons between two-footed and four-footed animals are deceptive, but the main object of these exercises is to demonstrate how difficult it is to stand or walk on a narrow base of support. The balancing exercise on a rail is only possible for man, with his superior intelligence and conscious self-control; in fact, some of us will never be able to stand on a rail, one foot in front of the other, while looking around; however, a four-footed animal finds it just as difficult to follow without wavering a perfectly straight and narrow path, and if the rider has not developed an acute sense of balance, he will not feel the horse deviating from the straight line. Novice riders are quite unaware that a horse may be swaying from side to side, or moving more or less sideways.

The horse also has at his disposal two mechanisms for the control of balance: an extrinsic one and an intrinsic one. He cannot of course, like us, lift his arms aside, nor can he bend his body, but he can keep his feet under his wavering centre of gravity and, in so doing, swerve from side to side of the straight path; alternatively, he can broaden his base of support by placing his hindfeet to the side of the line followed by his forefeet, thus moving more or less sideways. This sideways movement is normal with most animals and is particularly striking in the dog; it corresponds to the human walk with feet turned out, which increases stability but at the expense of speed and agility, and spares the muscles but to the detriment of joints and ligaments. Usually, however, the ridden horse uses one hindleg only, placing it like a walking-stick at the side of the track of the forelegs (*falling out* with a hindfoot). To help us to feel this falling-out with a hindfoot, at the beginning we should have an assistant on the ground who can draw our attention to it. The horse can also use his neck as a stabiliser, which he does by leaning on the bit. When a horse leans on the bit, whether he is moving hurriedly or sluggishly, it shows that he is not in equilibrium; at times his forelegs, at times his hindlegs are carrying a disproportionate amount of the load. Whereas our man on his rail would just step off it if he felt his balance impaired, the horse, to save himself, has to keep his legs under his wavering centre of gravity; if it gets too far forward, he hurries his steps; if it gets too far backward, he slows his pace to a shuffle. The same signs of instability continue to show for a long time with some horses in the lateral movements, in this case, the support being taken on one rein instead of both.

Good hands are essential to help the horse discover the strength to balance himself without outside support. Time and again, we realise how difficult it is to obtain just the right effect from the half-parades, which should merely assist the horse to recover his equilibrium. If we exert a continuous pulling action, the horse will snatch at the reins or lean on the hand; if our hands are unsteady and incapable of maintaining an even rein tension, the horse will hesitate in his forward movement. If he is to accept the bit, our hands must be neither unsteady nor rigidly set, but must passively maintain a smooth connection with the bit through the reins. It is perfectly natural for the horse to seek the assistance of the bit to balance himself. The support which he tries to find through the bit and the reins on the rider's body can be likened to the balancing aid used by tight-rope walkers in the form of a pole or an umbrella; it is a form of extrinsic control of balance. If the rider uses his reins merely to control speed, rather than for the purpose of obtaining an elegant head and neck carriage, he is helping the animal to learn how to preserve its poise by the proper use of its own muscles.

As regards the intrinsic mechanism of control of balance, I really do believe that the only way to understand the horse's problems is to practice gymnastics on our own feet; they will not only help us to develop a better sense of balance, but they will also show us how much muscular activity and mental concentration are required to achieve perfect pose. Flexion of the haunches, collection, lightening of the forehand, straightness, impulsion, animation, suppleness are all equally important features of the ultimate end, which is the achievement of this poise, and they must be developed concurrently. However, the gymnastic exercises of the manege which have been devised to improve each element will remain fruitless so long as the horse has not learnt to balance himself efficiently with a rider on his back at the natural gaits. Collecting aids may be necessary to achieve this end, but they must never impair the paramount essential, that is, impulsion. A tactful rider is a rider who can feel and maintain accord between desire to go forward and equilibrium. The art of the good trainer resides in his ability to educate the horse to dispense with extrinsic balancing aids. It is by straightening the horse's natural inflexion to one side that the trainer teaches him to use his intrinsic controls of balance, but he will never demand more than the horse's present state of mental and muscular development permits.

Firstly, however, the horse must learn lateral balance. If we are not yet very sensitive to any wavering from a straight line, we must choose a fixed point, a tree or some other object, towards which we direct the horse in as straight a line as possible. We need to concentrate to feel whether the croup is deviating to one side, causing the horse to move more or less sideways, or whether he is veering by following an instinctive tendency to move in one direction, usually the right (the circling instinct is discussed in Chapter 3).

Our ability to correct these tendencies will depend mainly on our ability to produce impulsion. By aiming at a given point, we automatically improve the horse's ability to move straight on straightlines. A horse that cannot move on a narrow track cannot be said to be balanced; he can only maintain a straight course by staggering unsteadily from one leg onto the next. When we come to the advanced dressage movements, the piaffe for example, if we feel effort and resistance, we should ask an assistant on the ground to observe whether the horse is setting his hindfeet further apart in that movement than at the walk and is appearing to become fatigued; if this is the case, the difficulty is due less to the effort of flexing the haunches, than to a lack of balance which causes the horse to support himself for a longer period of time on one diagonal than on the other. He sways with his croup and his hindlegs get tired; he then places them further apart, but his forefeet step so closely together that they risk treading on one another and injuring their coronets. The cure for the swaying of the hindquarters is resumption of forward movement, and less flexion of the haunches. In forward movement, the period of support of each diagonal is shortened and the horse need not resort to a widening of his base of support. We ought to know that, originally, the piaffe was nothing other than a gymnastic preparation of the hindquarters for the leaps in the airs above the ground of the High-School; it was not an object in itself.

I have mentioned the piaffe, but in all the gaits it is essential to have sufficient impulsion for the horse to be straight enough to be able to remain easily balanced on a narrow track. We must teach ourselves to remain constantly aware of balance, to become so attentive and sensitive to the state of balance of the horse that we feel uncomfortable whenever the hindlegs develop a force which cannot be felt to pass straight between our own legs.

There is a further reason for practising balancing exercises on the ground; they will help us to realise how much energy we waste and the strain which we impose on our muscles, tendons and ligaments when we do not keep our body properly poised above our feet; they will also help us to understand the real purpose of the gymnastic exercises to which we submit the horse when we school him in dressage. If the manege figures evolved in the past fail to produce the results which we expect, it may well be because our horse has not yet acquired sufficiently good balance; once we realise this, we will start using those same figures with a perception which considerably surpasses the requirements of mere craftsmanship.

Achievement of lateral balance is only a first stage, but it is on this achievement that all further progress depends. The development of balance in the sagittal plane takes much longer and is much more difficult to achieve; this balance in the sagittal plane is what we call equilibrium. It is the rider who teaches the horse to carry him in such perfect equilibrium that he, the rider, can maintain his vertical position with ease at all gaits; a peak of perfection is reached when he feels completely undisturbed by the horse's motion even if he had just imbibed a whole magnum of champagne. He must imagine himself in the position of an urn full of water poised on the head of a graceful woman; every ruffling of the surface of the water shocks her into adjusting her deportment: this illustrates how carefully the horse has to learn to carry his rider.

How can we presume to expect our horse to achieve such a fine sense of balance if we do not try to acquire it ourselves? It will certainly never suddenly come to us accidentally after months or even years of merely hoping, and it is not enough to understand the importance of balance in theory; it is only when we genuinely attempt to preserve our balance by suppleness and poise rather than strength of grip that we realise how difficult it is to distribute our weight equally on both seat bones; a crooked seat, unequal pressure on the stirrups, excessive dependence on the stirrups, sideways inclination of the upper body, hanging on the reins are all faults which we will never correct so long as we remain content with a theoretical understanding of the meaning of poise.

I cannot prescribe a programme of work which will teach the horse himself to acquire this perfect sense of balance. As with all other things, we may have to use very firm aids at the beginning, but as the horse learns, by the repetition of our influences, to respond more promptly, our aids will become less obvious. Let me take another example from the circus: a man, standing on a ball, tries to get it to move in a certain direction. At first, in his efforts to stay on the ball, he sways in all directions, over-compensating for imminent

An inexperienced but talented jumper, over-estimating the height of the obstacle *(above)*; the experienced jumper *(below)* has learnt to judge the size of the obstacles accurately and makes no more effort than necessary. Fritz Thiedemann on Godewind demonstrates a good jumping style, forearms well extended and hindfeet tucked up.

Experienced jumpers learn how to get out of trouble in critical situations and how to correctly estimate the size of obstacles. Kathy Kusner on High Noon *(above)* and T. Brennan on Kilmoon *(below)*.

A confident child rider *(above)* shows an independence of hands and seat which the adult novice rider finds so difficult to achieve. Ponies can be clever jumpers *(below)*.

The purpose of horse trials is to prove that the horse is obedient, well-trained and well-ridden. The cross-country phase over solid obstacles demands great courage on the part of horse and rider; the risks are great.

loss of balance, until he can keep a central position and remain upright. Finally, he will be able to move the ball as he wishes by hardly visible actions of his legs and body.

It is in a similar manner that the rider balances his horse with the aids at his disposal, until the horse himself has learnt to balance the rider; the latter will increasingly find himself in the role of a pole, a central axis from which all movements proceed and towards which they constantly return. A rider who feels as well as he comprehends the co-ordination of the driving aids with the restraining aids, who never urges forward to the extent of driving the horse onto his forehand, nor restrains enough to spoil or completely destroy impulsion, will always be able to maintain constant, fluent forward movement. Balanced between the alternating forward urging aids and the restraining ones, the horse finally learns to adjust his own centre of gravity to the centre of gravity of the rider; horse and rider are then transformed into a completely united system and with improved collection can remain poised on a progressively decreasing area of support. With enough mental concentration, it is possible to refine the aids to such a degree that the horse can be made to move his body backward and forward without ever lifting a limb from the ground. In the course of schooling, we will teach the horse to poise himself progressively on a narrowing base of support, and, as his equilibrium improves, our corrections become less frequent and less noticeable and he becomes more manoeuvrable. Finally, our aids become purely mental influences, and our own body and the horse's body will have become one completely integrated, animated system.

I need hardly add that sense of balance varies between horses as much as between human beings, nor that the equilibrium required of the cross-country horse need not be as highly developed as it has to be in the case of the dressage horse. In the case of the cross-country horse, good control of balance will come with the development of muscular strength by exercise; the superior poise of the dressage horse is also acquired by development of muscular strength through exercise and appropriate gymnastic movements, but it depends also on perfect body proportions and natural elegance of movement. These qualities are rare and it is not a coincidence that top-class dressage horses are always horses with excellent conformation. The length of the limbs in relation to the length of the body is most important: long bodies on short legs, or short bodies with long legs will always have balancing problems. The dressage horse especially needs very good hindlegs: it is not only their shape that matters, but also their position in relation to the body because of its influence on the whole form of the horse. Horses with crooked limbs, like humans with mis-shapen legs, will have some balancing difficulties and, therefore, all horses with sickle hocks or bowed hocks, or who twist the limb around the hoof or wobble on their hocks must be excluded as potential dressage material. A horse with naturally favourable aptitudes for dressage will place his hindfeet fairly and squarely on the ground in order not to teeter on them, but to support safely the weight of the body. If we develop the habit of examining carefully the position and the movements of the hindlegs of all horses, we will notice that no two horses use their hindlegs in the same way. However, in order to form a reliable judgement of a horse's aptitude for dressage, it is not enough to develop an eye for the movements of the hindlimbs: we must also have the ability to put our knowledge to the test by riding the horse, and it takes years of riding before one can have enough knowledge, skill and experience to entirely trust one's judgement.

In conclusion, I repeat that teaching the horse to become horizontally balanced cannot be done in one lesson, nor form a distinct phase of his training; it is a fundamental element of his whole training, just like relaxation, carriage and elegance of movement; rider and horse will always have to continue striving for perfection, but very few will achieve the ideal: a complete blending of horse and rider into one body that moves with the lightness of a bird.

POISE

In horsemanship, poise is so often mentioned that I believe that some clarification is needed, even for riders who understand that balance, equilibrium and poise are generally synonymous terms. But while balance merely implies a state in which no one part overweighs another, equilibrium implies, as balance does not, a tendency to return to the original position after a displacement of weight, while poise means perfect balance or stability of equilibrium, equality of weight in all directions. It used to be believed in years gone by that horses cannot naturally move in horizontal balance, that is with the weight distributed equally over all four legs, without the restraining influence of the reins, because the weight of head and neck causes five-ninths of the total weight of the animal to be supported by the forelegs. The principal purpose of training, therefore, was to compel the horse to distribute his weight equally on the forelegs and hindlegs. To this end, he had to be collected, that is made to engage his hindlegs, or "flex the haunches", and carry his head and neck high. These superficial observations were of course misleading, but for a long time they resulted in the most grotesque contortion of the bodies of horses and riders. It is not so very long ago that horsemen believed that if a horse were to jump safely, he had to land on the far side of an obstacle on his hindlegs first, or at least at the same time as on his forelegs; the rider had to assist the horse by leaning backward himself. The horse's natural way of landing was presumed to be injurious because it put too great a stress on the forelegs. Yet, despite this, horses would persist in touching the ground with their forelegs first when they were racing or hunting, thus inconveniently disproving the theory! It should be evident that we cannot apply the laws of statics to bodies animated by their own intrinsic forces. Other theorists then came along to prove that only the forward seat conformed to the laws of dynamics. But principles which apply to the design of man-made machines cannot be applied to nature's creatures; they will only agree to put their strength at our disposal when we have the tact to get their will to conform with our own. At the beginning of training, it is agreement of views that ensures the horse's obedience to our aids and makes him controllable. Nowadays it is understood that we cannot force the horse to distribute his weight equally on all four legs by holding his head and neck up; he is not a rigid mass with a fixed base of support and neither is he just a balanced beam with separate weights at either end. The horse, on the contrary, is a vital force with a will of its own. He must be trained to submit to the will of the rider and serve the purposes of his master. Eventually, horse and rider must become one single, completely integrated body.

A rider who has had the good fortune to be taught by a good schoolmaster of a horse and who has no prejudices, will have found out through experience that a well-balanced horse is usually relatively short-legged and of a rectangular form, with powerful shoulder muscles and a deep chest which makes him appear heavier in front than behind. On the other hand, long-limbed, short-bodied horses, of a square or tall build usually have poor equilibrium; but there are no hard and fast rules. Equilibrium is the result of good general muscular development and we cannot put a horse in a state of perfect equilibrium by enforcing a transference of weight through harsh, corrective measures. Like all the other aspects of a horse's education, his balance can be improved only gradually by exercise and schooling, and the art of training lies in the ability to ensure constant improvement.

If the reader has had the patience to follow me on the subject of balance, he will have understood already that the horse has to be trained, mentally and physically, to move efficiently with a rider astride; he will also realise that by leaning forward or backward or sideways he cannot help the horse to develop so-called poise. The rider's centre of gravity must always be drawn downward towards the horse's centre of gravity; his posture must be adapted to circumstances and to the stage of training of the horse, and if it is necessary sometimes to lean forward, the buttocks must not be lifted high above the saddle, but must slide backwards towards the cantle in order to avoid overloading the forelimbs. A good sense of balance and feel of the position of the centre of gravity is as essential for race riding as for dressage riding, and for training the novice horse as well as the advanced show-jumper or dressage horse.

However, we can choose between a passive use of our weight, when we keep our own centre of gravity as close as possible to that of the horse, to form with him a sort of centaur; or, an *active* use of our weight to displace the horse's centre of gravity, whereby we sit further forward or backward in the saddle.

For example, if we push our seat slightly backward, behind the normal common centre of gravity, an attentive, schooled horse will, of his own accord, tend to flex more the joints of the hindquarters, lighten himself in front and automatically adjust his equilibrium to balance the load. This manner of obtaining collection is only possible to a rider who has an upright, relaxed, firm posture and a deep "vertical" seat. But, if instead of remaining in the "vertical" seat, the rider drives his buttocks forwards (while keeping the upper body upright), he will push the centre of gravity forward and the horse will lengthen his stride . . . unless his muscles are insufficiently developed, when this pushing effect will only cause him to hurry as his centre of gravity rolls forward.

We can use these displacements of weight to shorten or lengthen the strides, to speed up or slow down the beat. This technique, which is useful for racing, is indispensable for show-jumping. However, beyond the narrow limits within which it is effective, the so-called driving seat produces the very opposite of the desired result; it nips the horse under the saddle, presses his back down and impairs the movements of the hindlegs.

A badly understood forward seat, a forward tipping of the upper body, even a forward inclination of the head, cause a considerable amount of the weight of the rider to fall in front of the centre of gravity and will have the effect on the horse of a forward pull, putting him on the forehand and causing him to hurry with quickened, shortened steps instead of increasing the scope and elevation of his action. And as for the slack and crooked rider, he has the same disturbing effect on the horse's balance as a rucksack insecurely strapped to the shoulders of a man ski-ing down a hill.

For the novice rider, the best way of learning to feel the common centre of gravity of the horse-man system is to ride at all gaits, in either the upright or the forward seat with eyes closed, and following a straight line. Aspiring show-jumpers can acquire a remarkably good understanding of the forward seat and of the ducking of the body that accompanies the movement of the horse as he jumps, if they practise lying prone on a grazing horse (buttocks on the cantle, chest on the pommel), with their eyes shut as if they were sleeping. It is astonishing how easy it is, in this position, to feel the situation of the centre of gravity and to adapt to any change, but the position is so comfortable that there is a danger of really going to sleep; much about the seat for jumping can be learnt by practising this exercise regularly.

GAIT

If you stand on a promenade and watch people passing by (walking, strolling, marching, hurrying, tramping, shuffling, waddling or plodding), who would you choose to dance with? Not many would pass muster. We ought to be just as critical when choosing a horse. Horses, like humans, have a characteristic manner of moving, a gait developed in youth and, hence, habitual. When a horse moves in the manner expected of a good saddle-horse, we can be certain that his gait has been improved by education. Style is acquired by education and habit and it is no exaggeration to talk of an art of moving. Essentially, the training of the horse is a school of movement; good control of the limbs is the basis of improvement of all the gaits.

Learning to move well is even more difficult for the horse, with his four legs, than it is for man, with his two. Man does not acquire the art of walking efficiently without difficulty, especially as he usually only wants to learn after he has reached maturity. How to place the heel and sole of the foot lightly on the ground, toes to the front; how to roll over the whole width of the ball of the foot and over all the equally loaded toes; then to straighten the ankle joint, keeping the knee bent and putting the weight of the body on this supporting leg; next to straighten the knee and hip joints of this leg to propel the body forward and clear the ground. When the hip is lifted by the supporting leg, each step can be 10 cm longer than when the hip does not participate in the movement. Supple hips, which are indispensable for dancing, impart grace to the walk as well. I am not, of course, recommending the feminine wriggle which is supposed to have sex-appeal. Each foot should be placed almost straight in front of the other; only the walk on a narrow track ensures efficient propulsion; walking with the feet apart is detrimental to impulsion because it produces swaying. People who are not used to walking in the manner described above may at first suffer some soreness of the muscles of the back, the buttocks and the abdominal region, but this soreness eventually disappears as the muscles become stronger; flat-footedness too can be cured by correcting the gait.

The practice of walking well is exceptionally good physical training; it teaches good posture and eliminates the ugly, excessive rotation of the trunk with a useless, exaggerated swinging of the arms. The act of walking becomes a pleasure and, because the weight of the body is entirely supported on one leg at each step, we could remain standing for as long as we wished on one leg only. The military walk on the other hand is a march which is quite the contrary of a good, effective gait.

As we develop an agreeable and effective gait, we also develop an eye for good movement, which we will need to have if we are to become knowledgeable judges of horses. All horses can be recognised by their gait, and a pleasing, effective, powerful action is something that only a relatively small number of horses have.

If we have to judge horses frequently, we must have a plan which will prevent us from overlooking blemishes or unsoundness but we must be as methodical in our examination of action as in our examination of the body and limbs. Knowledge and experience will suggest the order of our plan; it must give us a clear picture of natural or acquired tendencies of lameness or disease.

Here is a typical plan:

1 Note any fault of conformation or sign of lameness.
2 Observe general outline of the horse standing and in action.
3 Watch the limbs in action.
4 Examine the forelegs carefully.
5 Examine the hindlegs.

Anybody can recognise lameness in one leg and with practise will be able to identify the lame leg easily; but only a very experienced person will be able to decide whether a stiff gait is due to equal lameness in both forelegs, or whether a short, jerky action of the hindlegs signifies weakness of muscles or worn out joints. The layman must be able at least to recognise, by sound as well as by sight, irregular steps and uneven rhythm and must learn to appreciate a lively, energetic gait, or a feeble, listless one; a more detailed examination ought to be left to an expert because even excellent horses can give a poor show when they are incompetently led or, worse still, when they are badly ridden. On the other hand, horses can be drilled or provoked by excitement to move in an extravagant manner that can give a totally false impression of energy and may conceal lameness.

As horses must be judged with a view to their suitability for a particular purpose, equal attention must be paid to conformation and to action; one has to observe control of body and limbs, outline, gait, flexion and extension of joints, stableness of limbs, straightness of action. The moment he starts to walk, a horse must show a desire to go forward. He must appear to grow in stature and must point the toe towards the spot on which it is going to tread.

However, energetic movement must be the consequence of good muscular development and we ought to beware of a horse in poor condition showing extravagant action. Further more, we must see the horse walking and cantering as well as trotting: presence and energy must show in all the gaits. We must draw an imaginary line running from back to front along the length of the horse's body at the standstill; if the horse is young, the line must remain horizontal at all the gaits; if he is fairly advanced in his training, it ought to slope upward towards the forehand, but if it runs downward, it shows a horse on the forehand, with a wrong carriage, poor sense of balance and poor gaits.

When we observe the movements of the limbs, we must look out for energy, impulsion and a regular beat. Long strides are not always a sign of good movement; foals, for example, always have a long stride; their hindfeet always leave an imprint well in front of the imprints of the forefeet because they have disproportionately long limbs to help them keep up with their dams and the rest of the herd; a foal's long stride cannot, therefore, be taken as a token for the future. With mature horses, the length of the stride is always proportionate to the length of the limbs. A long stride, if it is listless, is a symptom of sluggishness or weakness; a short but energetic stride is capable of considerable improvement, providing the horse possesses good overall muscular development; as the horse becomes stronger, his propulsive power will improve and his steps will always be long enough to ensure satisfactory performance. For riders of little experience, short striding horses are much easier to school and, by learning to lengthen the stride, they will also learn to ride better. However, the horse must be robust; if the stride is short, because the feet are plucked up hurriedly, this can be due to bad conformation or to the presence of pain in the back or the limbs.

Good action can be either rounded or sweeping. With the rounded action, the knee remains slightly bent at the highest point of the trajectory of the hoof; while with the sweeping action, it is completely extended at that same moment; in both cases, the length of the stride will depend on the freedom of movement of the shoulders and on the power developed by the hindlegs. Horses with a rounded action generally flex their hocks more and lift their hindfeet more, in contrast to horses with a sweeping action who tend to graze the ground with their feet and to flex their hocks less. Horses with a rounded action have particularly broad hocks, which enable them to move well at all speeds. The sweeping action usually appeals more to spectators, but the rider knows that the performance of a horse with a sweeping action will depend very much on momentum; in collection, the hocks lack the strength required for elevation, and the beat will tend to be blurred. The two different types of action indicate different aptitudes and although a good trainer will be able to obtain excellent results from both types, he will have to proceed more carefully in the schooling of the horse with a sweeping action and will have to devote more time to muscle-building exercises; the horse will have to be taught to work actively at a slower speed and will have to be denied the opportunity to revert constantly to his natural tendency to hover.

Initially, a horse with a sweeping "daisy cutting" action will gain ground faster than a horse with a rounded action, because there is a longer moment of suspension in the trot, when all four feet are off the ground; a horse with a rounded action will not at first show a distinct moment of suspension in his trot, but eventually this will come as a consequence of increasing strength. In the sweeping action, the thrust of the hindlegs produces a long and low trajectory and horses with this sort of action seem to be preferred nowadays for dressage, because this action looks more elegant, but it is not easy to transform it into a more rounded, shorter trajectory. The horse with a naturally rounded action is by nature better able to collect himself and the thrust of the hindlegs can develop elevation more easily; therefore, dressage with its gymnastic exercises, is easier for him.

When viewed from the front or the rear, the forelegs of a well-made horse should move on a perfectly straight line towards or away from the observer; this presupposes perfectly straight forelegs; however, perfectly straight forelegs are rare and they do not play the same predominant role in the choice of a saddle-horse as in the choice of a stallion. If the toes point slightly outward or inward, showing a tendency toward dishing or plaiting, we should get the opinion of an expert, because brushing or crossing the forefeet can depend very much on condition as well as conformation, and also on the skill of the rider and its importance depends on the use for which the horse is intended.

A good appreciation of the shape and, especially, of the action of the hindlimbs, is more difficult because riders can distort both if they disturb the natural movement and, consequently, spoil or destroy impulsion, but one should look to see how the horse places each hindleg as it comes to support the weight of the body; if it does not give a secure support, the other hindleg will have to precipitate its own movement to safeguard balance. Again, the supporting leg can be thrust aside to give a broader base of support, or, if the horse is base-narrow (that is when his feet are too close together in relation to the hips) the toes may be turned out. Restricting reins are frequently the cause of various forms of distortion of the normal pattern of action of the hindlimbs; it is always by avoiding correct engagement of the hindlegs that a weak or lazy horse resists his rider and loses impulsion; he evades the restraint in front by going wide with his hindlegs, whereas an energetic horse will jog when he is held back by a restraining hand; both faults are rooted in the same cause.

It is not easy to decide whether a defective action is congenital or acquired, but an experienced horseman can visualise, by examining the stationary hindlegs, the pattern of action that they should produce and will be able to decide whether an unsatisfactory action is inborn and, therefore, cannot be corrected, or whether it is due to bad riding and can be improved.

Unimpeded activity of the back muscles is also essential; we judge whether the back functions properly by noticing whether the rider can sit smoothly or whether he is jolted by the movement. As the back connects hindquarters and forehand, a defective action of the hindlegs is inevitably reflected by defective activity of the back muscles; the lifting and propulsive effect of the hindlegs is transmitted to the forehand by the back, which must be elastically braced to ensure effective transmission; transmission will be impaired if the back is either arched or hollowed stiffly, or also if it is slack and shows a snake-like movement or, but more rarely, a wave-like motion that conjures up the picture of a caterpillar. While the stiff back jolts the rider, the slack back does allow him to sit comfortably, but the locomotive power of the hindlegs fails to produce impulsion, the drive escaping behind the saddle and consequently, as there is insufficient impelling force, the horse must pull himself forward by the forelegs.

Impulsion, engagement, following with the hindfeet in the track of the forefeet, tracking up, all these terms are really synonymous and we ought to use only one word. Hindlegs are said to follow when they can be seen to swing forward powerfully in the traces of the forelegs; however, the motor is at the rear; impulsion must be felt and not just seen; the hindlegs do not follow the forelegs, they drive them forward; therefore we ought to talk only of impulsion. The position, shape and action of the hindlegs, obviously, have a determining effect on impulsion; the horse must lift his hindfeet up positively, reach well forward with them, and put them down on a straight line, which neither wriggles nor wavers.

If we know how to judge the mechanics of movement of the hindlegs, we can spare ourselves the many disappointments which are the consequence of selecting for dressage a horse with a defective action of the hindquarters.

Impulsion must always be preserved, and for this purpose we ought to understand the exact meaning of movement on one track and movement on two tracks. Now, how can the normal forward movement of a horse be on one or two tracks? We are taught that a horse can move on two tracks if his body can be sufficiently inflexed to allow his hindfeet and forefeet to mark two distinctly parallel lines on the ground, and that he moves on one track when his hindfeet step in the traces of the forefeet because his body is straight. This is not sufficiently clear.

Single track is the prescribed, narrow path that a horse must follow in dressage tests, along straight lines of a course, when turning corners, performing circles and serpentines; any straying from this track is counted as a fault due to negligence or incompetence. What confuses people is the vague use of the word track, instead of trace.

If we stand at the corner of a dressage arena, where a judge sits to evaluate the straightness of the horse on the straight line, or his proper inflexion on curved lines, we may observe that the hooves of the oncoming horses can leave two, three or four traces on the ground. The hindfoot of one side should step exactly in the trace of the ipsilateral forefoot. A perfectly straight horse going "on one track" traces two very close parallel lines on the ground, but the perfectly straight horse is a rarity and deviation from absolute straightness is often seen. There are five different ways of moving:

1. Two close parallel traces: the horse is straight, moving on one track.
2. There are three traces on the ground because one hindfoot does not step in the trace of the ipsilateral forefoot, but is placed to the side.
3. There are three traces, because although the hindfeet step on two close parallel lines, one forefoot is out of line.
4. Fore and hindfeet are equally wide apart: two traces, but not a narrow track.
5. The horse is moving more or less sideways, and three or four traces can be seen according to the degree of crookedness; one hindleg is shirking its supporting role by stepping aside.

Only a perfectly balanced horse can move straight, tracing two closely spaced straight lines on an unwavering straight course, and can be said to be moving on one track. Horses with a defective sense of balance place one foot aside, usually a hindfoot, to widen their base of support.

In two-track exercises, when the horse moves simultaneously forward and sideways in an inflexed posture, shoulder-in, counter-shoulder-in, travers and renvers, impulsion cannot be satisfactory if the drive developed by the hindlegs is not in line with the forelegs. If the horse yields to the firmer pressure of one of the rider's legs without inflexing his vertebral column, he will move more sideways than forwards and will be making four traces. Since forward movement is insufficient, impulsion is insufficient. On the other hand, two traces can be seen, but the forelegs are on one line and the hindlegs on another; the horse's acrobatics may be impressive, but again he is moving more sideways than forwards, hence without sufficient impulsion and the movement does not conform with the fundamental principle that natural movement must be preserved; it is an artificial movement which is always damaging to the joints. In all movements in which the horse is inflexed around the rider's "inside" leg, the driving force of the hindlegs must be felt by the rider to pass between his legs, under his centre of gravity, and the driving force must be directed along a line that passes between the horse's shoulder joints.

In all the two-track movements required in dressage tests, lateral displacement is excessive and impulsion insufficient if the drive of the more loaded and flexed inside hindleg is not directly in line with the diagonal foreleg. The horse's inflexion may correspond with the direction of the movement, as in the half-pass, the travers and renvers, or it may be opposite to the direction of movement, as in the shoulder-in, but in both cases the inside hindleg is the major driving one. It bears the greater share of the task of balancing and propelling the mass. If the inflexion of the horse is insufficient, its propulsive force will partly escape between the forelegs, but this is the lesser fault.

With increased inflexion, the main driving hindleg is aligned with the diagonally opposite shoulder joint; in this case, the foot of this hindleg follows in the trace of the diagonally opposite forefoot; in the shoulder-in, the inside hindfoot would be hidden from the observer at the corner of the arena, by the outside foreleg; in travers, the outside hind would be hidden by the inside fore. Indeed, only three legs are visible and the horse is making three traces. Although it may be necessary sometimes, during schooling, to compel the horse to move sideways more than this, or to inflex him more so that he makes four or, eventually, two traces, this cannot be done without impairing impulsion and regularity, riding to music will easily prove this fact. (We should not confuse hip and hip-joint, shoulder and shoulder-joint. The hip-joint is 10 cm closer to the midline of the horse's body than the point of the hip; the shoulder-joint is about 5 cm closer to the midline than the point of the shoulder.) For the novice observer, however, it is sufficient to be able to see that lateral movement remains within the limits of natural movements because he will be able to see only three legs; if he can see four legs, the hindfeet will be making two separate traces beside the traces of the forefeet, because the horse is asked to inflex more than his suppleness permits; all that one can say is that he is moving forward and sideways with a twisted neck. A rider who wants to acquire a feel for correct inflexion must be helped, at first, by a person on the ground who can observe the movements of the limbs, until the rider can dispense with this assistance because he has learnt to feel whether he has correctly positioned his horse or has "overshot the mark"; one must concentrate especially on feeling the direction of the force of the main driving hindleg.

Teaching lateral movements with inflexion is not the same thing as teaching a horse to move forwards and sideways by yielding to the increased pressure of one leg. While shoulder-in, travers and renvers must always be ridden with impulsion, making a horse yield to one leg is useful for controlling excessive impetuosity; it prevents the young or the spoilt horse being able to use his strength effectively to run away with his rider and so puts him under the latter's dominance. Any exercise in which the horse yields to the leg, but is not inflexed, can have no place in dressage tests, although it is appropriate to an examination of a rider's competence. In all "lateral" dressage movements, there must be impulsion; for this reason inflexion should never exceed natural limits and there should never be greater distance between the tracks of the forehand and the hindquarters than the width of the breast; more than this causes impulsion to be lost and the movement cannot be considered to be natural; neither can there be impulsion when the horse moves sideways without being inflexed throughout his whole body.

The half-pass also is sometimes executed in such a manner that the force of the hindlegs cannot impel the forehand; the horse crosses his limbs and moves more sideways than forward; a horse can indeed be trained to trot from right to left, and vice-versa, or even to trot backward and sideways, which amounts to training him to come completely "off the bit". However, if the half-pass is to remain a natural movement, the horse must move forward with impulsion as well as sideways, and must be inflexed on the side of the lateral displacement so that the line of force of the hindlegs passes between the shoulder joints, thus effectively driving the forehand. If the lateral displacement is enhanced to the detriment of the forward movement and if the horse is not inflexed, the limbs may cross impressively and the movement may be spectacular, but the fact remains that it is not natural movement but sheer acrobatics.

All movements which are a travesty of natural movement must be called impure gaits and when a horse's gaits are impure, it shows that he has not learnt to move freely forward but has just been manoeuvred in all directions. He may be able to perform accurately the movements of a test, but at the difficult moments of change of position and speed disregard of elementary principles will show up in the form of a variety of blundering movements: uneven, tense, hurried, choppy steps, or uncertain, hesitant, wobbly steps. Gaits are impure when one hindfoot or both (going wide behind) do not follow in the track of the forefoot so that they need not bend at the joints; they are impure when the hocks are snatched up in the collected paces; they are impure whenever the horse hurries in the extended paces. Impurities can occur occasionally during a dressage test because of a fleeting moment of inattention on the part of the horse, which the rider ought to have sensed and forestalled before having to suffer the consequence; more often, the horse will have learnt by experience that he can turn the situation to his own advantage and resist the honest engagement of his hindlegs. This brings us back to the root of the trouble: hands which yield too late or insufficiently and so prevent the free forward swinging of the hindlegs. When impulsion is impaired by heavy hands, a horse that is too docile to try to resist the bit will develop instead habitual gait impurities. The latter must, therefore, be grouped with other forms of resistance to foward movement: such as tongue over the bit, crossing of the jaws, grinding the teeth, hollowing the back, and so on.

An impure canter is assessed differently. The canter must look and sound like a three time gait; the T–T–Tm sound of pounding hooves in wartime when a messenger galloped on the pavement in the night will never be forgotten by anyone who has heard it. However, in dressage tests, we often see a distinct four-beat canter when the collected canter is required; it is then the rider who is at fault; he is confusing change of speed with change of rhythm. In order to show the three beats of the canter, the gait must remain animated, the leap with all four feet off the ground must be sustained, the canter should not degenerate into a running action.

I have deliberately said that the canter must "look" like a three beat gait; in reality, it would be terribly uncomfortable if the three beats of the canter were "felt" with each stride; it would remind me of my first dancing lessons, when I strove so hard to accompany the three-quarter rhythm of a waltz with three quick steps while my less agile partner struggled to follow me with her three slower steps; we should not try to feel the three beats of the canter. We can excuse a young horse if his canter is a quick succession of beats, but with a schooled horse, neither three nor two bumps should spoil the pleasureable feeling of rocking which the horse gives us when his hindlegs are strong and supple. Some very experienced horsemen will judge the "feel" of a horse's canter by watching the rider instead of the horse's feet, but for most people it is better to watch the feet; we should never see more than three hoof-beats.

As I have explained, the forms of impure gait described above must be imputed to the deficiency of the rider; now we will examine defective forms of the trot which are either innate tendencies, or can be attributed to excessive muscular tone, although they can be just a habit that the horse has acquired. Three striking examples of an impure trot are hovering, scurrying, and bouncing. These are all actions which frequently impress the complete tyro, but experienced horsemen know how difficult it is to obtain, in the first place, genuine forward movement and, eventually, powerful collection and extension from horses that display these idiosyncracies.

Hovering is a form of trotting in which a horse springs from one diagonal to the other without first properly flexing his hind joints; there is an upward thrust produced by the natural elasticity of muscles, tendons and ligaments, and a period of suspension, but no effective forward propulsion; the stride covers very little ground and, at the summit of its trajectory, the hindfeet do not point the toes toward the spot upon which they will land. The action is elevated, but stilted and ineffective; novice riders enjoy it because the resilience of the hindlegs allows them to sit on the horse's slack back as comfortably as in a rocking-chair. Horses that have got into the habit of hovering hate to change their speed; they feel insecure when they do so; they are like engines that heat-up as soon as a certain rate of revolutions is exceeded.

The scurrying trot is also a trot with stiffened hocks, but with the difference that there is no spring at all; the body is propelled forward by the rapidly alternating strokes of the diagonals; speed is gained by momentum as the mass is constantly projected over the forehand. In the scurrying trot, the hindlegs straddle; it is an action which is very difficult to correct.

An ugly result of such impurities of the trot is a marked swaying of the whole body, for frequently the forelegs straddle as well as the hindlegs. Yet, astonishingly, horses with these awkward actions continue to be purchased to be used as saddle-horses.

In the case of a young horse of an energetic temperament, one would not be unduly concerned because excitement often produces excessive muscular tension, but one needs to be experienced to be able to judge a horse's constitution when he is excited. An experienced horseman would always try-out a horse that hovers until fatigue sets in and the horse has calmed down (an energetic horse will have presence even at the halt); he can be cured of his habit by being constantly made to change the speed of the trot, but for a long time he will always have to be driven forward to deny him any opportunity to fall back into his habit.

The bouncing trot, on the other hand, is a bouncing off pronouncedly flexed hindlimbs with an explosive extension; the swing of the hindlegs is not sufficient to ensure effective forward propulsion. The limbs overwork, the back is rigidly hollowed, the neck held up; it is an action that is considered elegant in a carriage horse but which is highly unsuitable for a saddle-horse.

Only a few words need to be said about the gait called the "pace". Some horses are natural pacers, others must be trained. In the Middle Ages, ladies' palfreys were trained to pace, but nowadays pacers are only trained for racing. The sort of irregular amble of the jogging horse is really a form of bridle-lameness.

Bridle-lameness is not an unsoundness; it is, indeed, a vice. The bridle-lame horse "nods" as if lame in a shoulder; the intensity of the lameness can be surprising and the vet may try to discover some cause for it in one part or another of a limb; in a bad case, the horse will move with such a hollow back as to suggest damage to this part. However, a typical sign of bridle-lameness is that it occurs only when the horse has a bit in his mouth, and then he goes lame whether he is being ridden, lunged or simply led; lameness disappears when he is led by a head-stall without a bit or when he is let loose.

Horses learn to become bridle-lame if clumsy attempts are made at

Properly relaxed rider and horse *(above)* at the walk on a loose rein. *(Below)* Young horse at a medium trot, showing impulsion and relaxation.

Powerful movement *(above)* without excessive tension; *(below)* the ease of a relaxed horse at the gallop.

collection without due concern for straightness, or also if collecting gymnastics are practised for which the hindlegs are not yet ready. Energetic horses will then get into the habit of making a shorter step and giving a stronger push with one hindleg (always the same and usually the left) than with the other; this is felt by the rider as an increased tension of the left rein and a slackening of the right, as if he had a heavy load in his left hand and nothing in the right. On the other hand, lazy horses will pretend to be lame in the right hind; the left hind will make a normal step, the right one a weak and short one in order to avoid reaching out to the bit with the right side; the horse appears to jog with the right diagonal (left hind, right fore). This form of bridle-lameness resembles lameness in the left shoulder if the horse is held straight by means of side-reins and is made to circle clockwise on the lunge; it does not show when he is lunged anti-clockwise. This pretended lameness will disappear on the clockwise circle also if the horse is allowed to move freely and to turn his head slightly outward.

There is yet another form of bridle-lameness, more apparent at the walk than at the trot, in which the horse leans on the hand while refusing to obey the legs; he will either make a shorter step with the left foreleg, leaning on the left hand, or a shorter step with the right fore, avoiding the contact of the right hand.

Bridle-lameness occurs when one tries to make horses execute dressage movements before they have developed basically correct forward movement, in which they neither hurry nor lag; the lameness does not occur at a fast, extended trot, nor at a slow trot if the horse is allowed to float, in a weak, vaguely passage-like manner; it happens at the working trot or when the rider tries to make the horse work actively in shortened steps; the horse will then drag his hindlegs, lower his neck and head over his right fore, which will then have to make a shorter step and this is how the horse avoids stretching the right rein. The real cause of the lameness becomes clear when he is frequently made to change his speed by lengthening and shortening the strides of the trot.

Bridle-lameness is a form of resistance to the bit, a form particularly difficult to correct because it is a vice, rooted in the temperament of the horse; furthermore, he learns to exploit the lameness when he is already fairly advanced in his training and has already tried many forms of resistance.

Two methods can be tried to cure the habit. The first consists in riding forward on loose reins, until the gait has once again become perfectly regular, both hindlegs working with equal energy; the second method is more effective, but open only to knowledgeable, very capable riders, who have the ability to compel the horse to go up to the hand with flexion at the poll, and to maintain a light but positive tension of reins; who can make a horse so obedient to the aids that he will not dare to hurry nor to hang back; the regular sequence of the hoof-beats will be restored as soon as the horse continually accepts being driven into the bit.

Even if a veterinarian is capable of proving his diagnosis by riding the horse himself, he ought to remember the mysterious workings of the rider's mind before mentioning the possibility of bridle-lameness; he will rarely be thanked for his perspicacity or for his advice, that one should learn to ride before attempting to school a horse. Most riders prefer to be told that a horse is unserviceable rather than to admit to their own incompetence; even modest riders, willing to accept advice, will rarely be able to cure the vice when their own inveterate habits have produced it.

Jogging is also a vice, a hideous and exasperating one, also usually linked to temperament. Jogging is trotting with such short steps that the jogging horse just manages to keep up with a walking horse. It can happen when an energetic horse with a long stride has to stay level with a slower horse and has to be continually slowed down; in this case, it is a vent for impatience. In contrast, a slow horse will jog to keep up with a longer striding companion. Jogging turns into a habit if the rider is inattentive or incompetent and, once the vice is established, it becomes almost impossible to get the horse to stretch the reins and to obey the aids. Jogging and hovering are related habits and it can be said that jogging is bridle-lameness on all four legs.

Correcting habitual jogging taxes severely the patience of the rider. Again, one must be able to control the hindquarters and get them to produce normally long strides; a horse inexorably made to yield to the increased pressure of one leg cannot possibly jog; even when normal rein tension is re-established, the shoulder-in will have to be resorted to for a long time before the horse can be allowed to proceed on one track; the shoulder-in position and absolute obedience to the impelling influences of the legs will, eventually, enable one to nip in the bud any further attempt at jogging.

We should not mistake for habitual jogging the occasionally

tripping gait of a keen, but still unbalanced young horse, learning to respect the impelling influence of the rider's legs at the walk; he does not understand that he is expected to lengthen the stride of the walk but thinks that he is being asked to trot. There is, unfortunately, no other way of getting the horse to understand that he must walk with energy, except to urge him on until he starts tripping; if he is attentive, then he can either be checked with the hand, or driven forward into a regular trot. Tripping steps show willingness; jogging is resistance to the legs that order trotting, and to the hands that order walking.

The whole object of training, not only at elementary level, but also at advanced level, is to give the horse an elegant and effective technique of movement. We must know and be able to feel what we really mean when we talk of improving the gaits. It is pointless to repeat, day after day, changes of gait and changes of speed within a gait, while always letting the horse get away with the same faults of deportment and the same irregularities of gait. The purpose of gymnastic schooling is continual improvement in freedom, and lightness of movement, balance and grace together with increasing development of sensitivity and obedience to the rider's desire for changes of speed or direction, in order to transform, eventually, the sport of riding into an art of movement. It is all a matter of establishing a suitable accord between propulsive force and retarding force, a combination of forces which we call impulsion. We must acquire the art of developing impulsion by continually making adjustments of speed, so that the horse never hurries nor holds back; hurrying is a wrong manner of propelling the mass, holding back is a wrong manner of supporting it; wrong, because in either instance the horse does not flex the joints of the hindlegs sufficiently and does not work elastically with his back muscles. In the first case, the horse has an excess of weight on the forehand and runs by loss of balance; in the second case, he holds his weight back, and shuffles; there is not enough thrust. Self-carriage is a balanced state between running and holding back. It is obvious that to get a horse to attain self-carriage, the rider, himself, must have a perfect sense of balance; he must be able to feel that he cannot maintain his deep, steady, vertical position effortlessly in the centre of balance, unless the horse uses his hindlegs effectively. However, the horse will not be able to control his speed and balance as one would wish before he develops better muscular tone and has learnt to obey us. This brings us back to our starting point on the treacherous road along which it is we who have to lead the horse in progressive stages, so that he gains, eventually, perfect control over his body and limbs.

The more the horse is endowed by nature with energy and good conformation, the more skill the rider will need to achieve the objects set above. It is never easy to exploit natural gifts without marring them, to keep in check an abundant flow of energy without impairing the fluency of the movements, to develop full impulsion, freedom of movement and self-carriage and yet not let the horse get the upper hand.

Are the piaffe and the passage natural gaits? Surely, a horse that performed, of his own volition, a genuine piaffe or passage, would be a freak of nature. Though we do sometimes see horses spring and bound with excitement, more or less on one spot, passage and piaffe are schooled gaits, conventionalised representations of the natural walk or trot, and not merely a controlled form of prancing. They must evolve smoothly out of the natural gait and decline back to normal just as smoothly. It is also important to develop the passage from the piaffe first, and only later the piaffe from the passage. In these schooled gaits, the horse's balance must be so perfectly established that he can dwell easily on each diagonal pair of legs in turn and with perfect poise as he alternates the diagonals. The pseudo-piaffe, with a choppy rhythm, a hollow back, a nodding head, raised croup and legs stepping on the spot but behind the vertical shows a horse that is not well-balanced. Piaffe and passage must be developed from a high state of collection, so that the horse can find a firm support in each pronouncedly flexed hindleg; although he moves almost on the spot, he must give the impression of wanting to go forward; the curve of his freely elevated neck must be bowed to the utmost possible limit, his haunches flexed must be like an archer's bow and his back must be elastically braced also. It is only if the back is arched that the haunches can properly flex. It is unflagging impulsion in collection, on unwavering straight lines, with increasing development of the strength and suppleness of the hindquarters and progressive shortening of the steps to a hoof-length which eventually produces piaffe and passage. If the steps are shortened more than this at the walk, the gait will lose its typical features: perfect symmetry and the well-marked four-time beat; the walk is impure whenever the steps are hurried, the beat indistinct or irregular. The hindlegs must be well-engaged, the hocks deeply flexed and the forehand raised as a result of the lowering of the hindquarters. The horse must have become so responsive to the precisely attuned, alternately stimulating and restraining aids, so calm, so willing, so perfectly poised that not a suspicion of his weight can be felt by the rider's hand.

The development of the manege or High-School walk must now be included in the daily gymnastic lessons; all the figures of the manege, shoulder-in, half-pass, serpentines, turns about the haunches, stepping backward and forward, will have to be repeated at this gait, with animated, half-length steps, the purpose of the exercises being the development of accentuated beat, perfect poise and muscular tone to ensure stability on each hindleg in the piaffe. Meanwhile, the rider's feel for rhythm, suppleness and balance will also improve so much that, eventually, without consciously willing it, he will obtain a piaffe in perfect diagonals in which the horse will clearly detach his hooves from the ground, and later a passage. This has been aptly described by a famous German horseman, Count Westphalen, as: "One hundred kilos in the legs, milligrams in the hands." A maxim which gives some idea of the power required by the horse to perform these difficult movements.

First the manege walk, then the piaffe, then the soft-passage, in quarter-length and half-length steps, finally the true passage with energetic steps: this is the rational progression which will help the horse to remain perfectly balanced in extreme collection. Because of the scope of the movement, the passage requires more power and stability than the piaffe; isolated passage-like steps which do not evolve from the piaffe nor decline into the trot cannot be said to be an honest passage. We sometimes see some impressive, bouncing strides in dressage competitions, which are full of energetic motion, but they cannot be described as the beautiful passage of the High-School horse. The artistic merit of the movement can be judged by the seat of the rider; if the passage is an expression of extreme collection in perfect balance, it is impossible not to sit deeply in a perfectly vertical position; so often, however, we notice the rider trying to avoid being jolted by the back of the horse by lifting himself out of the saddle, or gripping to stick to it.

Even if piaffe and passage are just artistic representations of natural movement, they must never be caricatures of nature. It is a misunderstanding of the art of dressage to practise them for their own sake and to make them the sole object of specialisation, so that they degenerate into acrobatic stunts. They are important gymnastic exercises for the horse, corresponding to knee bends and somersaults which human gymnasts perform to improve their strength and balance. They have a place, like the manege walk, in the daily gymnastics of the advanced dressage horse; but a horse who can do a piaffe and a passage, must also be capable of doing an extended trot of such elevation and reach as to make him appear to fly above the ground; powerful movement should be the end product of all gymnastics. If the horse proceeded from the piaffe into a stiff-legged, hurried hound-trot, the piaffe would be a clownish act and the horse would look as ridiculous as a young man collapsing with exhaustion after skipping for a few minutes.

The gaits cannot be free and regular if the rider is a disturbing influence or if the horse is not fluently submissive; the horse will always remain over-tense so long as he is held in a straitjacket. The length of the strides and the rhythm can vary in all the paces, but the movement must always remain fluent; the muscles must continue to work elastically if we do not want the horse to resist by hurrying, pulling or hanging back. Flexion at the poll must be the result of overall elastic muscular tension.

To teach himself to feel how much he can demand, the rider should count the number of steps to the minute. At a free and active walk, the rate of the beat ought to be 120 to 130 steps per minute; a slower rate can only be achieved if the horse can collect himself as, otherwise, the movement would be sluggish. A regular extended walk at a rate of 90 steps per minute or less is a revealing test of a rider's feel. The rate of a good working trot is 160 steps per minute; 180 steps per minute already compels the horse to shorten the propelling phase of each step and to elevate the forehand; this is the best rate for teaching the horse to move in self-carriage. The rate of a racing gallop is approximately 140 beats per minute; of the working canter, 100 to 120. If the canter is not to deteriorate into a quick succession of four beats, less than 100 beats per minute requires the horse to be well advanced in his schooling and capable of collection. The rein-back also can be hesitant and too slow, or too quick and unco-ordinated. The rider ought firstly to learn to obtain four separate backward steps (four half strides), each step being made with the same hindleg, before he can demand four consecutive steps (two backward strides), because this will teach him to feel the movements of the hindlimbs. Learning to stand still is also education in movement; a horse with too much weight on the forehand is incapable of remaining still at the halt.

In conclusion, I will repeat that all resistances, whether they are felt by the hand or expressed by a crooked tail carriage cannot be corrected by any other method than regulating the gaits; furthermore, one should never undertake to correct the faults of a horse before one has acquired an exceptional feel for the purity of the gaits.

SPEED: BEAT AND STRIDE LENGTH

The importance of a regular, well-marked beat cannot be overstressed. The slightest irregularity has to be penalised in advanced dressage tests; in the elementary schooling of the horse, regularity of the beat is essential to the improvement of the natural gaits.

As soon as the regularity of the beat is lost, the steps become uneven. The movement can be so hesitant that it stops, or so hurried that it degenerates into a kind of totter. The essence of regularity is of course briskness and the opposite of briskness is sluggishness, but briskness must not be confused with speed. If a horse maintains a good posture, we can assume that his movement is sufficiently vigorous, regardless of speed.

A dedicated rider will try to improve his own sense of rhythm by checking the beat with a stop-watch which he can wear on his wrist. The number of steps to the minute at a normal walk is between 110 and 130. One begins with a walk of 110 even steps to the minute then one gradually proceeds to increase the speed to obtain a medium walk of 130 steps of equal length to the minute. The number of steps to the minute in the trot can be between 120 and 180; the rate of the canter can be between 100 and 140 beats per minute. In any one of the gaits, the slightest irregularity of the beat ought to disturb the rider as much as a dancing partner who has a poor sense of rhythm. Checking by the stop-watch, one strives to maintain a set speed. Extremes of quickness or slowness will, obviously, never be within the ability of any but the most remarkable artists.

The horse, however, will not be able to maintain a regular beat of his own accord before he has mastered his flight reflex. What is the flight reflex and how does it affect rhythm?

The flight reflex is an automatic interchange of impulses between the central nervous system and the limbs. It is not always a sensible reaction to danger; in an extended sense, it is an automatic response to any kind of emotional upset. Anything which makes an irritating impression on the senses of the horse provokes a change in the activity of the limbs, causing them to make agitated, irregular movements. As a result of more than a thousand years of domestication, the horse has become a more or less tame creature, estranged from nature; his flight reflex has therefore become purposeless. A wild horse behaves like all other herbivorous, unpredatory beasts; if his attention is caught by a strange object, he stops in his tracks, examines it from a safe distance and, having identified it, will settle on the wisest course of action; ignore it if it is not at all dangerous; circumvent it cautiously if it is not too dangerous; rush away as fast as possible if he fears it, or attack it if he thinks that it is vulnerable. The flight reflex of the wild animal is intelligent behaviour. But domesticated horses have lost the ability to appraise strange and possibly dangerous situations sensibly; one can say that the flight reflex cuts off all communication between the higher nervous system, located in the brain, and the lower nervous system, situated in the spinal column, which determines purely reflex actions. Furthermore domestic horses react by running away, not only when they suspect danger in a strange object, but also when they are perturbed by something to do with the rider; it can be the unsteadiness of his hand, the severity of the pressure which he inflicts on the mouth with the bit, the restlessness of his legs, the muddling effect of his aids, or the disturbing influence of his position on the horse's balance. Disorderly limb movements and irregular beat can be imputed to any one or all of these factors. Faltering, shuffling or hurried steps are, in fact, vestigial remnants of the atavistic flight reflex. But as the horse gradually learns to trust his rider, he gradually also learns to dominate his reflexes. We must educate him not to fear our influences on his body, but to understand and obey them, even to accept them gratefully as a reassurance.

The old type of manege was excellent for this purpose, because it eliminated all exterior sources of distraction, so that the horse could concentrate his attention entirely on the rider. But in most modern riding schools, there are too many people moving in the gallery, bent on fun or business, not always disciplined; there is far too much noise. It is all very well if we want to accustom the horse to the bustle of indoor competitions, but the conditions are most unfavourable for teaching an alert, intelligent young horse. The design of the horse's eye gives a very wide range of vision at distance, but a horse will always start at the sudden sight—or sound—of an object appearing so closely that he cannot examine and recognise it; and even after he has recovered from his fright, he will continue to be distracted by surprising movements and noises and will not be able to give all his attention to his trainer. We would expect university students to ignore the noise of a barrel-organ playing outside the windows of a lecture room, or the sight of some idiot making faces behind the lecturer's back, but not children; in similar conditions, how could a teacher hope to keep the attention of infants in a primary school?

And so, it is growing trust in his rider and experience of the world which will eventually liberate the horse from his flight reflex. This cannot be achieved quickly, by constraint or by exposing the horse, in the shortest time possible, to every conceivable kind of impression. Calm and rhythm cannot be drilled into a horse's nervous system; yet rhythm is a requisite of effective movement, as much as it is of tuneful music. The regularity of the beat is bound to be impaired whenever the horse's mental composure is ruffled, as when his posture and movement are hampered by forcible means of restraint.

Except in the most advanced dressage tests, the horse will be required to quicken the beat whenever it is prescribed to shorten the steps. This is logical; as the speed must remain constant, the steps have to be shortened in time as well as in space. A slower beat is pardonable whenever the steps must be lengthened, but if the beat in the short steps is slower than in the long ones, it clearly denotes a loss of impulsion. Slow, unsteady, wavering, passage-like steps are faulty when a shortening of the stride is prescribed in a test; one wants to see a quick and lively beat.

But to satisfy the much more stringent requirements of an artistic performance, the beat may not change when the speed has to change; to fulfil this condition, the horse must be able to support a large amount of weight alternately on one hindleg and the other for a longer fraction of time than in the normal, working gait; he must therefore be able to flex his haunches pronouncedly; in other words, he must be capable of an advanced degree of collection if he is expected to slow the speed by slowing the beat. On the other hand, tremendous energy is needed to swing the limbs effectively in the extended trot, and normally one would allow the horse to quicken the beat, as this would lessen his effort; but, in artistic dressage, the beat may not vary on the short and long sides of the arena; it is the length of stride which varies. The difference between short steps and collected steps must be perfectly understood. For the short steps, the beat must be quick and the horse must be in "horizontal balance". Collected steps, on the contrary, must be very composed and the forehand must be elevated because of the deep flexion of haunches; these steps are steps of the High-School, because impulsion is directed more vertically than horizontally.

Finally, in an ideal state of complete unity with the horse, the rider will be able to command the movements of the horse's limbs almost without thinking; the pair will move in quick, short steps, or long bounding strides, or slow, graceful steps, in perfect harmony with a tune and with enchanting elegance. This is dancing on four legs.

To prepare the horse for the difficulties of real collection, we must start by teaching him to shorten his steps and quicken the beat.

To maintain a trotting speed of 160–170 steps to the minute on a large circle, the horse will have to move with short and lively steps; with a particularly impetuous horse, it may be necessary to push him outward on the circle, which helps to hold within limits the propulsive force of the hindlegs. On the circle, the mass has to be more securely supported by the hindlimbs; this compels the horse to start arching his back, and this, in turn, gives him a more satisfactory posture. When resuming a straight course, the rider must ensure that the speed remains the one which he wants, and not one just of the horse's choosing; the horse must neither propel himself forward too much, nor slow the speed by leaving his hindlegs "behind", or by hovering with stiff hocks; to prevent one or the other of these occurrences, the circle will have to be either enlarged or made smaller. Circular lines make it easier to develop impulsion without causing rushing, and they also deprive the horse of the possibility of avoiding the action of the bit whenever the speed has to be regulated by the hands. The critical moment is always the return to a straight course; this is when the horse will try to alter his posture and to use his limbs again for their more normal propulsive function, which straight lines favour. It is in this case that leg-yielding or, at a later stage, the shoulder-in render such signal service; whenever the horse tries to rush, he must immediately be put in one or the other of these positions, which enable the rider to set inflexibly the speed that he desires; they both prevent excessive impetuosity as easily as the device of enlarging the circle. Gradually, however, as his strength and understanding improve, the horse will learn to compose himself on straight lines as well as on circular ones; with the development of the muscular strength of his hindquarters, he will eventually become able to collect himself.

From the point of view of our own education, changes of speed are an excellent test of our sense of balance. It is our sense of balance that must tell us if the hindfeet alight as they should, just beneath our seat, which means that the horse is carrying himself properly; it is also our sense of balance that tells us if impulsion in the shortened steps is really fulfilling its requisite supporting function, so that the thrust of the hindlegs ceases to produce the slightest feel of heaviness on the hands with increased tension on the reins. We should be able to sit up easily, with our buttocks so deeply sunk into the saddle that the two feel as if they were glued together. Changes of speed will not only give us the feel of impulsion; they will also teach us how to produce it. A balanced horse, moving with impulsion, neither hurries nor holds back; impulsion is neither excessive nor insufficient forward propulsion.

A brisk beat makes the horse spring off the ground, prevents resistance, fosters energy and gradually transforms the effect of the force of the hindlegs; this will result in less forward propulsion and more upward propulsion.

Learning to prescribe beat without impairing impulsion is an important part of a rider's education. Riding to music helps, providing the music is suitable; the beat of the tune must be clear; but regarding the choice of beat, there are two conflicting opinions, though both are correct: one can choose to ride all the movements, in all the gaits, with the same beat, or choose a tune that varies between lively-energetic and slow-collected; however impulsion and springiness must not suffer, and every stride in all movements must be the same.

In advanced dressage competitions powerful extension can never deserve good marks if the beat becomes irregular; but even during schooling it would be harmful to let the horse feel that he can get away with just one uneven step; it would be letting him feel that he can have his own way, and soon he would take further liberties; the uneven steps would become more and more frequent, the horse would gradually become more and more resistant to any form of restraint and all his gaits would deteriorate.

But although regularity must eventually be infused into the horse's blood we must also develop attention and obedience to the different forms of action of our aids; the horse must learn to understand whether we require him to change the rate of the beat or to alter the length of his stride. Our sense of rhythm may be a gift of the gods; nevertheless we will always have to remain consciously aware of the beat and the length of stride when we have to influence the speed. Using the legs unthinkingly and insensitively to hustle the horse, or braking with stiff shoulders, arms and hands are pernicious habits which show ignorance of the most basic principles of horsemanship.

TRAINING: STYLE AND FORM

At all gaits, the horse must have style. The opposite of style is a certain looseness of body and limbs that produces shambling gaits. Talking about a horse's movements, this sort of looseness is called disunity. Both the effectiveness of our aids and the steady improvement of our horse's performance depend entirely on our own sense of style, posture and balance.

If certain stables, trainers and jockeys enjoy long runs of successes, it is not because they always get the better horses, but because trainer and jockey know their job. It is a great shame that so few jockeys get the opportunity to school the same horse long enough to be able to imbue him permanently with balance and style; during the race, there is little that a jockey can do to balance a horse that has not been well-trained.

Show-jumpers must also be taught to develop a good cantering and jumping style, if we want them to jump safely and to maintain their form. A horse should never be made to jump high or at speed before his style is confirmed, and this principle is supported by the fact that some horses with a tremendous jump will clear impressive obstacles on some occasions but will have twenty knock-downs at another event; their results always remain a matter of chance. If his style has not been polished, a show-jumper cannot be reliable; a constant form must be established before consistent performance can be expected.

This principle applies, of course, to all forms of athletic riding; in whatever direction we intend to specialise, progressive training must gradually develop the muscular fitness, stamina, and breathing technique of the horse (and of our own).

The most successful method of training for this, appears to be "interval training". It has been practiced for a long time with remarkable results by long distance runners in Finland. Their hilly country has compelled them to break up, during training, the overall distance of a run into short lengths, with intervening brief pauses to pay off the oxygen debt. The universal superiority of Finnish long distance runners produced the theory—since then confirmed by observation and experiments—that interval training taxes the nervous and locomotive systems less severely than the traditional methods of developing speed, because it promotes the growth of a larger capillary bed; and an intricate mesh of blood capillaries is essential for the rapid dispersal of carbon-dioxide and lactic acid produced by extreme muscular exertion. I am convinced that highly-strung horses would perform much better in racing if more trainers could be persuaded by scientific arguments to adopt interval training methods. It is for the same reason that I consider, as I stated in an earlir part of this book, that hunting is good for young thoroughbreds destined for racing; the frequent checks help to dispel excitement, and furthermore, they provide a form of interval training. It is not sufficiently realised that pulling and excitement are often signs of physical weakness, which disappear when muscle, heart, and lungs have been strengthened by progressive training.

In the long distance conditioning exercises that we were subjected to in the cavalry between the two world wars, we had to gallop for periods of 25 minutes, and ride or lead our horses at the walk for five minutes between every period of galloping. Eventually, our horses would be so fit, that they could keep going for many hours at an average speed of 25 to 30 km per hour, with 55 minutes of galloping with intervals of 5 minutes walking.

For horses destined for the sport of dressage, endurance training must also be systematically included in their programme of work, and the sooner the better. This sort of exercise counteracts the strain on the joints of gymnastic schooling. The difficulties of dressage can be avoided if the muscles are developed by free, natural movement, before abnormal flexion of the haunches is demanded. But improvement of style at every pace must continue to be included in the daily routine of work of even the advanced dressage horse; in much the same way as do pianists who never discontinue the gymnastic limbering up of their fingers every day, even when they have become celebrities.

For the horse, exercise is necessary because muscular strength is needed not only for effective movement, but also for effective athletic posture. Satisfactory performance does depend absolutely on a good body carriage.

Once again, I illustrate my meaning with an example from human activity. Standing on the head, or standing on one leg in the vertical or horizontal body position, promotes much more disciplined body control than running, or throwing and lifting weights. This is because the limb muscles (the extrinsic muscles) are strengthened by activities which utilise the friction of the ground (running, leaping, climbing, throwing); whereas the muscles of the trunk (intrinsic muscles) can only be developed by posture improving and balancing exercises. In all sports, the effective use of the limbs depends upon the stability of the body; therefore, it is logical that good postural habits should be acquired before strength of limbs is developed towards any particular use. This principle, which ought to underlie all systems of training for human sports, applies just as much to the training of horses.

In the vocabulary of sport, the word "form" is used to describe a combination of muscular strength, speed and style; it can also refer to the degree of fitness, or condition. It applies to the degree of preparation of the individual for a special performance; he can be "in poor form", "good form", "top form", and his performance can be predicted accordingly. The form of a subject can remain at a steady level for a certain length of time; it can improve or deteriorate, but neither man nor horse can be perpetually in top form. The art of training consists in getting the horse up to top form, in time for the ultimate performance, and seeing that he maintains his form up to the day of the event.

And so, the word training can mean two things; it can either be applied to a method of educating the horse to become obedient and to improve his style; or to a system for bringing him by diet and exercise to the required state of physical efficiency for a race or some other athletic feat.

In the second sense, we must distinguish between training the young horse—to give him the physical exercise which will help him to reach maturity with healthy, strong bones and muscles—and training the mature horse to get him fit. However, a fit, mature horse is a very powerful animal that will need a lot of work and a fit, experienced rider; he has reserves of energy which he must be made to use and it is not always easy to manage a horse in such fit condition. Fat, soft horses are a different proposition; their early morning freshness quickly vanishes after a few minutes of lungeing, by which time they are relaxed, docile and suitable for peaceful hacking and teaching novice riders. This must be the reason why so many horses are too fat.

All riders ought to realise that fatness and flabbiness in horses is as unsightly and harmful for them as it is for humans; they ought to be able to recognise suitable condition and know how to get a horse fit. But they should also know that a fit horse needs a fit rider and a lot more work than is generally realised.

DRESSAGE

Horsemanship is a science with technical terms of its own, but many of these technical words are not very appropriate and it is time that some of them were revised.

Dressage, for example, is a word derived from the old French word "dresser", a verb meaning to tame an animal and teach it to perform tricks. When an elephant stands on one leg; when a lion gently holds his trainer's head between his jaws, resisting the temptation to bite it off; when horses at liberty perform a perfect drill—this is dressage. Circus trainers have cleverly exploited the natural imitative instinct of animals to teach them to perform unnatural actions. In this sense, dressage is teaching by frequent repetition and using, if necessary, mechanical devices to enforce obedience.

Although some circus training methods are based on sound animal psychology and are used by a number of acknowledged masters of equestrian art, we do not like to think of the art of dressage (as it is practised, for example, by the Spanish School of Vienna) as the skill of taming animals and teaching them tricks. We prefer to think that we are educating and "schooling" horses.

So dressage can mean a method of training horses to show them in hunter classes, to compete in jumping or dressage sports, to give artistic displays or to perform circus acts. The word should not have been included in the horseman's vocabulary.

Teaching is developing the horse's intelligence so that he learns to understand and obey us. Training is making him repeat certain movements until he performs them automatically; mechanical means of persuasion have to be employed because no attempt is made to develop the horse's mental attributes.

We must believe that the horse has some intelligence and that he is capable of understanding us. We do not want a dumb, mechanical instrument; what we want is a trusting, obedient, attentive and spirited friend and servant. If we are not prepared to believe that the horse has a mind, we cannot pretend that we are educating him.

Though there are still as many unsympathetic "trainers" as genuine "teachers" in the horse world, a large section of the public is unaware of any difference. However, a knowledgeable observer knows that if a rider has to make use of all sorts of artificial aids, it means that he is incapable of teaching a horse to stand and to move in freely acquired balance, and that the rider himself does not understand the meaning of "influences" or "aids". He has never reflected on the scientific, psychological premises of education. To begin with, he starts off with a wrong conception of lungeing work when he ties the horse's head down with side-reins, in the belief that by restraining the front end and urging from behind with a whip, he will be teaching the horse collection. While mechanically enforcing obedience and imposing an artificial form, the trainer destroys the horse's strength as well as his spirit. Eventually, with much assistance from whip and spurs, he will make the horse jump obstacles, will wrest flying changes of lead by suddenly shifting his position, and will rehearse ad nauseam the figures and steps prescribed in a dressage test; but the horse will move with a stiff head carriage and a rigid back if he has never been allowed to move freely. With a certain amount of agility, an insensitive rider can impel a horse's legs to make the movements of the piaffe or the passage, but he will never get the horse to flex his haunches or to show, in the transitions from one gait to another, the requisite upward or forward impulsion.

It cannot be denied that mechanical methods of training do enable some riders to score successes in show-jumping, eventing and even dressage competitions. This speaks only for the talent of some horses, who manage to accommodate themselves to any kind of mechanical restriction, providing that the rider is consistent and has the intelligence to make his intentions clear; some sort of amicable agreement can then be established.

But a genuine teacher is a superior person altogether. He knows how to combine traditional taming and training methods with modern psychological knowledge; he develops relaxation, balance, a regular beat and obedience to the aids to produce, eventually, a pleasing picture of harmony of carriage and movement, and of docility. His basic object is the production of what used to be called the reliable campaign horse. Such a horse would be able to perform a novice dressage test with surrendered reins on the long sides (60 m) of a dressage arena without alteration of carriage or speed and would then proceed to jump fluently a small course of obstacles. It is only after this essential foundation has been securely established that specialising for anything, show-jumping or dressage, can be contemplated. But we never hear "campaign riding" mentioned nowadays. In the past, this was the name for the basic education of all horses, whether they might eventually become general purpose saddle-horses, competition horses or High-School specialists.

It is not invidious to argue that competition dressage and artistic dressage are different things. Real connoisseurs of the art of the High-School know that the type of horse suitable for the sport of dressage is not designed for the movements of the High-School, and that the converse is also true; few, if any, Lipizzaner can satisfy the stringent requirements of modern dressage tests, and the thoroughbreds or cross-breds preferred for the sport of dressage are not built to perform (without detriment to their joints) the extremely elevated airs of the High-School. Yet some people refuse to understand that there should be a difference between advanced dressage and High-School dressage.

Advanced, competitive dressage tests must include all the "Airs on the Ground", while High-School dressage includes the "Airs above the Ground". It's difficult to imagine a Lipizzan capable of making a fluent transition from the high springs of a High-School trot into a flying extended trot; to put his feet down on the precise spot towards which his toes point at the highest point of their trajectory (a requirement of truly artistic movement), he would have to make bounds covering a distance of 10 m. A dressage horse must be seen to want to go forward; elevation, for him is of secondary importance; it should be only sufficient to help him to develop impulsion and speed. But for the High-School horse, elevation is the important thing, and forward propulsion must be only sufficient to help with elevation; the propulsive force of the tremendously powerful hindquarters must be contained, to be delivered in a predominantly upward direction; there must also be impulsion but its effect is at a different angle with the horizontal. While the impulsion of the dressage horse is facilitated by momentum and a measure of rapidity and briskness, the leaps of the High-School horse must be produced by sheer muscular effort; the strength required to project the body more upward than forward is incomparably greater. Impulsion in the piaffe and the passage of the High-School, or the leaps of the Airs above the Ground, needs such a development of thigh muscles that the High-School horse can be compared with the human weight-lifter.

Despite this, one would like to see some resemblance between High-School dressage and competitive dressage. The same principles must be respected in all forms of horsemanship, but it is in the sport of dressage that they ought to be most staunchly supported, if we do not want it to be a mere travesty of the art. Ideally, of course, these principles ought also to be respected in show-jumping; and the training of hunters and show-jumpers can be just as interesting or difficult as the training of dressage horses. Haphazard clearing of big obstacles is no more pleasing to watch than an accurate but dull dressage performance by a horse with a shortened neck and rigid back. Instead of being mechanically trained to jump, horses must be educated to be sensible and to develop a good style, just like human athletes, so that instead of tearing round a course, they learn to judge speed and to increase it sufficiently at the right moment to clear an obstacle safely. That would also be dressage.

But the horse world continues to apply the word "dressage" to any other kind of riding that is not jumping or galloping across country, instead of thinking of it as an education for all horses, which must be completed before they are required to specialise. Dressage (with a capital D) must never become an end in itself before a horse has received a broad primary education; if the word continues to be mentioned in a disparaging sense, it is because some people cannot see the difference between good and bad "Dressage", between a mechanical performance and an inspired one. In its proper sense, dressage is a combination of education, physical training and gymnastic development of muscles that must make every horse a pleasure to ride.

Though dressage tests are sometimes interesting to watch, they are more frequently intensely boring, and a lot of the time the public disagrees with the judges. The system of judging by awarding points is often blamed, but a system of numerical evaluation of movements can be neither more nor less fair than any other in which judges are free to express their taste; it is well known that two witnesses of the same event never see or describe it in the same manner, and to some extent the points system does avoid too much vagary; unfortunately, it compels judges to look out only for faults and to pay so much attention to detail that they cannot take in the whole picture. So, while spectators are carried away by their enthusiasm for a particularly attractive display, judges are too busy noting every fault and slight inaccuracy to realise the overall quality of the picture. If the rules compel the judges to mark favourably a faultless execution of a test by a docile but dull and wooden horse, they should not expect a public, who are sensitive to beauty, to agree with their verdict.

There are two ways of appreciating a good test. In certain eyes, it is the faultless performance of prescribed movements at a determined speed, in an acceptable form; then all the judge needs to do, is watch the horse's feet. For others, it is an artistic display; it must give aesthetic pleasure and the judge ought to be allowed to express his preference.

A fair system of judging ought to take artistic merit into account as well as technical skill and reward inspiration as much as accuracy. This is the system used for judging skating competitions.

It might be possible to divide dressage competitions into two phases. The first, free-style, with marks for relaxation, style, form, balance, rhythm, impulsion, purity and elasticity of the gaits, suppleness and submission, elegance of the rider, smoothness of the ride and correct application of the aids. The judges would have to evaluate the grace and harmony of the performance, and the public could be treated to a display of dancing horses.

In the second phase, the technical skill of the rider and the obedience of the horse would be demonstrated by riding prescribed movements at a determined speed of so many metres per second; the rider would be able to concentrate entirely on precision without having to worry unduly about elegance.

Thus the rider would be required first to reveal his level of education by showing what he believes to be a picture of unconstrained, regular and pure gaits. After this, he would have to demonstrate his technical skill by performing with precision the prescribed movements of a test.

If such a system were adopted, and if Phase I counted for more than Phase II in the final score, we would not continue to see, as we so often do, awkward, irregular movers, blatantly restricted by their riders, gaining higher marks than others that move with grace but lose points on account of trifling inaccuracies.

Admittedly, much work is needed to prepare a fit horse for the accurate performance of a difficult test. This is however, no excuse for the mechanical, unimaginative exercises, as tedious to watch as to perform, which often pass as dressage. It is time something was done to revive public interest in the "art of dressage" and genuine artists ought to be given a fairer chance.

The suggested system would also take away from "Dressage" the aura of superiority that it has arrogated to itself, although in its present form it rarely suggests that horsemanship is an art.

Normally, all that we are offered is the spectacle of a succession of horses of good conformation, with naturally good gaits and a reasonable degree of suppleness and submissiveness performing a set of identical movements; it is impressive drilling, but if that is all that dressage is supposed to be, it would be even more impressive as a test of obedience if, instead of performing alone, horses went in groups and were also required to jump a small course of natural obstacles or, at least, to gallop in formation. This would show that a dressage test is not an end in itself.

Furthermore, I do not think that movements which properly belong to the High-School should be included in the sport of dressage, not even in the advanced tests. There should be two different kinds of competition. The first, tests of obedience for sporting horses, which would include only natural gaits, in horizontal balance. The second, tests of artistic merit, in which properly elevated, collected movements would have to be performed. In the first category, a passage with little elevation but with a lot of impulsion would be as acceptable as a true, elevated passage, but the piaffe would not be included; the shuffling, fidgety movement which we so often see bears no resemblance to a piaffe of the High-School.

In the present situation of dressage, most of the people who can get to the top are those who have the finances necessary to purchase horses with exceptional conformation and a natural brilliance of movement. Real artistic merit is not rewarded. Artistic dressage will perish, unless opportunities are created which would encourage more riders to take it up.

THE NATURAL METHOD

This modern expression for a system of training first promulgated in Italy is so appropriate that it is difficult to understand why it has been so variously interpreted by knowledgeable horsemen in different countries. Caprilli and his followers applied scientific observations and principles to the training of horses for cross-country and jumping, and developed a system which rapidly took the Italians to the summit in show-jumping. The world sat up and took notice. In Germany, in particular, Baron Waldenfels was the first to recognise the advantages of the method; he modified the Italian seat and developed a jumping style which gives very precise control. However, the forward seat continues to be wrongly interpreted by many riders and its fiercest protagonists and antagonists are those who understand it least, while the usefulness of cavalletti work and the advantages of giving a horse complete freedom of head and neck carriage continue to be hotly disputed. Caprilli, an unquestioned master of the forward seat, could help a horse to balance himself and could regulate his speed, while keeping a deep seat, and letting the horse use his neck freely; but many advocates of his method teach that the rider must lean forward over the horse's neck to avoid burdening his back, that the hands must be held low, midway along the sides of the neck, and that the stirrups must be so short that the buttocks become the highest point of the body. They believe that it is possible to train a horse to become an obedient show-jumper or eventer just by giving him the experience of jumping over the greatest possible variety of obstacles. It is true, of course, that an indifferent horseman does less harm in a forward position than in a classical position, in which he is inclined to hang on and provoke resistances which he is unable to destroy.

Obedience is the crucial thing, but horses trained by the so-called natural method become disobedient if more is demanded of them than they are capable of achieving, or if the rider's clumsiness and his mistakes disturb them; obviously, we will never know whether a horse is perfectly obedient until we face him with a difficulty, but, for a long time, he should be allowed to enjoy jumping easy obstacles, in an unforced attitude, at the speed that suits him best.

Intelligent training by the natural method does establish a sound basis for specialisation towards dressage as well as show-jumping, although the success of the method depends on being able to train in surroundings which resemble the natural habitat of horses; results are unsatisfactory when the method is used in maneges. The natural method belongs to the out-of-doors. The theory is that a horse will become straight and balanced if his strength is developed by natural exercise, and that all the schooling figures—which so many riders enjoy and consider to be essential—can be dispensed with. In the natural method a horse must find out how to balance himself without any assistance from the reins, and the walk and gallop are preferred to the trot. The rider uses his reins only to maintain rhythm, balance and a regular speed, but he never allows the horse to find support from the bit; he can hold his reins in one hand, supported on the mane, which is an effective method of preventing hanging-on and too much use of arm strength.

At the beginning, the speed is moderated by "taking and giving" hand actions which cheat the horse of any possibility of taking a hold; most horses quickly come to understand the meaning of these actions. At a later stage, when the horse has established a balanced gallop, so that the rider can sit upright, rein contact is alternately offered and abandoned, but this must not affect speed or rhythm, nor cause any change in the rider's position.

The secret of success lies in maintaining determined forward movement, which obliges the horse to swing his legs powerfully and to make long, bounding strides; it is speed that ensures straightness. Although the hand interferes only to check any attempt at running away, the parades can be energetic and supported by a firmly braced back. The muscular tension produced by the swinging of loins and hindlegs at the gallop enable the rider to feel and easily maintain a suitable speed, should he feel a loss of energy, betrayed by a trailing of the hindlegs or a swaying aside of the hindquarters, he must urge the horse on and straighten him by placing the shoulders in front of the evading hindlegs. These interventions may have to be frequent at the beginning, but eventually incipient crookedness can be nipped in the bud and the gallop can be straightened without recourse to greater speed.

It is only when the horse is able to walk, trot or canter on a straight and narrow ridge, or in the trace of a cart wheel that he can be considered to be straight; and he can be considered to be balanced when he allows the rider to sit upright and when his speed and rhythm remain unaltered as the contact is alternately established and surrendered.

The underlying principles of training by the natural method are, therefore, identical to the principles of traditional schooling; they are relaxation, straightness, balance, submission, all those qualities that allow a rider to sit upright and to control impulsion without difficulty. The traditional method seeks to achieve these objects through collection; the difficulty resides in obtaining collection without destroying impulsion. On the contrary, the natural method aims at obtaining collection, eventually, through the development of impulsion; the ability to collect—which is essential for surmounting big obstacles and for the difficulties of advanced dressage—is believed to be acquired by the horse through improved balance and control of forward movement. In the natural method, the horse first learns to move in good, effective style over uneven ground and natural obstacles; the suppling of the haunches by manege work comes at a later stage. This is logical, and the order of priorities is reversed only by riders who misunderstand dressage training.

However, even if one believes in the natural method, there must come a stage when the horse will have to accept a tension of the reins to contract elastically the muscles of his back and neck; without this tension, it would be difficult to regulate the speed with sufficient precision in dressage and show-jumping. For this purpose, the gallop is also the most appropriate gait, because it is easier to compel a horse to swing his back and put enough tension on the reins if one can make him move faster than he is naturally inclined to do.

This, however, applies to all the gaits. It is only by making a horse work harder than he would of his own accord, that we can make him use his back muscles properly and relax his poll and that the rider can maintain a steady tension of reins. But the tension of reins must never be rigid; some head movement must be allowed at all the gaits and the rider must acquire a sensitive feel for this, in order to be able to determine with precision the length of every leap of the gallop by acting with rhythmical parades in harmony with the forward swing of the hindquarters. A fixed hand, with an inflexible tension of reins, induces the horse to pull, "to gallop into the ground"; a steady hand receives impulsion, fosters or limits it and never prevents the horse from galloping in elastic bounds that can be easily lengthened or shortened.

That is the essence of the art of training and the rider can use any method he prefers, providing that the final result is a straight, supple and willingly submissive horse.

3 Outline

The front of the body of the horse ends at the mouth and the tension of muscles of tongue and jaws affects the whole carriage of the horse. Here lies the key to the relaxation of the muscles of the poll which enables the rider to have the horse in hand. The tendon of the sterno-maxillaris muscle (sternum to the lower mandible) inserts in the fleshy parts of the masseter muscle (muscle of mastication); the sterno-hyoid muscle and the omo-hyoid muscle join the tongue to the sternum and shoulder-blade respectively. By stiffening these muscles, the horse resists the action of the bit, stiffens his neck and poll and pokes his nose. Knowledge of anatomy helps to understand why the movements of the neck affect not only the movements of the forelimbs (through common points of insertion of muscles on the shoulder-blade), but also the movements of the hindlegs (through related muscular ties along the back and the croup). In all displacements or attitudes of the body, the whole musculature is involved, so that it is not possible to form the horse by imposing a desirable shape on an isolated part of the body, such as the neck for example. Whenever we try to establish the form of the horse's body, we must start by thinking of the hindfeet. Above them, the forward swing of the hindlegs will put an elastic tension on the muscles of the back and the neck; the elastic tension of the back muscles holds the neck up in a graceful arch; all this gives greater freedom of movement to the shoulders, by relieving them of some of the load which they normally support. Here, a lightening of the pressure of the bit must be interpreted by the horse as permission to go forward, while, in response to intermittent pressures—half parades—he must yield by relaxing his jaws, flexing at the poll, lightening the forehand and so collecting himself. A rider who, instead of opposing the activity of the whole muscular system, knows how to harmonise his actions with the horse's movement, is rewarded by the horse's acceptance of the bit and the smoothness of the movement. A pleasing carriage of the head implies proper functioning of all parts of the body and must result from overall muscular development and progressive training over a period of years.

Need I say again that to be capable of training a horse to carry himself well, and of feeling, as well as seeing, improvement or worsening of carriage, the rider must start by educating himself.

Xenophon put it this way: "When a horse has been trained to carry himself of his own accord, to show presence at all times, he gives the impression that he enjoys carrying a rider."

We must think of forming the horse in the same way as we command his movements: from back to front. Head and neck position will then develop an established form, as if they had been cast in a mould. We do not try to set their form; we must wait until the horse has developed enough strength to balance himself properly in all his gaits, and then produces it of his own accord. Carriage is a consequence of balance. A body cannot hold itself up properly if it has not got firm muscles. This applies to humans as well as to horses, and no rider should forget this fact. When we train a horse, instead of thinking of moulding him into a cast, we must develop his balance; we must use our reins only for this latter purpose, and not to give head and neck a fixed position. Position of head and neck must be related to the horse's state of muscular development and degree of training. When he can balance himself without any intervention from the reins, just by reacting to the influence of the rider's seat, he has perfected a state of equilibrium which we call self-carriage. This is the dream of all riders.

An arching of the neck that does not correspond to the general condition of the body is what so many riders try to produce, but it is not correct carriage. Correct carriage implies arching of the back by elastic tension of muscles; lightening of the forehand; unimpaired engagement of the hindquarters; suppleness of the joints of the hindlimbs; and impulsion. All these will help the horse to carry the weight of the rider and are essential conditions of submission; but head carriage must correspond to the conformation, the degree of training and the objectives of training of the horse.

Horses who have to jump obstacles and gallop across country must be allowed free scope of neck movement for safety. On uneven, difficult terrain, an inexpert rider ought to abandon all tension of reins and leave the horse free to look after himself; any restriction of neck movement impairs the horse's safety.

On the other hand, elevation of the forehand is a requisite in dressage, but we speak of "relative" and "active" elevation.

Relative elevation is the result of training and improved weight-carrying capacity of the hindquarters. Even with old remounts, the strength and suppleness of the hocks has to be improved by exercises. In relative elevation, the top neck muscles are under strong tension and help to support the back, giving it the elastic tension which makes the movement comfortable for the rider. The neck is not shortened; its underline is concave, though it can be straight with a high degree of elevation; the nose is approximately vertical.

In contrast, active elevation is produced by shortening the neck muscles, to hold the head up; the neck is compacted, shortened and S-shaped; the cervical vertebrae are one above the other, and the underline of the neck is convex; the horse becomes "ewe-necked" and pokes his nose. As the functional connection between back and neck is disrupted, the trot jolts the rider out of the saddle. It is obvious that it is relative elevation that we want.

Forced, active elevation of the head and neck inhibits the driving capacity of the hindquarters, and so does exaggerated inflexion of the neck. By deliberately holding a horse's head up, we depress the base of the neck and in so doing also hinder the activity of the hind-quarters. A knowledgeable and skilful rider will sometimes use this method to dominate an excessively impetuous horse, and will then make him work in side-steps until he carries himself properly with relaxed neck muscles.

When they choose a horse, novice riders are always influenced by the way in which he carries his head. Head carriage is a good indication of a horse's docility or intractability. Certainly, when an elegant head carriage is accompanied by calm, rhythmical and roomy strides, it does show that the horse is suitable for pleasant hacking. However, this limited understanding of the role of the neck induces many riders to commit the worst possible fault, which is to interfere with the hands to produce a set head position. They manage to get the horse to flex at the poll either by sliding the bit to and fro in the mouth ("sawing") or by constantly closing and opening the fingers; because of their preoccupation with the position of the head, their hands are never still. This activity has an effect only on the mouth; it does produce a curved outline of the neck—providing the rider has tactful hands—and the horse can be made to understand that when the fingers close tightly on the reins, he must stop. But an obedient horse, who has learnt to respond to this command, will halt abruptly by braking with his forelegs. Constant fiddling with the reins achieves nothing more than an arching of the neck; the parts behind the saddle, loins and hindquarters, escape the action of the reins and, besides this, the continually busy hands interferes with the regularity of the motion of the limbs.

On the other hand, many ignorant and unsympathetic riders resort to side-reins, running-reins and systems of pulleys to lower the horse's head, so that he is held in a sort of straitjacket. A sufficiently cruel and persevering use of these gadgets will demoralise and subjugate the most head-strong horse, so that he can then be ridden safely even by a beginner learning to sit; but does the horse look then as if—to quote Xenophon again—he enjoys carrying a rider?

Side-reins, running-reins and other devices, such as pillars, which enforce an arching of the neck can impose flexion of the haunches. However, all these instruments betray to a knowledgeable person the incompetence of the rider. They can be useful, at a certain stage in the rider's education as they can save him from having to work hard; it would be a mistake to deprive him of these orthopaedic aids as soon as he has learnt merely to sit and steer, if he is so used to them that he would be helpless without them; but they must be discarded as soon as possible. The amount of energy that the rider spares himself by using such devices must be compensated by commensurate skill and feel because the effect of the hands is multiplied tenfold by these gadgets. Recognition of this fact and the disastrous ultimate consequences of the use of contraptions have caused most of them to sink into oblivion. When we see a rider resorting to them again because of his incompetence, we can expect to see him "riding the horse into the ground" within a very short time. Artificial aids of this kind are no substitute for skill and knowledge and, if a rider is prepared to sink deeper into a morass of ignorance, he will eventually discover that using them tactfully is more difficult than learning to ride effectively. Only very clever horsemen can afford to use these systems without risk of doing more damage than good.

To impart to a horse the sort of presence pictured in Xenophon's words, we must be able to distinguish between the aids which determine a certain rate of speed and the aids for forming the horse into a certain shape. However, it must never be forgotten that it is by improving the horse's balance that we gradually improve his outline.

It is always because of laziness (or weakness), or freshness and hypertension that a horse refuses to make the necessary muscular effort to move in balance, and at the beginning the rider will have to intervene frequently to restore equilibrium. However, the horse can effectively oppose the parades if these occur during the propulsive phase of the movement of the hindlegs. It is essential, therefore, for the rider to learn to feel the moment when he can intervene. The right moment is the split second during which the hindleg is flexing while supporting the mass; the precise instant at which the half-parades are most effective is when the advancing hindfoot is touching down. It is because this phase is so distinctly felt by the rider in the canter that it is the best gait for teaching a horse to carry himself in balance.

In all the gaits, the horse can maintain a balanced, dynamic posture, only if all his muscles function equally and effectively in their proper role. A balanced posture favours the good development of muscular power and harmony of movement; conversely, both needless expenditure of energy and insufficient activity weaken all the muscles, but particularly those of the neck, back and croup.

The unavoidable conclusion is that the only useful exercises for improving head carriage and strength are those which simultaneously improve balance and posture.

REIN TENSION

All horses must eventually learn to stretch the reins and none are incapable of doing so. To form the horse into the shape that will give the rider complete control, a certain tension of the reins is essential. However, it should not be forgotten that horses are not all made the same; we will never be able to effect a radical change in the shape of a body and we cannot expect to mould two horses into an identical form.

When a horse suitably stretches the reins, the bit should rest comfortably on the bars of the mouth and/or the tongue. A jointed snaffle is supported more by the bars of the mouth than by the tongue; a half-moon bit rests only on the tongue; a grooved curb bit rests on the tongue and lightly on the bars; a bit with a high port rests only on the bars. The degree of leverage of a curb bit then depends on the adjustment of the curb chain and on the length of the cheeks.

The horse can impart to the reins any measure of light or strong tension.

With a light tension, the bit just rests in the mouth, supported by the relaxed muscles of the jaws and tongue; the mouth is then slightly opened, but the lips remain closed. The "chewing of the bit" (which is not a rhythmical masticating action) is a sign of relaxed activity of those muscles by which the horse seeks to maintain all the time the feel of the bit. These small, invisible movements stimulate the secretion of saliva which then shows as a little froth on the lips. The smooth effect of the actions of the hands depends entirely on the relaxed activity of the mouth, which is transmitted to the muscles of the poll and neck, so that they also work in a relaxed manner. A horse is said to bridle nicely when he flexes at the poll, so that his nose drops almost to the vertical; he is then "on the bit" or rather "in hand".

At the beginning of training, neither a tightly constricting cavesson nor a dropped nose band should ever be used because they would interfere with the freedom of movement of the lower jaw. Any restriction of this freedom will destroy the confidence of the young horse, prevent him from relaxing all the other parts of his body and will provoke his resistance. Thoughtless constricting of the jaws in the early stages of training is the most common source of persistent stiffness of back and neck muscles. A riding instructor who admonishes his pupil against holding the horse in with unsympathetic hands, but who tightens the nose band to prevent any movement of the lower jaw, betrays his ignorance.

It is essential for the horse to stretch the reins to the same extent on either side. Here is the opportunity to warn against a very common fault which has disastrous consequences; it consists of opposing, with the outside rein, the lateral flexion demanded by the inside rein. This inflicts painful pressure on the outside bar of the lower jaw, which the horse tries to avoid by thrusting his lower jaw toward the side of the bend and, frequently, by rotating the head laterally, so that the outside ear is lower than the inside one. True, the rider must maintain a certain tension on the outside rein and, in the later stages of training, it is entirely with the outside rein that the rider determines the degree of lateral flexion of the poll; however, the tension of both reins must remain the same on curved lines as on straight ones and, therefore, the outside hand must always advance to the same extent as the other hand retracts.

An excellent method of teaching a novice rider the feel of even tension on both reins consists of winding the divided reins around a short whip, while making sure that they are of even length and separated by about 30 cm. The rider must hold the reins between the middle and third finger of each hand, with his thumbs forming a roof over the whip. The centre of the whip must be held exactly over the mane. The rider will find it easy to see how much the outside hand needs to go forwards and the inside hand to come backwards, if he is to maintain an equal feel on both reins during circles and corners: every time he fails, one rein or the other will become slack. However, the horse used must be well-schooled, in which case there is no better way of teaching the rider that the reins are used to indicate direction but that it is with the legs that one imparts lateral inflexion to the horse's body.

The suitable degree of rein tension depends on speed. In the collected gaits, because of the high degree of suppleness and sub-missiveness of the horse and the lightness of the forehand, a very light, hardly noticeable tension of reins is appropriate. On the other hand, a firm tension of reins is necessary when great speed is required—as in racing—because it helps the rider to determine the degree of arching of the loins and the scope of the strides of the gallop and of the leap over fences. So while we want the horse to be very light on the hand in the elevated movements of the High-School, conversely, we require him to make us feel a very positive tension of reins when we want to gallop fast and clear the big fences of a steeplechase course. These are the two extremes; but, between the two, there are infinite degrees of "elastic tension" which gives the rider the feel of being connected to the horse's mouth by rubber bands. This is the sort of tension which is desirable in all sporting uses of the horse and, particularly in dressage, where the essential requisites are that the horse be active, obedient and perfectly balanced. There are as many degrees of elasticity of rein tension as there are degrees of elasticity of muscle. Only a perfectly trained horse (in the widest sense of the word "training"), in completely established balance and form, can be safely ridden at speed with a hardly perceptible tension of reins. Nevertheless, this is the sort of tension that we need for show-jumping.

Whatever the degree of tension, the horse must always be "on the bit", which means that he must keep a contact with the rider's hand through the reins; yet, the natural movement must never be impaired. And, to allow the freedom of movement of the neck, essential to the establishment of a firm, dynamic posture, the hands must passively maintain a steady tension. The horse shows that he trusts the hands when he goes forward "on the bit", neither pushing against it, nor coming behind it—always trying to regain contact with it when he feels the hands advancing, but without any loss of regularity of movement and balance.

Inappropriate tension of reins is always detrimental to balanced dynamic movement as well as to the sensitivity of the mouth. While too much tension incites a horse to pull, one that is too light encourages him to develop the habit of going behind the bit; both faults teach him to be disobedient; either to hold back or to hurry and get excited, or to move crookedly, generally disregarding the aids and escaping control. Once this has happened, the horse will have to be completely re-educated by a quiet and knowledgeable rider, who will be able to re-establish genuine, regular forward movement. The only way to overcome all the difficulties attending resistance to rein tension is to re-establish the regularity of the movement. Before the reins can be used again for any other purpose than regulating speed, calm, even and determined forward movement must be completely established.

There is almost unanimous acceptance of the fact that a relatively firm tension of reins is desirable for the sporting horse, but the tension of reins suitable in dressage is the subject of endless controversy in the columns of specialised journals. Some writers argue that, at a peak of perfection, no tension of reins can exist, because tension implies a certain dependence on the reins for balance, a "fifth leg" which the dressage horse must dispense with as much as a High-School horse; an accomplished dressage horse should move in self-carriage. Self-carriage means: that the tension of reins is reduced to almost nothing; that the horse is almost on the point of being behind the bit, but is moving with impulsion, at the speed and in the direction wanted by the rider, with an arching of the neck which indicates elastic support by the back. A horse that holds himself with elegance, of his own accord, while appearing to enjoy carrying the rider on his back, and who does not lose his presence and rhythm when the rider surrenders and then re-establishes positive contact with the mouth through the reins, can be said to be in a state of self-carriage.

However a rider who concentrates solely on the influence of the horse's movement on his seat will be able to recognise at every instant whether the movement—be it on one or two tracks—is or is not correct and will not need to think about the tension of the reins; though the lighter the tension can be, the better. If a horse can perform a dressage test from beginning to end with genuine impulsion, in perfect rhythm, posture and submissiveness, on a practically loose rein, he proves an accomplished education; he has nothing more to learn. Though he may occasionally have to be reminded through the reins, firmly if need be, that he must continue to concentrate on working diligently and maintaining his carriage, the reins are not needed for any other purpose. It is through the varying effects of seat and position of the rider that he senses whether or not he is allowed to lower his head and neck. However, this is the ideal, the highly skilled dressage horse, perfectly in tune with his rider, obedient to the slightest indications, whose industriousness does not have to be demonstrated by the tension of the reins.

Nevertheless, for the novice rider and the young horse alike, a sufficient tension of reins indicates satisfactory impulsion; still, tension must never be a constraint which the horse resists by tightening the muscles of his jaws, poll and neck. Throughout the entire period of a horse's education, the rider will have to promote and sustain balance and regular forward movement, but his final object is a horse that can dispense with the assistance of the tension of reins; however, like everything else, progress has to be gradual and our first concern must be to inspire the horse with confidence in our hand, so that he freely goes into his bit. It is impossible, of course, to define an adequate tension of reins, but we should, at least, know that: firstly, if a horse is lazy and, consequently, does not stretch the reins, we cannot control him; secondly, if he has been properly trained to go calmly and with impulsion, the tension of reins will vary with the speed; thirdly, if he is a High-School horse, in perfect self-control of his equilibrium, it is with a thread of silk that our hand is connected to his mouth.

FLUIDITY

It is through our aids that we transmit our orders to the horse. The horse must be attentive to them and must unresistingly let the impulses of the aids *flow through* his whole body, from front to rear, rear to front, from left to right and right to left. A "fluid" horse is elastic and compressible, easily flexed and inflexed. This ungrudging submissiveness to the aids is what Germans call "Durchlässigkeit", fluidity.

In a crude sense, obedience is a matter of determination on the part of the rider. Any unspoilt young horse can be urged to move onward

Self-carriage of the Camargue horse, customarily ridden on a loose rein. This is
maintained . . .

. . . even in short, rapid turns at the gallop.

by the whip, or halted by a more or less skilful or energetic use of the reins; he can also be turned one way or the other by strong use of hand and leg on the same side of his body. However, between obedience and fluidity there are many shades of difference, and a fluently submissive horse is like a flexible channel through which our own impulses flow smoothly.

There are two diametrically opposed methods of developing the sort of pliancy which in a horse is called fluidity.

The protagonists of the first method are interested initially only in the activity of the hindlegs; providing that the horse is going with impulsion, therefore stretching the reins, they make no attempt to set the position of head and neck, and fluidity is eventually achieved by constantly adjusting speed and balance. Finally, when the horse is perfectly obedient to the legs, they develop the pliancy of the head and neck with skilful hands, always ready to yield. They build "upward and forward" by regulating the forward movement.

There is a second method which consists, at first, in stretching the muscles of the top of the neck by inducing with the reins a lowering of the neck and head; when this object is realised, the difficult task of lightening the forehand must be achieved by developing collection. Still, it is essential for the rider to be able to feel whether impulsion is satisfactory. Success in both methods must depend on the rider's feel.

In dressage, however, a horse cannot be said to be fluid unless he carries himself with an arched neck, a relaxed poll, supple hindquarters and shows impulsion. Fluidity in the sagittal plane allows the rider's parades to be conducted through the horse's body as far back as the hocks, compressing the joints of the hip, stifle and hocks.

If one could imagine the horse's body to be cast in a rigid mould, intersected by a line A – B the parades would travel through this tube from the mouth to the hip joint and the horse would have to step backwards, unless he was prevented from doing so by the pressure of the rider's legs; a horse obedient to this pressure would have to increase the flexion of the hind joints. We could also imagine a rider firmly fixed to the horse, so that a white line C – D intersected A – B at a constant right angle. The backward tipping of C would have to produce rotation of the whole system about the point of intersection of the two lines, with elevation of the forehand and lowering of the croup.

However, neither of these two lines is rigid. On the contrary, they are flexible in all directions. If they were rigid, brute force is all that would be needed to compel the joints of the hindquarters to yield to compression; however, the joints are protected by a system of nerves and ligaments which allows them to resist compression, besides providing a mechanism which ensures that smooth, precise movements are produced.

The arching of the neck is the result of a constant tension of the muscles of the topline, an elastic tension, in which all muscles are constantly returning to their original length, but are never slack. Similarly, the tension of reins must also be constant. However, the arching of the neck is useless to a rider who cannot also command the arching of the back by determining the swinging of the hindlegs. When the bow behind the saddle is firmly braced, as in collection, the same tension of muscles is continued through the back muscles to the neck, which is then naturally elevated and arched by intrinsic forces; it is under these conditions that the rider's parades can be effective. In the absence of overall elastic muscular tension and satisfactory impulsion, the rein effects stop at the saddle; though the mouth, the poll and the neck yield, the horse is shortened only in his neck and overbends. He can also resist by refusing to engage his hindquarters and by stretching the reins.

Therefore collection cannot be obtained by shortening the reins and pulling with the arms; the parades are not properly an activity of the hands but rather a change of distribution of the rider's weight, which he executes by imperceptibly drawing himself taller, without leaning backward.

Obtaining collection is certainly the greatest difficulty of dressage and the origin of the difficulty is invariably the weakness of the hindquarters. Extreme flexion of the hocks is tiring and soon produces soreness of muscles. If the horse is obedient and the rider unsympathetic, every step in collection will punish the horse for his obedience. Eventually, to obtain relief, the horse must straighten his hocks, but then he is no longer submissive. For him, it is much easier, much less effort, to fight the rider's hands than to yield to the compression of the hind joints. Irregularities of gait, stiffness of back, neck, poll and jaws are all resistances that can be traced back to a stiffening of the hocks; the final result is that the parades do not flow through to the hindlegs and are therefore ineffective.

Yet though we may know that the source of all difficulties can be traced back to stiffness of the hind joints and that all other resistances are secondary effects, we still cannot dismiss them as being of secondary importance. It takes time to feel the movement of each hindleg, but until that feel is developed, all riders ought to have at least a theoretical understanding of the mechanical effect of the parades and of the mechanics of locomotion. Unless they understand that natural movement must be allowed to flow undisturbed, they will never comprehend the symptoms of and reasons for resistance and know how to cope; still more important they will fail to understand that their own actions may be the cause of the horse's resistance.

It is easy to think of responsiveness to the parades as obedience to the hands and it is too often forgotten that the foundation not only of impulsion, but also of trust in the hands and acceptance of the bit, is obedience to the legs. It is never with force that one controls a horse. It must have been their particularly sensitive hands that inspired Simon and Haase to compare the ring of muscles connecting the hindlimbs with the jaws to an electrical circuit carrying a continually flowing alternating current. They imagined the bit to be one of the terminals on this circuit, not, it must be emphasised, a point at which the flowing current stops, as this must be a continuously flowing force, but merely a point (or one of many points) of connection to the circuit.

Responsiveness to the legs cannot be established if the horse feels that the free swinging of his hindlegs will be disturbed or hindered by a brake in his mouth. The force developed by the hindlegs must be allowed to be released in forward and upward movement. If we think of it this way, it is easy to understand why a well-trained and perfectly balanced horse is so easily upset by a rider who has had experience only of unbalanced horses, heavy on the hands; his insensitive hands will, sooner or later, cause a submissive horse to boil up and, according to his temperament, run away with the rider or stubbornly refuse to move. This behaviour is always caused by the rider's insensitive opposition to forward movement. Hands always allowing the energy to flow in a forward or upward direction and skilfully parrying at the right moment any forward loss of balance are hands that preserve obedience to the legs. This applies to racing, hunting and show-jumping as much as to dressage. Conversely, constricting hands that hold the horse in a vice, pull his head in, shorten and weaken his neck, will disturb the smooth flow of the movement and destroy obedience to the legs.

When the rider concentrates on being relaxed and sits perfectly centrally and deeply in the saddle, he will be able to feel the force of the movement of the hindlegs and the direction in which it propels the horse. One can even imagine the movement as an electrical current and realise that the propulsive power generated can only be controlled and directed if the rider is central on the line of conduction and the current passes, as it were, through him. He cannot be on such a centre line if the line of the imaginary electrical force or current from one hindleg or the other passes to the side of his seat. A crooked horse, therefore, cannot be precisely conducted. It does not require much imagination to comprehend that one must never bend the line of force with the strength of the arms; it must be directed by the aids in such a way that one is always on the centre line of the conductor. Thus, if the driving force is felt to pass to the side of this centre line, the horse must be straightened in his neck and the forehand must be placed in front of the straying hindleg, so that once again the rider is in the middle. This is the only way to control the motor force and to direct it without weakening and distorting it. The line of force must remain unbroken.

If we can think of the aids as electrical impulses it is easy to understand that things must go wrong when the conductors carrying the force or current and their controllers are out of harmony—not in unison. We must always be able to preserve the continuity and direction of the force. If the current fails to pass through the controller or the control fails to operate in the correct manner and at the appropriate moment confusion must result and fluent submission cannot be expected. Neither should the force of the current be weakened or distorted by our aids, nor should the horse's resistance to our aids harden or unduly weaken this force. We must be able to bring the terminals closer together or draw them further apart at will by bracing or relaxing the bows in front and behind the hand, though never by force, never by inflexibly opposing a horse's resistance and inexorably preventing the flow of energy from the hind-limbs along the lines of conduction. The terminals at either end must never be absolutely fixed and, even if only one is fixed, greater resistance rather than better submission is the likely result of the rider's inflexibility. If we try to fix the front end, the horse will lock the muscles of the jaws, poll and neck and if we try to fix the rear end, the horse will resist by stiffening his hindlegs during the supporting or the propelling phases of the movement. The only moments during which the rider's parades can be effective are when the extremities are in a position to yield, that is during the phase of shock absorption and support—of the hindlimb. In the lateral movements, the horse can obey the sideways driving action of the rider's leg only while the corresponding hindleg is off the ground; still, it is only if the poll and jaws are relaxed that the reins can prescribe the direction of the movement. In any case, the rider can never influence the movement if he acts on a hindleg at the moment when it is using the resistance of the ground to propel the mass.

Imagining the movement of the hindlegs as generating an alternating electrical current which passes along the conducting lines on which the rider (or controller) is placed, helps us to understand why the aids must be synchronised with the alterations in the current. This must continually flow and not be interrupted before it arrives at a terminal; only then can it be reversed. If currents of equal force flowed in opposite directions, they would collide midway, damaging the conductor and throwing the system out of order. If one force is much stronger than another, the weaker force soon becomes exhausted, but the stronger force is also relatively weakened. Smooth conduction and preservation of energy are possible only if the current can run freely backward and forward between two poles; if it is allowed to flow freely forward, all the force developed by the hindleg arrives at the bit as softly as a ball bouncing against a wall of foam rubber; the energy is immediately sent back to be absorbed equally softly by the hindleg as it bends at all the joints; the hindleg then extends, returning the energy forward and the rider's hand must yield at this moment to allow the free flow of impulsion. This interplay is most easily felt at the canter because both hindfeet touch the ground almost simultaneously. At the trot, the rider must first learn to ride on one hindleg (rising trot) to influence the flexion at the joints of that leg, but once he has acquired a deep seat he will be able to feel quite easily the movements of each hindleg. It is this interplay that teaches the horse to submit to the parades and become more fluid—impulsion must always be the primary consideration.

It is only when one hindleg tends to extend more vigorously than the other, thus threatening equilibrium, that the rider executes a well-timed parade which delays its extension and gives the less active hindleg time to engage properly. But even the mildest of parades inflicts some discomfort to the horse, so he eventually discovers that it is less unpleasant to make the effort necessary to remain well-

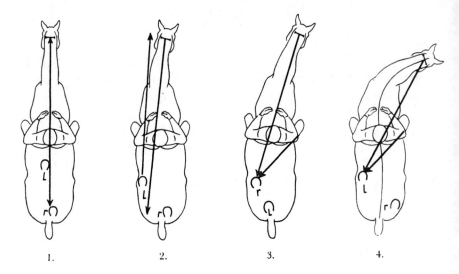

ABOVE AND OPPOSITE PAGE Movement of the horse's head and neck: *L*=left; *r*=right.

1. Correctly, the lines of force and the rein effects pass through the rider's body: the horse is straight, balanced and moving on a narrow track.
2. The action of the left hind is excessively propulsive; the foot is not engaged toward the centre of gravity; consequently there is too much tension on the left rein and not enough on the right. Line of force and line of action of the rein are left of centre; the rider is obliged to sit more heavily on his left seat bone and is inclined to hang on to the left rein.
3. Leg-yielding. Inflexion created by right lateral aids; the horse can yield to the predominant pressure of the rider's right leg and moves obliquely left and forward. The right leg of the rider guides the advancing right hind of the horse to come in front of the left hind; the horse is inflexed right through the seat and position of the rider. The effects of the rider's right hand and right leg converge and produce a displacement of the mass sideways and forward; the rider's left leg controls the sideways displacement, preventing the horse from crossing the hindlegs and rushing or stumbling in the displacement. Resistance to the action of the right leg of the rider is counter-acted by half-parades with the left rein; the horse is in a position in which it is impossible for him to develop the propulsive effect of the hind legs; propulsion is thus effectively extinguished.
4. The rider is trying to get the horse to yield to the pressure of his right leg but is acting during the propulsive phase of the movement of the right hind, when the latter is not in a position to obey. The rider is merely pulling on the right rein and bending the neck; the horse is disunited; the hindquarters are turned to the left; the left hind cannot support the mass. This is not yielding submissively to the leg.
5. Forward displacement toward the right, the horse inflexed toward the right, looking in the direction of the movement: travers position. The rider's left leg drives the horse's left hind forward, in front of the right hind; it is the rider's right leg that produces the inflexion; his hands allow this inflexion to spread to the neck and poll.

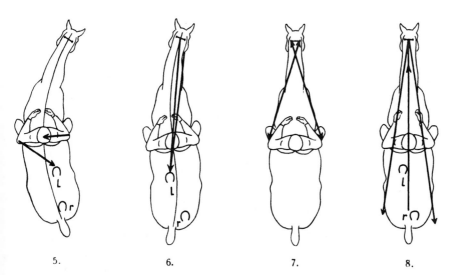

5. 6. 7. 8.

6. A horse with a pronounced "S" disposition of the body. In this case, to correct the twisting, a diagonal effect can temporarily be used (right hand acting on the horse's left hind); as soon as the horse is straightened, both hands act in the direction of the left rein to oblige it to perform its balancing function better and restrain its propulsive effect; the aids are similar, in fact, to those for a turn on the haunches.

7. A diagonal effect (left leg, right hand, and vice-versa) recommended by some instructors for getting the horse to stretch the outside rein in turns. This is absolutely illogical. In all turns, it is to the movement of the hind legs that the rider must remain attentive; if his left leg engages the left hind, his right hand must allow the inflexion to extend through the length of the horse's body and neck; if the inside leg of the rider is opposed in its effect by his outside hand, he will merely shorten the horse in his neck and constrict the movement. Pliancy extending from the mouth to the girth is not genuine fluent submission; the limited aims of these actions are to accustom the horse to "chew" the bit in a quiet and regular manner; as soon as this result is obtained, the hands must become passive.

8. The rider's hands are set wide apart, so that there is some backward traction on the reins; the hands are helpless in limiting the propulsive effect of the hind legs. The horse cannot be expected to submit.

This detailed examination of the interaction of the horse's movement and the rider's actions should not make us forget that the horse is an articulated system that must function as one unit. Our final aim is to become united with that system. Fluidity is just one element of this unity, made up of so many interrelated parts or elements that it requires deep study to comprehend it perfectly. Without theoretical knowledge, we cannot recognise our mistakes or the reasons for the horse's resistance to our actions, but knowledge is not sufficient; we still have to learn to feel the movement and discipline our reactions.

balanced. The more moderate we are in our demands, the better we will succeed in undermining resistances, in getting a horse to moderate his impetuosity, in teaching him to carry himself in improved dynamic posture; all this is fluidity. Very gradually, we obtain a quicker response to the half-parades and an increased flexion of haunches without restricting the swing of the hindlegs by senseless opposition to the forward movement.

FLEXION OF THE POLL

At each step of the walk, the head and neck of the horse regularly swing in rhythm with the movement of the forelimbs; there is an upward swing each time one forefoot advances and a downward swing as it touches the ground, though if the horse stiffens his neck, the movement will not occur. The movement is the result of the attachments between the muscles of the top of the neck and those of the scapula and back above the vertebral column, and, below it, between the ventral muscles of the neck and the muscles of the forelimb. The three big muscles on top of the neck insert not only on the spinous processes of the thoracic vertebrae, but also on the scapula which, therefore, must participate in the overall movement of the back and neck. When a forelimb swings forward, the upper end of the scapula is drawn backward, exerting a pull on the taut muscles of the neck, and the head swings up. On the ventral side, the neck and forelimb are connected by the mastoido-humeral muscle. This muscle originates on the mastoid process and the wings of the atlas, where the splenius is inserted. At its lower extremity, the mastoido-humeral muscle is inserted in the anterior surface of the humerus and the fascia of the shoulder and arm. When the head is lifted, the stable base of action of the mastoido-humeral muscle shifts to its upper, anterior attachment, and the contraction of the muscle draws the forelimb forward, thus increasing the scope of the movement.

In the young horse, freedom to swing the head and neck is essential to the freedom of movement of the limbs and must never be restricted by the reins. With sensible training, the muscles of the neck develop in bulk and strength and can then perform their function without the assistance of the downswing of the neck. Nevertheless, even a well-trained and well-ridden horse, when he suffers from fatigue, will use the swinging of the head and neck to pull his body forward. Though this passive downswing of the head is largely caused by gravity, the rider feels that the neck is being pulled down by the mastoido-humeral muscle and the forelimbs.

To preserve freedom of movement, the rider should never try to suppress the swinging of the head and neck with resisting hands; but it is at the walk, on a semi-tension of reins, that he needs to be particularly careful; a good walk depends on strong and freely functioning neck muscles.

The swing of the head and neck plays an essential role also in obedience to the parades. Flexion of the poll, essential to smooth control, can only be obtained at the moment when the muscles of the neck naturally relax their tension; if the rider's hand opposes the natural movement, it not only prevents the forward swing of the forelimb, but also causes the horse to resist by stiffening his neck muscles.

With the young horse, the rider must deliberately accompany the movement of the neck. Yet, although this swinging is natural and remains a lasting tendency, it can be exaggerated. The exaggerated arm swing of human beings in the walk is an unnecessary movement which tends to twist the trunk and restrict the swing of the legs; it is a symptom of lack of tone of the lumbar muscles and of poor co-ordination. Similarly, with the horse, an exaggerated swinging of head and neck indicates a certain lack of muscular tone; in a mature body, it indicates persistence of childish habits. As the horse improves in strength and balance, the swinging of head and neck should be reduced, but until a horse has achieved a perfect state of balance he will not be able to keep his head and neck perfectly still. Instead of trying to prevent the exaggerated swinging of the neck with the reins, the rider must realise that it is a sign of weakness and give the horse the opportunity to develop his muscular strength by rational exercise. Reducing the movement of the head and neck should be done by improving the horse's balance and not by fixing the hands.

It is only by carefully accompanying the movement of the head and neck that the rider learns to control his hands so that they remain in passive contact with the mouth. Providing the horse stretches the reins confidently—the length of the stride can be determined by more or less advancing the hands in harmony with the movements of the limbs.

However, when he is in the saddle, each hip of the rider in turn is carried forward by the back of the horse as a result of the propulsive action of the horse's hindlegs, and the hand must move forward to the same extent to accompany the movement of the head and neck; this gesture is exactly the opposite of the reflex swinging of the arms in the human walk. A very good exercise for learning to discipline oneself consists in walking with the hands in a rein-holding position, as if one were driving a horse with long reins. Learning to move hands and hips in harmony with the movements of the horse's limbs requires a lot of concentration and self-control; however, it is an effort which we must make if we want to be able to control the horse without provoking opposition on his part to our actions.

STRAIGHTNESS

A naturally straight horse does not exist. All horses are congenitally "crooked", in the sense that their spine is more concave on one side than the other, or that it has a more or less permanent "S" shape. This curvature is sometimes believed to be due to the position of the foetus in the womb, but there is no evidence to support the theory; it is invalidated by the fact that the young of multiparous animals are also crooked, the dog being a particularly striking example. Uneven development of both sides of the body is usual with human beings also.

It is more reasonable to ascribe this uneven control of body and limbs to the fact that all movements which serve a particular purpose are always executed in the same manner and that this manner becomes instinctive; any particular action would always produce the same movement. During growth, the body adapts itself to the performance of certain instinctive movements and, consequently, develops unevenly. Later in life, will-power—in the case of man— and constraint with animals, can modify postural habits, with the result that movement becomes more effective and easier.

Why the right side of the body and the right limbs are stronger than the left in most living creatures is a question which will never be quite convincingly answered. However, it is a fact that bilateral skill can be improved by exercise.

These long-held beliefs do not provide us with a satisfactory explanation of the phenomenon. A different one has occurred to me, suggested by personal observation and study of the movements of humans and animals, experience of gymnastics and a life-time of riding. I believe that it would help in solving the problems of straightening the horse.

All humans and animals show a tendency to walk in circles if they are blindfolded or deprived of points of orientation, as in the dark of the night, in thick fog or in a dense forest. Walking in a perfectly straight direction necessitates constant correction of deviation with the help of the eyes. The "circling instinct" is very noticeable in young children and young animals, and in the early stages of life it is no handicap because it always leads the infant back to his starting point whenever he becomes disorientated in his first exploration of the world. It is surely a mistake to attribute this circling to uneven muscular development; the reverse must the be case: the circling must be the cause rather than the consequence of uneven development. This instinct is most probably linked to the labyrinth of the inner ear which provides an important part of the information which assists the balance and posture of the body. The tendency to move on a circular path, always in the same direction, remains inconveniently strong with some adults, while others have succeeded in correcting it. This fact can be proved by trying to keep to a straight line when walking with the eyes closed, and opening the eyes occasionally to observe by what extent one has deviated from the intended direction. It is possible, however, to prevent deviation from the straight, even with the eyes blindfolded, by making short, quick steps and carefully placing each foot directly in front of the other. Walking on such a narrow track is an invaluable exercise for developing an acute sense of balance. The circling instinct is also responsible for vertigo; nobody who has learnt to control this instinct will continue to suffer from vertigo, but anyone who has retained it to a marked extent will feel anxious when compelled to follow a mountain path in a direction opposite to his normal instinct. Such a precarious sense of balance can even cause fainting.

Right-handedness is very marked in dancing also and can be observed in oneself or others on any ballroom floor when revolving right-hand or left in the waltz. The same feeling can be noticed in the exercises preparing the pirouette.

The puzzling crookedness of horses is probably due to this little known and, in this matter, insufficiently considered phenomenon. Therefore, crookedness should not be imputed to some inherent stiffness or to uneven muscular development and the aim of straightness need not be pursued by tedious repetition of gymnastic exercises purporting to equalise the suppleness of both sides of the body. Rather should the rider think of educating the horse to master his reflex and learn to co-ordinate his movements.

On the basis of these observations, there are good reasons for tackling the difficulty of straightening the crooked horse in a different manner than is usually prescribed. It seems useless to try to get the horse out of the habit of hanging on to the left rein by the method of "taking and yielding" with the left hand; this only encourages him to return time after time to his original position. On the contrary, whenever the horse slackens the right rein and hauls on the left, he must be put on a course which will oblige him to stretch the muscles of the right side of his body and come up to the right hand. He must be made to punish himself severely for hauling on the left rein, until he eventually gives up his hold and stretches the right rein. It is by forcing him to circle in a direction opposite to his instinctive one for a sufficient period of time that his imbalance can be corrected. As soon as he willingly stretches the right rein, he must be ridden forward on a straight line, with an even tension of reins, but any attempt to take a hold on the left rein must immediately be punished in the same manner. The circling instinct must be eradicated by persevering long enough with corrective exercise on the circle.

One should not assume that any rider can quickly and easily teach a horse to move straight. Knowledge of the importance of developing balance must underlie all gymnastic training, of the rider as well as the horse, but very few horses are so evenly developed that they can be taught in a short time to use the limbs of either side with equal energy. The development of perfect straightness is a very difficult task. In this respect, the slightest improvement or deterioration must be noticed without delay and the schooling programme has to be planned accordingly. But there is more than one symptom of crookedness and the whole subject must be thoroughly studied.

With the majority of horses, the vertebral column is slightly convex towards the right side in the thoracic region. There are then compensatory curves behind and in front. It is only too willingly that these horses yield to the indications of the right rein and resist those of the left rein by contracting the mandibular muscles of that side and thrusting the jaw to the left, while turning the neck and croup to the right. When a young horse refuses to stretch the right rein, slows down or may even refuse altogether to go forward on the right circle, while on the contrary he hurries and leans on the left rein when asked to circle left, it shows that the natural tendency to move crookedly is becoming more pronounced. The most usual and most futile reaction of riders is to use only the hands to destroy the resistance, which, like all others, must of course be opposed by directing the hindquarters also.

With the crooked horse, the hindfeet do not follow in the track of the forefeet. On circles in one direction, they follow a smaller path than the forefeet and, in the opposite direction, they make a wider circle. He can easily be made to increase the radius of a circle right, but getting him to decrease it is difficult. Exactly the reverse happens on a circle left.

A crooked horse also causes the rider to sit crookedly. As the majority of horses are bent to the right, the majority of riders have a tendency to slide to the right. An experienced rider knows that he must put more weight on the left stirrup to help himself to maintain a straight position; a novice rider, knowing nothing about crooked-ness, will allow himself to load the right stirrup more than the left and this causes the saddle to slide to the right. At the rising trot particularly, the left stirrup will feel shorter than the right and this can mislead the rider into lengthening it by one or two holes. Although this may put his seat bones again in the centre of the saddle, it forces inflexion to the right at the waist. As the rider gets used to this faulty posture, the horse's crookedness increases; whereas increasing the loading of the stirrup on the convex side of the horse's body—the left side in most cases—obliges the horse to use his left hind to support better the weight of the rider and is one of the best methods of equalising the movements of the hindlimbs. Therefore, if a riding instructor, observing his pupil from the rear, notices that he inclines his upper body toward the right, he should know that the horse is crooked. It is the horse that must be corrected, because the rider will only be able to sit straight if he succeeds in straightening the horse. On the other hand, an experienced rider who knows that he sits straight must always check on the even length of his stirrups when he schools a young horse. If he then feels that the left stirrup has a tendency to slide toward his heel, he will recognise this as a sign that the horse is not perfectly straight. This is a symptom to which few riders pay sufficient attention.

So, how does one straighten the horse?

To start with, one should never worry about straightness before the horse has developed active forward movement and has learnt to stretch the reins confidently. However, the gymnastic suppling exercises—circles, serpentines and figures of eight—with lateral aids can begin as soon as the above requirements are satisfied; on the curved lines of the course, the horse must learn to inflex his trunk in response to the pressure of the rider's left leg and to accept the pressure of the right leg instead of trying to evade it by bending in front of the withers. When he has learnt this lesson, the lateral movements with inflexion produced by lateral aids are introduced. It will be found that the intervention of the inside rein becomes unnecessary as the horse learns to inflex his body by stretching the muscles of the outer side and thus stretches the outside rein of his own accord. He will then be on diagonal aids.

A horse is said to be straight when he is equally responsive to both the rider's legs, can inflex as easily to one side as the other and when his inflexion extends continuously from head to tail. The hindlimbs then follow in the track of the forelimbs and the rider can sit straight.

Inflexion is so often misunderstood. It should be realised that it is the inside leg, and not the inside hand that creates inflexion. Furthermore, the maximum possible degree of uniform inflexion should just allow the rider to see the mane and its underlying elastic nuchal ligament "slip" to the left or right side of the neck. The inflexion in front of the withers must never be greater than the curvature of the whole body. If the rider pulls backward with the inside hand, the neck and head turn, but the outside hind cannot follow in the track of the forehand; this disturbs the regularity of the movement and can give the horse the habit of bridle lameness or of moving crookedly.

Leg yielding, and the more difficult exercises in lateral movement with inflexion of the whole body, are used not only to equalise the elasticity of muscles on both sides of the body, but also to prevent the horse from running away in reaction to the pressures of the rider's legs. A knowledgeable rider will use the lateral movements to enable him to keep the horse under control while demanding animation; the movement will remain flowing and regular. On the contrary, an uninformed and tactless rider will use his strength to bend the neck of the horse and, in so doing, will spoil the fluency and regularity of the movement; in his hands, a quiet horse will lose all desire to go forward, while a temperamental horse will become hectic.

It is fairly easy to teach a horse to yield to the pressure of the inside leg at the girth; it is much more difficult to get him to obey the pressure of the outside leg by moving forward and sideways with the concave side of his body on the side of the direction of the movement, as in travers and renvers. No horse would ever assume this position naturally, except occasionally if he is turned out and goes for another horse with his teeth, while ready to defend himself with his hind hooves. It is for this reason that yielding to the leg and the shoulder-in are taught before travers and renvers. When a horse can move in travers and renvers with unimpaired impulsion and regularity, one can assume that he is not only straight, but also perfectly submissive.

The vertebral column of all horses makes a sinuous movement during motion; the croup swings right as the head and neck swing left, and vice-versa. One makes use of this reflex to make a horse engage his left hind. He is placed with his right side against a wall, and his head is turned slightly left; the wall will prevent the hindquarters from moving right, while the position of head and neck helps the rider to control the activity of the left hind. Though the serpentine movement of the vertebral column is easy to feel from the saddle at the walk, it is particularly striking when one drives a stubborn young horse in long reins. To avoid going forward, the horse will constantly try to turn or veer away from the straight course, by turning his hindquarters to one side and his head to the other. To keep him moving in the direction wanted, one must turn the head the same way as the hindquarters. By keeping a careful watch on the hindquarters, turning the head immediately in the same direction as soon as they are seen to sway to one side and thus zigzagging for a while, one learns to thwart immediately every attempt the horse makes to change course. An un-schooled horse has great difficulty in moving more or less sideways with an inflexion toward the direction of the movement and this is what prevents him from persisting in his resistance. Long-reining is a very good way of teaching the rider to understand these reactions and to develop the quick reflexes he will need if he finds himself in a similar situation when mounted.

The serpentine motion of the vertebral column in the horizontal plane is not the only one which we should know about. In the vertical plane also, every movement of the head sets in action a series of reflexes. A horse can lash out with both hindlegs, only if he is free to lower his head and neck. If the head and neck can be forcibly held high, the horse will be unable to kick back with both hindlegs; this is essential knowledge for any rider who has to cure a horse of the habit of threatening other horses with his hind hooves or lashing out at them.

To return to the serpentine reflex; some reputedly incorrigible horses, that one rider after another has vainly tried to manege will have learnt to twist themselves in a perpetual "S" shape which has enabled them to evade all controls that their riders could think of. Although they willingly turn their head and neck right when the rider pulls on the right rein, in doing so they turn their hindquarters the other way. On circles, the hindquarters sway out to the left to such an extent that the horse will stumble or fall. Many riders are blissfully unaware of this perversity and will happily go hacking on such a horse, cautiously tacking to and fro to avoid a conflict. It is when one tries to re-school the horse that one will have to contend with every imaginable kind of resistance as soon as he is made to keep his hindfeet in the track of the forefeet. Usually, he will try to run away when one inflexes him left and will refuse to go forward, or even rear, when one inflexes him right. There is only one remedy, which is to get the horse into the habit of stretching the right rein, but the means of achieving this end must be perfectly understood and the rider will need a lot of patience. To start with, the horse will have to be taught to yield to both legs, without any consideration of head and neck position; one must eventually succeed in steering him with the leg aids alone. The reins will have to be kept loose, only gathered up occasionally to give a mere indication. Eventually, when the horse relaxes—when he has stopped snorting, when his breathing has become calm and when he is getting lazy—one can direct him on a large circle right with the help of the right rein only; the left rein must continue to hang slackly. The horse is then driven outward by the right leg of the rider.

At first, he will constantly attempt to make the circle smaller by inflexing his head and neck right and turning his hindquarters left; still, with his right leg, the rider must continue to urge him forward and maintain the forehand in front of the hindquarters. To start with, the tension on the right rein will have to be very light and increased very carefully. Finally, the horse must accept this tension and straighten himself by stretching the right rein. It may take a long time to get to this stage and, having got so far, one will have to continue riding with a tension only on the right rein. However, one must now try to get the horse to change the direction of the circle by

All horses are naturally crooked. The gymnastic work involved in lateral movements aims at promoting agility, obedience and straight movement. Richard Hinrichs on the Andalusian stallion Lebreo demonstrates the left half-pass.

Piaffe, according to the French conception. Pronounced flexion of the hocks is not desirable in the case of horses of thoroughbred type because it is detrimental to the fluentness of the movement. The relaxed depth of seat of the rider is exemplary.

A smooth passage *(right)* showing expansive strides and impulsion directed forward and upward. The passage evolves from a perfectly balanced piaffe. Karin Schlüter on Liostro. *(Below)* The Spanish trot, nowadays rarely seen except in the circus, is obtained by activating only the forelegs. The natural co-ordination of limb movements is disrupted and there is no connection between hindlimbs and forelimbs. V. Busch on Pontifex.

In the dressage horse *(above)* impulsion results in low, ground-covering strides; *(below)* a Lippizan horse shows that impulsion directed upward and forward is characteristic of the breed. Riding Master Lindenbauer at the passage.

yielding to the pressure of the left leg and turning left; obviously, obedience to the pressure of the left leg will have been established already. At first, the horse will continue to displace himself toward the right, looking in the direction of the movement (as in a renvers), but he will not persist for long. After a few hesitant steps, he will resign himself to inflexing around the rider's left leg, stretch the right rein and turn left. Still with a tension on the right rein only, the horse will then be made to yield to the left leg to enlarge the circle and will thus be guided by the diagonal aids: right rein, left leg. Finally, he will be guided by the right rein and the legs on serpentines, figures of eight, turns about the haunches, at an active walk, with steps of even length, and correctly inflexed in both directions. Thus, in the changes of direction, the right rein will be alternately the inside rein and the outside one—the left rein remaining inoperative. This is an extremely difficult lesson, but with a very spoilt horse the method must be persisted with for a long time, first at the walk and later at the trot. In a way, the trot facilitates the task, because it is easier to maintain forward movement and activity at this gait than at the walk. With a particularly obstinate horse, this corrective work can only be done in a manege, with the help of the walls; furthermore, one may have to resort sometimes to the left rein if, for instance, the horse decided to run away or turned his neck so much to the right that the situation became dangerous. Once the habit of stretching the rein has been firmly established, the vice of persistent "S" twisting will not occur again; one will then be able to proceed with schooling in the normal manner, with even tension on both reins, to obtain eventually equal elasticity of both sides of the body and both hindlegs.

In some cases, however, a horse will oppose all corrective measures by sticking his tongue out and refusing to go forward. When this happens, the only remedy possible is riding forward on straight lines with moderately slack reins. This, of course, is a return to the most elementary method of all and, in a way, the most difficult, which consists in riding forward at all the gaits without letting the horse find the slightest support in the left rein, until he has learnt to move regularly and to carry himself in balance by making the necessary effort. The rider will have to keep both legs constantly in contact and use suitable actions of each leg to produce regular steps and prevent the swaying of the croup to the left. This swaying is the result of dragging the left hind and it is by quickening the steps that the tendency of the horse to twist his body continuously like an "S" can be eliminated. It will remain for the rider to feel when the horse is again ready to be ridden with an even tension of the reins.

The reason why I have gone into such detail on the subject of crookedness is that most riders have to ride crooked horses. The perfectly straight horse is such a rarity that his owner is seldom willing to sell him. Furthermore, if the rider understands the causes of this sort of irregularity and has studied the means of correcting it, he will be extremely attentive with a young and unspoilt horse; any tendency of the latter to turn the croup more to one side than the other must be immediately foiled. Even at the early stage of accustoming him to be led, but especially during the first weeks of riding, any inclination to hang onto the left rein that the horse might show must be frustrated. A horse that has acquired the habit of moving actively and regularly will remain straight for the rest of his life.

HANDINESS

Obviously, the horse must go where his rider wants him to go; he must obey the guiding aids. But, if one used the same aids with an un-schooled horse as with an advanced dressage horse, one would confuse him enough to provoke his resistance. In the training of the horse, every factor must be the subject of special attention and it is only gradually that they can be put together.

Systematically, and in successive stages, the horse must first be taught to change direction in response to unambiguous aids and to follow straight lines, then to move on circular lines; later, he will be taught to perform voltes, turns about the hindquarters and lateral movements and, finally, pirouettes. Although all the schooling figures serve the same purpose, which is continuously to improve balance and obedience on straight lines and in change of direction, an inflexible method of controlling direction does not exist.

Fluidity can only be inculcated by degrees within the broad frame of a plan of education and the aids must vary according to the stage of education. For the purpose of steering, it is in the final stage that the legs are completely substituted for the hands. Still, it must be emphasised that it will never be possible for the rider's will to prevail in setting the direction of the course unless the horse obeys the command of the legs by moving forward willingly. Therefore, the hands must never impair impulsion. If the propulsive force of the hindlimbs is more than suits the rider's purpose, the latter's ability to get the horse to go forward with animation when evenly inflexed in his neck and trunk is an effective way of controlling speed without impairing impulsion by shortening the neck with a rigid tension of reins. The traditional schooling figures, with frequent changes of inflexion, are designed to harmonise control of direction with impulsion: the one must not contradict the other, it must promote it. Again, impulsion and speed are not absolutely the same thing. Impulsion is constant readiness to go forward with free, natural movement, and must always be present, even in the rein-back. Though rushing and pulling certainly show desire to go forward, they cannot mean impulsion in the above sense, no more than jogging or running backward.

With a young horse, control of direction must be primitively simple; one turns him by drawing on one rein until the desired change of direction is accomplished; if he resists, the rein must be held shorter and the neck turned until the horse is compelled to obey by straightening his body. If, however, the horse turns too hastily, he must be straightened by the other rein before being directed once again by the first. At the beginning of training, there must be no question of producing a flexion of the poll by tension of the outside rein; this would completely perplex the untutored horse.

The tension of the outside rein in the turns, in the early stages of education, bewilders the horse and causes him to swing his quarters out and so he must continue to be led by one rein at a time until he can perform all changes of direction and large figures of eight without throwing his head up or altering his rhythm. Once this result is achieved, one can start teaching him to respond to the steering influences of the legs and one can let him feel the tension of the outside rein.

The novice rider should also be taught to guide the horse with one rein only. He will usually be surprised to find that he will succeed with a much lighter tension on figures of eight than on straight lines; this is because a beginner normally tries to keep a course straight by holding the horse back with both hands. It is a well-known fact that a horse relaxes his mouth and neck and therefore does not resist when he is guided by one rein only. If one hand yields when the other acts, changes of inflexion never give the horse the feeling of being restrained which would induce him to resist. In order to teach a rider the aids for directing the horse, one must first instruct him to ride on a course of shallow loops, which are progressively flattened, until he is able to maintain a straight direction without pulling on both reins at the same time. As the rider's feel improves, the horse will come to accept an even tension of reins and the pupil can then be taught to steer with passive hands, by the aids of seat and legs. The horse will have learnt to keep his neck straight in front of the withers without intervention by the rider.

If the reader has read all the preceding chapters attentively, he will not imagine that I am advising him to manoeuvre constantly on a serpentine course before going forward on a straight course. My intention here is to explain that control of direction is also a subject of continuous refinement, and that there are no inflexible rules applicable to all horses regarding control of direction.

As for the hindlegs, at the beginning of training, the only requirement is that they follow regularly in the traces of the forelegs. However, once the horse has learnt to accept the bit and let himself be guided in all directions easily, either by one rein or the other (or both), control of direction must be transferred to the locomotive organs, that is the hindquarters. On a course of figures of eight, the horse will be made to understand that he must inflex around the rider's inside leg in every change of position; in response to the predominant pressure of the rider's inside leg, he must swing his inside hindfoot forward, to place it in front of the outside foot. He must then be taught to enlarge or decrease the size of the circles and, next, to step forward and sideways by obeying the leg aids. He can be considered to be perfectly "between the rider's legs" when he can inflex as easily around the left leg as the right and when the steps in the lateral movements are perfectly regular in both directions. The rider will then be able to regulate beat and tempo at will and to forestall all resistances without inciting opposition by backward traction on the reins. As soon as the horse is perfectly "between the legs", so that his rhythm and impulsion are easily maintained in all the two-track movements, he can be steered entirely by the legs. The role of the hands will then be limited to the preservation of even tension of reins and balance.

For example, one rides on a circle, trying to guide the hindquarters with the legs. Until he has been perfectly straightened, the horse will try to move on a larger circle with the forehand than with the hind-quarters; when the rider attempts to lead the forehand in on the circle with the inside rein, the hindquarters turn outward and the rider must use his outside leg to drive them inward again. In contrast, a straight horse, who does not break the continuity of inflexion of his vertebral column and firmly stretches the outside rein, will allow himself to be easily directed as the rider places the forehand in front of the hindquarters. To enlarge the circles, the rider performs half-parades in the direction of the inside hind at the moment when it swings forward. Thus, the horse is directed on circles by getting him to turn about his inside hind with more or less the same aids as for the turn about the haunches. The inflexion is created by the legs and not by pulling with the inside hand. Although in the canter pirouettes, it is about the outside hind that the horse turns in place while continuing to perform distinctly the movements of the gallop with his limbs, this result is achieved in the same manner by gradually reducing the radius of the circle. At this stage, all turns must be made like fractions of wide or small circles at all the gaits, with the idea that they are turns about the inside hind. The simple turns about the haunches, correctly performed, are excellent for developing this feel. Once the horse has learnt to obey equally well the predominant pressure at the girth of the rider's right or left leg, and when the rider has understood that he must guide the horse by positioning the forehand in front of the hindquarters—which always determine the direction of the movement—the outside leg need no longer be used to prevent the hindquarters from turning out. Furthermore, once the rider has developed the feel of aligning the forehand in front of the hindquarters, he will stop worrying about subtle manipulations of reins. However, the ability to feel the movements of the hindlimbs can be developed only by long practise and ability to relax and can be considered to be established when the rider knows at every moment whether the lines of force pass under his seat or to the side and whether the forehand is correctly driven forward by these lines of force. The old motto: "Ride the horse forward and straight" should be completed thus: "In all turns, be sure that the horse is straight and think of inflexing him behind the saddle before worrying about inflexion in front of the saddle." By pulling with the inside hand, with opposition of the outside hand, one prevents engagement of the inside hind; the horse becomes disunited and cannot be controlled smoothly. In show-jumping, this is the cause of all such resistances as rushing, running-out and stopping.

In straight movement on straight lines, the horse must be straight from head to tail. Some dressage riders wrongly believe that there should be a lateral flexion at the poll, but inflexion which is limited to only one part of the body is unsightly and incorrect; it can only be produced by restricting the movement with excessive tension of reins. Furthermore, to ride straight, the rider must always look straight ahead, on a line passing between the horse's ears and, to be able to steer the horse with the legs, he must sit in the centre of the saddle with a straight body. There can be no exception to this rule: on straight lines, the horse must be uniformly straight, and in turns and movements on two tracks, inflexion of head and neck must never exceed that of the whole body; whenever it does, it must cause the hindquarters to turn out.

On the subject again of the turn about the haunches, this movement is so seldom performed correctly that one may wonder why it was ever thought of as a useful suppling exercise. If the movement is performed after a halt has been established, the inside hind remains fixed on the ground, forming a pivot around which the outside hind circles. The movement is correct if the horse is brought from a walk in shortened steps almost to a halt and immediately proceeds to turn around the inside hind, remaining in walk rhythm. The inside hind must continue stepping on the spot, making exactly the same number of steps as the outside hind revolving around it; the movement is just as incorrectly performed when the inside hind makes fewer steps than the outside one as when it remains rooted to the ground. With a horse well advanced in his training, the rider should try turning about the inside hind in 8, 12 or 16 perfectly regular steps. In this movement as all others, hesitant or hurried steps deserve a low score in a test. A rider who succeeds in getting the horse to bring his hind hooves closer to his front hooves in the turn about the haunches, will have succeeded in obtaining such a lightening of the forehand that he will obtain the piaffe almost without trying.

By studying the cause and the results of the horse's tendency to move with his body conforming more or less to the shape of an "S" and by experiencing all forms of resistance due to this tendency, the rider will develop his skill in the use of diagonal aids. However, all riders will go through a period during which they will try to correct the same resistance in an identical manner with many different horses, without thinking of improving their own skill. In this, they will have to help themselves. The best instructor in the world cannot judge from the ground whether a rider's actions are always correct and timely.

I have already explained that the rider must be able to feel the movements of the hindlimbs and that the horse must respect equally the right or left leg of the rider ordering him to place his inside hind under the mass of the body, and keep it flexed long enough to soften the impact of the movements on the rider. The rider also must have learnt to dominate his instinct to pull on the inside rein as if to bend the horse. He will have developed the skill of keeping the hands passive and of resisting and steering with the legs and seat; all his aids will proceed from the use of his waist.

Now, to master the skill of using appropriately the diagonal or the lateral aids, I recommend the following exercises.

One rides the horse in the open along the right side of a ditch or a footpath. The horse will start drifting to the right because his left hind thrusts him forward and sideways more than his right and, consequently, he will start leaning on one's left hand. One must remain composed. The wrong thing would be to pull on the left rein. Instead of this, one should feel that, as the right shoulder of the horse advances, his left side comes against one's left leg; this means that the left hind is coming into support. The steps of the left hind must be shortened by means of discreet half-parades in order to moderate the force of its thrust. These half-parades with the right rein, directed toward the left hind, must be done without force as it swings forward and must not last a moment longer than this. The horse will not respond immediately but he will certainly start turning about his left hind, rather as in a turn about the haunches, after the fifth or sixth step and will start moving back to the track. Much patience, practise and concentration are required to perform this exercise properly; however this is riding in order to learn to ride better. Riding along bridle-paths, meandering from side to side, persevering with shortening the steps of the left hind with half-parades on the right rein, one gets the horse to change his inflexion, the former inside rein becomes the new outside rein and the former outside hind becomes the new inside hind (when the horse drifted towards the right, the right rein was the inside rein).

Although the primary purpose of the half-parade with the right rein is to moderate the thrust of the left hind and develop the suppleness of its joints, one must not forget the right hind. It must be stimulated into greater activity, make longer steps, react to the rider's right leg. Either the rider's right calf or his spur must be used while the left shoulder swings forward. As the horse is straightened step by step without force, by the same aids one would use for a turn left about the haunches, one makes it impossible for him to continue leaning on the left rein.

Once the technique has been mastered at the walk, it can be applied at the trot. Impulsion should make things easier but the rider tends to get muddled by the quickness of the movements. It is easy, however, to overcome this difficulty by rising to the trot. It is important to start by riding with the right diagonal (left hind—right fore). At the top of the rise, when the rider's weight is entirely on the stirrups, his left leg presses against the horse's side. It does not matter whether one concentrates on the movement of the horse's shoulder, on the feel of the left leg against the horse's side or on the movement of the rising trot, but it is most important to perform the half-parade at the right moment. This is when the horse's right shoulder is forward and when the rider's left leg is on the horse's side. The right rein, or both reins, act in the direction of the left hind which is flexing, before the stifle extends. No horse can resist the effect of these discreet half-parades, providing that they occur at precisely the right moment of the stride. The technique is especially easy to master if the rider is careful to change diagonals every time he changes direction; left diagonal in turns to the right, right diagonals in turns to the left; half-parades either with both reins or predominantly with the outside rein, diagonally affecting the inside hind as the rider is at the top of the rising movement. If he holds his reins together and places his hands exactly in front of his body, he need in fact only think: right hind or left hind, as the case may be; this automatically produces the desired result. The method is, of course, exactly the same at the sitting trot and the rider must continue to be guided by the feel of the movements of the diagonally opposite shoulder and hindleg of the horse; he will, however, have to concentrate more because of the rapid succession of the movements.

In theory, control of direction ought to be more difficult at the canter than at the trot; in fact, it is much easier. The main difficulty is the right lead canter in which most horses have a tendency to hold the croup to the right. The best way to obviate this is to do a counter-canter on the left circle (right lead) until the horse assumes of his own accord a correct inflexion and the rider can dispense entirely with his left rein for guidance. However it is preferable to practise this out-of-doors because it is only if there is enough impulsion that the horse is perfectly straight at the canter. It is quite impossible to have a horse straight at a lolloping sort of canter.

As I have said, a rider who is not yet able to feel the movements of the diagonals at a sitting trot should rise to the trot and he can then improve his feel by changing diagonals every fifth or third stride, concentrating on feeling on which hindleg he sits; as he changes diagonals he should try to make the horse yield a little to his actual inside leg. However diagonal aids must never be used in leg yielding; only lateral aids (right leg, right hand and vice-versa). From the point of view of the rider, leg yielding is a good exercise because it helps him to feel if his horse is properly inflexed around his inside leg and responding properly to its pressures or trying to evade these pressures so that his movements become irregular; it also helps the rider to feel the difference between a sideways movement with inflexion toward the direction of the movement or against it.

All the above exercises teach the rider, not only to understand the diagonal aids, but also to understand the aids in general.

Lateral aids, right hand, right leg for example, compel the horse to place his right hind in front of his left hind, thus making his body concave on the right side. Yet, the left lateral aids must prevent the horse from reacting to the pressure of the right rein by avoiding forward movement and inflexion, and just running away sideways. This lesson must teach the horse to inflex uniformly from tail to head for the purpose of equalising the suppleness of both sides of his body and, eventually, making him straight. Lateral aids, providing that they are correctly applied at the right moment of the movement, are effective actions which no horse can resist. They can even be used with a considerable measure of severity, as a crude method of preventing the horse from running away in order to avoid the influence of the rider's legs; as has already been explained, a horse will never of his own accord move in the direction toward which his body is concave. With lateral aids, one can make a horse move forward and sideways, sideways only and even backward and sideways, providing that the aids are used in concordance with the forward movement of one hindlimb. Very little skill is needed.

In contrast, diagonal aids have a strong collecting effect. The different degree of skill required for lateral or diagonal aids is like, for example, the different degree of precision needed for carpentry and cabinet making. Diagonal aids deprive the horse of the possibility of avoiding the tiring muscular effort which collection requires by resorting either to sideways movement or to crookedness with too much turning of the head and neck in front of the withers; they compel him to keep his jaw, head, neck and back straight. The only possible ways by which the horse can resist them are rearing or bolting. With a tactless rider, diagonal aids can drive a horse into a frenzy if his hindlegs are not yet sufficiently strong to bear the effort of collection. The effect of a diagonal aid (right hand, left leg) on the horse's left hind is to cause it to support the whole weight of the body on bent joints, as in the turn about the haunches; in the latter movement, this is not so difficult, because the horse is not required to continue propelling his mass forward and upward as he must in the collected walk or trot. To succeed in producing collection without impairing impulsion demands enormous powers of concentration on the part of the rider. The more the left hind flexes, the more the right hind must swing forward—as is also the case on circles. It has already been explained that the right hind is usually lazy and avoids driving the mass forward by reducing the length of the forward swing; the rider, therefore, must not forget to activate the right hind while he slows down the movement of the left hind. The best way of overcoming this difficulty is to frequently change the inflexion, equalising the suppleness and strength of both hindlegs, straightening the horse and teaching him to stretch both reins to the same extent. Then one will need no greater strength of arm than that required to hold a cigar. In fact, for these exercises, the rider ought to hold the reins between forefinger and thumb, the thumb forming a roof over the finger. The other three fingers of the hand are relaxed and inoperative. It is with coaxing fingers that we get the horse to co-operate; not with aggressive fists.

THE MOUTH

An interest in bits should lead one to examine the lower jaw of a horse's skull and the bars of the mouth of hundreds of horses. Some bars are rounded, others are quite sharp. Sharp bars, being more sensitive than rounded ones, are suited by thick though light bits. They are particularly susceptible to bruising and it is not just the mucous membrane covering the bone that is delicate, for the periosteum itself is easily inflamed and subject to severe injury.

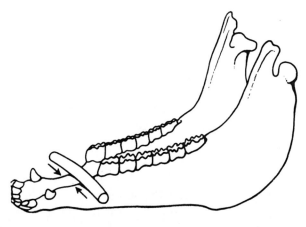

The bars of the lower jaw and the position of the mouthpiece. If the rider carries his hands properly, the curb bit rests on the tongue. The snaffle or bridoon always rubs the bars.

Following injury, an exostosis will develop in the region of bit pressure so that even sharp bars will become insensitive. Bitting difficulties can be expected when the bars have gone through a succession of injury, inflammation and repair. So, when choosing a bit, it is wise to first examine the bars of the mouth of the horse who will wear it. One must also note that mares often have rudimentary tushes which are not rooted in the bone, as they are in the male horse, but are loosely embedded in the skin or membrane; this often becomes reddened and painful around the tushes of mares, which should then be extracted.

Tushes start growing during the fourth year in males and females and it is during this period that one must be especially careful to notice any signs of inflammation. In the case of mares, they do not always break through the skin and can be felt for some time as sensitive swellings in the anterior third part of the bars. To prevent the bit from coming into contact with this delicate point while the tushes are piercing, it must be fitted as near as possible to the molars. However the hypersensitivity of the skin disappears once the tushes in males have taken root in the bone socket. But, although sharp bars and injured bars can cause bitting difficulties, the reason for resistance to the bit must usually be sought elsewhere.

Providing the bars are normal, a bit does not cause discomfort unless the rider's hands are heavy or unsteady. The excessive pressure of the bit on the bars inflicted by heavy hands produces different forms of resistance at the mouth but invariably causes the horse to stiffen his hocks. However the rider feels either a heavy pull on the reins because the horse throws his mass against the bit, or has to contend with the various ways in which the horse tries to avoid discomfort: for example, overbending to come behind the bit, or star-gazing to get above the bit. Freedom of movement is impaired and the steps are either short and hurried or long and lackadaisical as a result of the stiffening of the hocks. There are still other obvious resistances, such as tossing the bit, grinding the teeth, constant and rhythmical chewing; or passing the tongue over the bit or through one side of the mouth. Less frequently, the tongue is stiffly arched so that air is sucked in; the noise produced is similar to roaring, but contrary to roaring it occurs only when the horse is ridden and is bridled; the horse does not fight the bit when he is standing tacked up in his box. As the noise is not due, like roaring, to paralysis of the muscles of the larynx, it can be eliminated like other bitting difficulties.

Basically, however, the reason why riders experience all these troubles is that they do not use their legs properly and when they attempt to remedy the disorder by trying various rein effects, they confuse cause and effect. The first thing they must do is to establish a regular gait. Once the horse has submitted to the driving actions of the legs, the rider must carefully maintain a constant, even, passive and light tension of reins without worrying about the position of head and neck. Though he must avoid pulling backward, he must follow all backward movements of the head to foil the horse's attempts to come behind the bit. All forms of resistance to the bit disappear eventually when the rider succeeds in getting the horse to swing his hindlegs freely and stops fussing with the reins or holding the head in. Head and neck carriage will improve purely as a result of active movement and development of the right muscles.

The procedure is more complicated in the case of horses that have developed an insensitive mouth through the persistent habit of leaning on the bit, stiffening the jaws and using the sterno-mastoid muscle to lower the head and push hard against the bit. The muscular contraction and locking of the jaws must be overcome by all such means as active work in shortened steps, half- and full-parades, yielding to the leg on circles, frequent changes of inflexion, riding with tension on one rein only and riding out-of-doors on loose reins until the horse has learnt to carry himself without leaning on the hands.

However, on principle, the beat must be slowed down and the horse must be made to lengthen the stride if he hurries; conversely the beat must be quickened without concern for length of stride or position of head and neck if the horse holds back or hovers.

Passing the tongue over the bit or out to one side is a persistent habit, a vice in fact, that is very difficult to eradicate. It is developed when weak, easily dispirited horses are ridden by riders with heavy hands. The sensitivity of the bars of the mouth is destroyed and the horse becomes a hard puller. Again, the remedy is the same; a regular gait must be established.

Playing with the bit, on the other hand, is not a persistent habit. It shows a lack of attentiveness to the aids, a playfulness that stops as soon as the horse has learnt to concentrate on the rider and to carry himself properly.

Grinding the teeth is a habit that I have studied by riding as many horses addicted to it as I could find. In its worst form, it denotes stubborn resistance; in a mild form, it shows an argumentative disposition, in which case one can still get the horse to work satisfactorily. With many horses, it is a temporary symptom of resistance which even a good rider can provoke if he has to school a horse within too short a period of time. Occasional grinding of teeth in the course of training is always a sign that too much is being demanded.

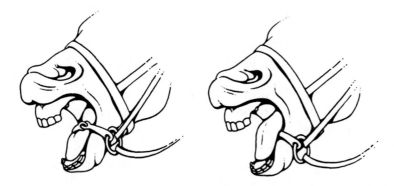

The horse seeks to evade the control by the bit by passing his tongue over it. For the sake of clarity, this vice is depicted with the mouth open.

The habit usually starts at a certain stage of schooling when a horse begins flexing at the poll. If the rider then tries to enforce collection before the hindlegs are sufficiently strong, the horse shows his annoyance by grinding the molars. The use of draw-reins by so-called strong riders is particularly pernicious. The resistance disappears quickly if a more sympathetic rider takes over but, if the horse is continually ridden by over-demanding riders with insensitive hands, grinding teeth becomes a vice. The noise produced is rhythmical but not necessarily consonant with the beat of the movement.

Again, grinding the teeth can be a symptom of hypertension which occurs when the horse is unable or unwilling to comply with the rider's demands for an increase of speed by lengthening the steps, or a decrease of speed by shortening the steps; if allowed to maintain his habitual beat and length of stride, he remains quiet. There is little joy to be had in trying to cure an old horse of the habit but, in any case, only a sensitive and knowledgeable rider can succeed; he may be able to loosen the cramped back muscles, restore the freedom of movement and the horse's trust in the hands.

Finally, the worst offenders are genuinely bad tempered horses, stolid animals who have always had the better of weak riders. They grind the molars on one side of the mouth, usually the left because it is the engagement of the left hind that they resist. They stubbornly refuse to exert themselves and persistently pull on the left rein. Their annoyance is displayed in the same manner when they are being led in hand and when one does up the girth, and eventually whenever they come in contact with anybody who has to handle them. In these cases, correction entails complete re-education; one must get the horse to fear the left rein, to the extent of coming behind the bit on the left side. A very skilful and ruthless rider may finally succeed in getting the horse to stretch the right rein.

The grinding of teeth of a placid horse with an argumentative disposition is sometimes so slight that an inexperienced rider may not hear it. This sort of horse is never stirred by anger or impatience and it is for this reason that he is incorrigible. He can be used with pleasure by unambitious riders for leisurely out-of-doors activity but he is totally unsuited to competitive riding. In dressage, grinding the teeth cannot be marked more leniently than other forms of resistance, such as irregular steps, stiffening, tail to one side and wind-sucking with the sheath.

Bridle-lameness has already been discussed and no more need be said about it, except that like all resistances to the action of the bit it can be cured by a good rider with sensitive hands.

Before considering the effects of mouthpieces in common use, we must understand how we influence movement with our hands and what effect is produced in the horse's mouth through the agency of the mouthpiece. A rider who has not given the subject sufficient thought, and who cannot control his hands, is not in a position to express an opinion on the effects of various kinds of bits on the mouths of various types of horses.

In the early stages of training, the rider acts with his hands according to the principle of hands without legs, legs without hands. As training progresses, seat, legs and hands are increasingly co-ordinated in their actions until finally such a perfect harmony is established between horse and rider that the link of the hands with the horse's mouth through the bit is needed only to give slight indications. At the beginning of training the hands are active; later they become passive; eventually, the horse is controlled by a subtle combination of seat, legs and hands. A well-schooled horse will have been educated to feel and understand indications given by the fingers of the rider. It is not just the horse's mouth that needs to be educated by the rider. The rider has to educate his own hands also.

There is no other way of slowing the speed with an untrained horse than by exerting backwards traction on his mouth, but these actions of the hands can succeed only on condition that the horse responds by flexing at the poll, relaxing his jaws and coming to a halt. We must learn to pull backward in a smooth, elastic manner with a gradual braking effect which must cease immediately the horse shows the first sign of understanding that by slowing down he is doing the right thing. A rider who has not got his hands under perfect control never yields soon enough and thus prevents the horse from understanding the meaning of the pulls on the reins, with the result that the horse stiffens his jaws and refuses to obey. Still, how else than by pulling can the rider communicate his intention to the horse if the latter is totally uneducated?

Sometimes, however, through no fault of our own, in response to the pull on the reins, a horse will lock his jaws, stiffen his neck and continue to move forward. In this case, it is senseless and futile to exert a continuous and stronger pull; it only incites the horse to pull harder and become more obstinate. The appropriate action, in this case, is described as taking and giving, which does not mean losing contact with the mouth through the reins at the moment of giving. This can be done with the arms only, but if one knows how to use the seat, it is more effective to come out of the saddle a little and lean forward to prevent the horse from taking a hold and then straighten the upper body to resist the movement powerfully. There is a whole range of possible actions in the face of stubborn resistance, between simple giving and taking and a passive opposition of the hands, held forward in front of the body, supported by the straightening of the back. In the latter manner, the horse is made to punish himself severely against the bit at the end of the downward swing of his neck and head. Whichever the choice of action, it must be sufficiently severe to frighten the horse against pushing hard against the bit. Active pulling and yielding must produce unconditional obedience in the form of a slowing of the speed or a total halt; it is an action which, however, is effective only when the movements of the rider's hands are exactly co-ordinated with the forward swinging of the horse's hindleg. If synchronisation is perfect, the horse cannot possibly resist; the giving and taking will have a compelling and calming effect on the horse. But if the pulls are effected during the phase of propulsion, the consequences are more disastrous even than continuous hanging on. The taking and giving can vary in degree between a smooth interchange of pulling and yielding and a strong tug followed immediately by a sudden yielding. The only way of gaining experience and skill is to ride as many horses as possible at various stages of training, not excluding spoilt horses.

Yet, we must eventually teach the horse to seek a constant contact with the rider's hand by keeping the bit steadily and evenly on the tongue and the bars of both sides of the jaw and applying an equal tension to the reins. This can only happen if the rider is also able to maintain this tension with passive hands. Continually active hands prevent a horse from learning to balance himself and are detrimental to impulsion. A good rider can, in fact, maintain a light and even tension of the reins even in the early stages of training young horses.

Keeping the hands still actually means passively maintaining the same tension of reins instead of perpetually trying various rein effects. Of course, it depends on the ability to sit still, undisturbed by the movements of the horse. If the rider has not yet developed a sufficiently deep and relaxed seat, or if the horse's movement is too rough to allow him to sit, the hands can be rested on the mane. The ability to keep the hands still comes with general progress in the skill of riding; conversely, a horse is always more comfortable to ride if the rider can keep his hands still, allowing the bit to rest smoothly on the tongue and bars, and never inadvertently tugs on the reins. It is unreasonable to expect a horse to be submissive when the tension of reins is erratic.

Again, there are degrees of stillness of the hands, from relative stillness to absolute stillness.

Relative stillness implies an elastic tension of arm muscles, relaxed elbows and wrists, absence of rigidity; it is not a complete immobility of the hands. It maintains some of the elements of giving and taking, so that the relaxed activity of the muscles of mastication and the nodding of the head are not entirely suppressed. It encourages supple flexion of the poll without enforcing elevation of the forehand or collection. This relative stillness is necessary at the stage when the horse is still uncertain of his balance. The reins are then frequently compared to rubber bands which are never completely slack nor stretched to their limit. If the rider surrenders all tension of reins, the horse knows that he can lower his neck and slacken the tension of his muscles. This sort of stillness requires a sensitive feel of the natural movements of the head and neck which the rider utilises either to lengthen the stride (with more extensive movements of his hands), or to shorten the steps by limiting the liberty of movement of head and neck.

Absolute stillness is complete immobility of the hands, held at the level of the rider's waist. This does not mean that thereby the horse's head and neck are held still. The hands can never in fact be absolutely still until the horse is very advanced in his training, when it is he who then makes the effort necessary to maintain a light and constant tension of reins and to carry the bit carefully. In other words, the horse must be capable of totally independent self-carriage and collection; of his own accord, he maintains his head and neck in a position of maximum possible "relative" elevation, completely still, with the base of the neck raised in front of the withers by the tension of the muscles of the top line. The amount of weight supported by the rider's hands could be measured in milligrammes, while still giving the rider control of the tremendous force developed by the hindlegs. It is the horse himself, at this stage, that avoids any jolting of the bit by carrying it carefully with his tongue and the bars of his mouth. Very occasionally and discreetly, the rider acts with the hand to warn the horse against a momentary lapse of attention.

Obviously, there are many stages in the transition from relative stillness of the hands to absolute stillness and it is only if the rider has gained complete control of the haunches through his position, legs and seat that he can demand collection with totally motionless hands.

Now, what about the controversial "*arret*"?

This is an abrupt sort of parade, which can only be executed with a horse that has achieved a state of total self-carriage and extreme suppleness of hocks. Even then, he may sometimes feel too full of himself or be suddenly surprised or frightened by some object and then try to force the rider's hand; occasionally also, the rider feels him becoming inattentive and about to risk losing his equilibrium and fluent submission. The *arret* lasts for a fraction of a second, the time it takes for one hindlimb to flex during the phase of support; its effect is psychological rather than mechanical. It can be used to warn a horse of a quick transition from a trot of maximum extension to one of utmost collection without change of beat. By means of two consecutive *arrets*, the rider can dictate the beat exactly as he wishes without having to increase the tension of the reins. The feel of an *arret* is most easily acquired by the rider when he tries to obtain the very short steps—half-steps—by means of which a collected horse is prepared for the piaffe. However, in contrast with half-parades, an *arret* must not slow the speed. The rider must merely influence the balance of the horse by slightly changing his own position, lifting his ribs, bringing his shoulders a little further back to cause the horse to shift his centre of gravity by flexing the haunches. The *arret* should be nothing more than a mild weight effect. The horse, of course, must be extremely advanced in his education and totally submissive because this action must never be coercive and the tension of reins must remain very light.

The firm tug on the reins, "the sock in the mouth", has to be mentioned. It can hardly be called an aid, but it is a punishment that is as necessary at times as the energetic but judicious stroke of the whip or the firm application of the spurs. When a horse bucks instead of obeying the legs by going forward, the rider must use the whip or the spurs with utmost determination to send the horse on; out-of-doors, the horse can then be allowed to gallop on, but in a manege it is not safe to let him do so; one must then resort to firm upward tugs on elastically taut reins or to the *Insterburger* (on one rein) synchronised with the leaps of the gallop. Providing these tugs are in phase with the forward swing of the hindlegs, the horse cannot resist for very long.

Usually, however, it is by a combination of passive resistance and opportune tugs—during the phase of suspension of the limbs at the gallop—that the rider controls a trained horse when he tries to get out of hand. During the propulsive phase, the hands must maintain a tension of reins sufficient to keep contact with the mouth.

In principle, however, it must be understood that it is by influencing the balance and posture of the horse that one slows his speed. One cannot expect an unbalanced and tightly constricted horse to be willingly submissive and the pressure of the bit will always provoke resistance when the rider is tactless and does not yield soon enough. Yielding, by passively following the movement of the neck in a forward direction, is the most important of all hand actions. All the rider's oppositions must proceed from a yielding action of the hands, and be as brief as possible to avoid provoking the horse's resistance by imposing a painful arching of the neck; the rider must be quick to yield again at the precise moment when the horse yields. Yielding must invariably and immediately reward the horse for his submission; eventually, he will understand that the rider intends him to maintain flexion of the poll without having to be constantly corrected. The reward, in the form of yielding with the hands, must be granted at the slightest sign of obedience and it is always better to be too generous rather than niggardly. It takes a long time to develop the reflex of yielding, even when one has understood its importance and tries most conscientiously. Frequently the resistance can be forestalled by yielding in anticipation, so that the horse discovers that the opposition that he was preparing himself to resist has suddenly vanished, leaving a disconcerting void and nothing to fight. Again, he cannot resist the hand that always yields at the moment when he propels his mass forward with his hindlegs.

Elastic reins promote elastic tension of muscles and persuade the horse that it is more comfortable to keep his poll relaxed. Though the hands must follow the movements of head and neck in all directions at the beginning of training, at a later stage they tactfully limit these movements and then they help the horse to improve his posture and to become fluently submissive. All transitions and half-parades subsequently become postural corrections.

The art of passively maintaining a constant tension and of yielding promptly, once acquired, remains with a rider for ever. Such a rider will be able to control speed in all the paces without spoiling impulsion. Though his hand always gives the horse "room to breathe", it never loses contact with his mouth.

Though anybody can ride with lateral aids, still the rider must learn to discipline his hands in turns and circles at the very beginning of his education. If he develops bad habits at this stage, they will remain with him for ever. Turning by pulling on one rein and tactlessly failing to yield sufficiently with the other produces a constricting effect. Should the horse refuse to obey the command to turn by leaning on the active hand, the rider can sit more heavily on the same side, so putting himself in a position that enables him to resist passively until the horse submits; the rider must then yield instantly. Alternately, he can yield first, and then let the horse jolt himself on the bit; or he can use an *arret*. Yet again, he can drop the rein which the horse hangs on to and ride forward until the horse stops trying to rely on it as a balancing aid. All these methods must teach the horse to support the bit centrally on his tongue, instead of crossing his jaws to push against it. The gentleness of the horse's mouth will reward a rider with a gentle hand.

Though this section concerns especially the effects of the bit, it must be stressed once again that the arching of the neck is subordinate to the firmness and suppleness of the hindquarters and that elevation of the forehand must remain relative. All the effects of the bit must extend through the whole system to the hindfeet, determining beat and stride, and improving balance and posture; they must on no account influence only the shape of the neck.

To return to the subject of bits, it should first be realised that their design is only relatively important. A good rider will manage a horse as well in one bit as in another.

Asked how many types of bits he knows, a knowledgeable horseman will only think of two: soft or hard. This, of course, is the correct answer, assuming that the rider has tactful hands.

More explicitly, there are unbroken mouthpieces with a precise action, and jointed mouthpieces that can move in the mouth, producing a less precise and less powerful effect. A curb bit, properly fitted, is not necessarily a severe bit; the severity is inherent in the rider's hand and not in the construction of the bit. Normally, it is carried on the tongue and there is practically no pressure on the bars.

In the hands of a good rider, who can feel exactly, in milligrammes, the degree of pressure of the mouthpiece on the lower jaw, when he (the rider, not the horse) yields, or acts or merely resists, then the curb, despite its unjointed mouthpiece, is the finest bit imaginable. No other one can give a rider so perfect a feel of the movement of the tongue of the horse when he quietly chews the bit.

The jointed mouthpiece, in contrast, can form a wedge in the mouth, clamp the lower jaw, press on the outside edges of the bars and slide on them, because it is not equipped with a curb chain which prevents it from being displaced. With a jointed mouthpiece, in the presence of resistance, the rider has to use cunning or strength. So, contrary to common belief, the so-called severe curb bit with its curb chain is the most gentle and effective instrument of all . . . in the right hands. Conversely, the jointed mouthpiece, usually called a soft bit, because it has an imprecise action does not give such unmistakable effects and can induce the rider to use more strength than necessary. However, curb bits are for riders with sensitive fingers; snaffles are for riders with fists. No one without perfect seat and hands educated to yield should ever attempt to ride on the curb; its action is too immediate. If the reins are attached to a snaffle, the rider can gesticulate as much as he wishes, or even hang on to the reins for dear life without driving the horse crazy. The curb, like the knife of the surgeon or woodcarver, needs to be handled with extreme precision. Only skilful hands can be trusted with sharp instruments. The snaffle is more of a blunt instrument that sometimes can be used with force, but blunt instruments can hit and miss and chop off a finger.

Francois de la Gueriniere (1732) is usually credited with the idea of using a bridoon with a curb, although Grisone (1552) is represented in a portrait showing him on a horse equipped with a double bridle. Seydlitz introduced it to the Prussian cavalry in the middle of the 19th century, at a period in history when horsemanship had ceased to be the exclusive privilege of noblemen and was losing its image of a sublime art requiring total dedication. The headlong charges of the modern cavalry necessitated a kind of mouthpiece that could be utilised by troopers with fists, strong arms and strong backs. The bridoon was such an instrument; it did not have to be used with more delicacy than a hacksaw, in contrast with a curb which must be handled as politely as knives and forks should be. If the rough trooper of modern history had been equipped with only one rein attached to a curb, his horse would have thrown himself over backward rather than move a step forward. He was therefore provided with a bridoon for the purpose of steering, and a curb to stop the horse promptly instead of galloping through the ranks of the enemy. So the bridoon was a concession to the clumsiness of the average recruit. It is a pity that so few riders, nowadays, attempt to use a double bridle: it teaches discipline; it stops one from hanging on.

The snaffle—with or without a dropped noseband—is used all over the world nowadays, except by Arabs and cowboys, and it is an appropriate instrument for novice riders and novice horses. A beginner does little damage to a horse with a snaffle and would never get his horse to move if he were armed with a curb. An experienced rider will also prefer a snaffle with a novice horse, because it cannot come into action so quickly and is thus less likely to frighten the horse. It is the perfect instrument for progressive transitions and for simple changes of direction and is less likely to impair impulsion. For this reason, when it is used to moderate speed or stop the horse, several half-parades are needed before it can complete its effect. Nevertheless, for advanced schooling, precise indication of stride and beat, smooth changes of speed, collection of the canter, riding with a snaffle demands so much attention as to become rather tiring. Reluctance to use the double bridle at this stage shows to what extent the art of horsemanship has regressed in this century. Most of the old masters have left this world; even if they were still alive, their services might not be in great demand, because so many people believe that anybody with natural talent can succeed without having to learn to ride. And there are no queues of eager pupils waiting to be taught by the few genuine masters of the art still alive.

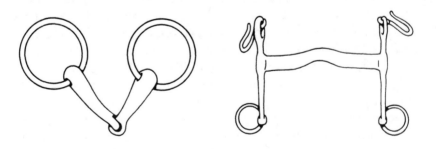

Snaffle bit *(left)* and curb bit *(right)*.

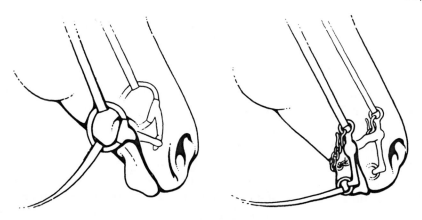

Position of snaffle and curb bit.

However, regarding the curb, it is the chain that maintains it steady and which must never be adjusted so loosely as to allow the horse to play with the bit. The length of the cheeks and the presence or absence of a tongue groove obviously allow of more or less leverage and precision, but this should not worry a rider with good hands. But a bit with a high port, which allows all the pressure to bear on the bars of the mouth, is an instrument of torture. Furthermore it fails to serve its intended function; the precise effect which the leverage of the curb normally produces is lost when one hard material acts on another equally hard one (steel against bone). A curb bit must be supported, at least partly, by the horse's tongue and if it is furnished with a high port, the horse's attempts to keep his tongue in contact with the bit result in a painful pressure against the palate, which forces the horse to keep his mouth open. The curb is basically designed to hold the lower jaw firmly between the mouthpiece and the curb chain, depriving the horse of any ability to avoid the effect of the bit so that, in a certain sense, the rider handles the horse by the lower jaw. The reciprocal effect of the activity of the muscles of the tongue and jaws on the whole posture of the horse, on the flexion of the haunches as well as the flexion of the poll is well known and is the whole point of being able to act with precision on the lower jaw. However, the range of action of the rider's hand is limited by the very precision of action of the curb bit and it can safely be employed only by a rider capable of sitting still and with a horse ready to yield promptly to the pressure of the bit.

Since the curb bit can only be effective provided that the horse holds his jaws straight, it is difficult to understand why one sometimes sees riders dividing the reins so that three are held in one hand, and one in the other. A bridoon rein should never be held separately from the curb rein on the same side or used independently from the curb rein. The horse must be ready to be ridden in a double bridle by which time all fiddling with one rein is futile and to be avoided. Bridoon and curb rein must be adjusted to the same length since the horse is supposed to have been sufficiently schooled so that it is not necessary to shorten or lengthen any rein for the purpose of steering him. The so-called French manner of holding the reins— hands held in a vertical plane, bridoon rein over the forefinger, curb rein under the little finger, both reins adjusted to the same length—is excellent for helping to feel the different effects of bridoon and curb. If the horse responds to the pressure of the curb by lowering his head, he feels the lifting effect of the bridoon; if he tries to avoid the action of the bridoon by poking his nose, he feels the increased pressure of the curb. The collecting effect of the curb and the elevating effect of the bridoon thus continuously alternate without any need for active intervention by the rider and the horse automatically learns to keep his head steady. The rider, of course, must maintain an equally steady hand with as light a tension of reins as possible, which can vary only by milligrammes. If the rein can be stitched together to the appropriate length, this frees the rider of even the effort of thinking about preventing one rein or the other from slipping from under his thumb and then having to re-organise himself. The reins will then form a loop which can be held with one finger and this will allow the rider to concentrate entirely on the effects of the bridle on the poll and jaw; he will discover how easy riding in a double bridle can be when one understands the principle.

For normal purposes, however, curb and bridoon reins should not be separated even by one finger; they must be adjusted to an equal length, held in either hand between the same fingers and allowed to slide together or be shortened together. This will prevent letting any rein become too tight or too loose.

The curb can be used alone—bridoon rein hanging—but only if the horse has established perfect self-carriage and impulsion; other-wise, he will soon overbend.

Once the horse is ready to be ridden in a double bridle, the reins should never be used again for steering; they are unnecessary for this purpose and, furthermore, resorting to them is against the principle that the bit must remain centrally on the tongue. The rider warns the horse of an approaching turn or circle by performing a half-parade with both hands in the direction of the inside hind and then indicates the turn by slightly rotating his rib cage to bring the outside shoulder forward.

Although riding on the curb only is not generally advisable, it can be quite revealing. If the loose bridoon reins remain motionless, it shows that the horse is straight and is maintaining his self-carriage happily, while they show that his balance and suppleness are less than perfect if they are seen to swing. A rider who desires perfection could occasionally try this test.

The Pelham is a rather harmless imitation of the double bridle with curb and bridoon. Even with a shallow groove for the tongue, the latter prevents too much pressure being applied to the bars of the mouth. Although the action of the Pelham is much less precise than that of the curb, it is much less likely to inflict pain if the rider is clumsy. With some horses, novice riders may fare better with a Pelham than with another bit. We are often horrified by the bits used

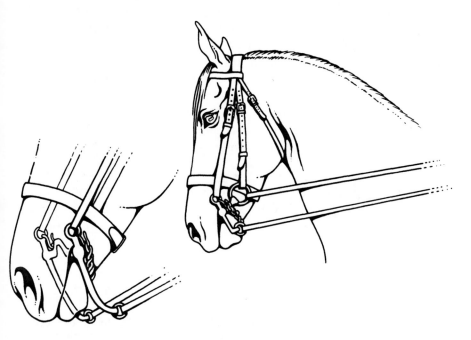

The longer the branches of the curb bit, the greater the leverage.

Pelham and Rugby Pelham.

by horsemen of the period of the Renaissance, with several joints to the mouthpiece, which meant that the jaw of the horse would have been tightly held between the curb chain and the bit. I personally do not think that they were the instruments of torture that they appear to be, though of course they would have been such if the rider were brutal. The placid and powerful but extremely heavy horses needed to carry a knight in armour were manoeuvred by the legs, or rather by very long, sharp spurs, and the lightest effect of the potent bits. Surely, no man would have had sufficiently strong biceps to stop those enormous horses with the help of a snaffle but one cannot imagine even a very placid horse putting up with the intolerable pain those bits would have inflicted if they were used roughly. For polo, the Rugby Pelham with a hard rubber mouthpiece, without a tongue groove but slightly arched to make room for the tongue, has many advantages; the curb chain gives it the precision and steadiness of a curb bit, while the bridoon rein helps the rider to steer the horse with greater ease. Some riders use a coupling to connect upper and lower rings to one rein; in polo, it is a concession to the necessity of steering

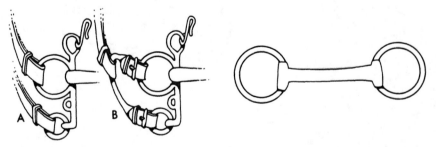

Pelham used *(left)* with four reins (A) or with two reins attached to a coupling (B), a dangerous practice. A rubber snaffle *(right)*, a good bit to prepare the horse for the curb bit.

with one rein and to the speed of the game. However, using a Pelham with two reins instead of four, in the hope of controlling a puller is a dangerous mistake. The horse may well obey its harsh effect at first, but gets used to it and gradually develops a totally insensitive mouth. In fact the worst injuries to the bars of the mouth that I have seen were caused by Pelhams used with a single rein. With double reins, it is quite a mild bit which can be used relatively early in the course of the horse's education. The advantage of the unjointed mouthpiece is that it compels the rider to learn to steer with his legs instead of hauling at the reins to turn the horse.

Most bits are nowadays made of stainless steel which is not guaranteed against breakage. The danger of the presence of an air bubble in the steel, which sooner or later will cause rusting of the mouthpiece or the rings, is greater than is generally realised. Some years ago, I was cantering peacefully on a bridle-path; suddenly the bit, which had been in use for a number of years, ruptured, hitting the horse in the mouth and so terrifying him that he leapt into a ditch half-full of frozen water, where I lay for many hours with a broken vertebra. Since then, I have heard of five similar accidents within my circle of friends, one of these during a dressage competition. The unpredictable breaking is caused by a defect in the material and not by the violence of the rider or the horse. I have never trusted stainless steel bits since suffering such an unpleasant experience.

A bit which is excellent for preparing a horse for the unjointed mouthpiece of a curb, is the Mullen mouthpiece made of firm though flexible rubber, with loose wire rings. As it must rest loosely in the mouth, it is better to use it with an ordinary cavesson nose band rather than a dropped nose band. Should the rider have a tendency to draw the bit through the mouth when he is asking for a change of direction, he can be allowed to glance at the side of the horse's mouth; all beginners learning to turn with the help of one rein have a tendency to pull too much on the inside rein and advance the outside hand more than they need. Letting them ride with this bit, without the dropped nose band, helps them to correct this tendency. Besides this, the bit lies on the tongue, preventing a beginner from hurting the bars of the mouth, as he can easily do with a jointed snaffle. It encourages a horse to relax his tongue and mouth. It is particularly suitable for horses that have been frightened of the bit by past rough treatment and it has a surprisingly quietening effect on strong pullers.

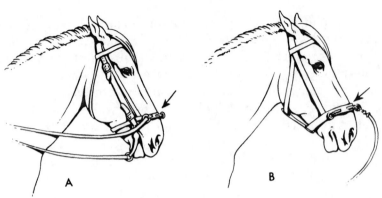

The cavesson works by exerting a pressure on the nasal bone. In southern France and in Spain, young horses are often trained with reins attached to the cavesson in addition to the reins being attached to the curb bit (A). Cavesson used for lungeing (B).

For the purpose of teaching beginners, the cavesson has fallen into oblivion. One forgets too easily that any kind of bit is unpleasant for a horse when he is ridden by a beginner. Furthermore, it is difficult to teach the beginner the feel of a quiet and steady tension of reins when the horse constantly tries to evade the discomfort caused by the hands of an insecure rider. It takes most beginners a number of years to learn to keep a steady tension of reins, and a cavesson with reins attached adjoined to a snaffle protects the horse's mouth against the jolts in his mouth unintentionally caused by the rider. The horse then confidently stretches the reins, thus teaching the rider the feel of the proverbial rubber bands, and is automatically rewarded for every flexion of the poll even if the rider is not prompt enough to do so himself. The reins must be adjusted to an even length, one attached to the cavesson, the other to the bit. When the horse flexes at the poll correctly, the cavesson rein becomes tauter and the bit rein looser and as the pressure of the cavesson on the nose is not painful, it does not prevent forward movement. The horse chews the bit as he should because the rider can never pull on the snaffle reins without pulling also on the cavesson and, if the horse tries to throw his head up to resist the cavesson, he then meets the unpleasant pressure of the snaffle. The interplay between the actions of the cavesson and those of the bit, comparable to the alternate effects of curb and bridoon, automatically teaches the horse to keep a steady contact with the rider's hands. All horses will go quietly when bridled in this manner because the beginner cannot then upset the horse by the erratic movements of his hands.

I have mentioned elsewhere the use of auxiliary reins for the purpose of producing an arching of the neck; here, I want to explain their effect on the position of the bit in the mouth. Martingales, side-reins and running reins are well enough known and can legitimately be used if a horse throws his head up and thus endangers the rider. Martingales and running reins hold the bit firmly on the bars of the mouth and so prevent the horse from pushing against it with his molars but they prevent the rider from yielding sufficiently promptly when a horse gives up his resistance. However, for a skilful rider, they can be of considerable assistance when he has to re-school a spoilt horse; but side-reins on the other hand should only be used for the purpose of teaching a rider to learn to sit. Nevertheless, all auxiliary reins show that the trainer or rider has insufficient faith in his ability to school a horse. They are not indispensable. Habitually resorting to them with every horse means that one prefers to admit one's incapacity rather than learn to ride.

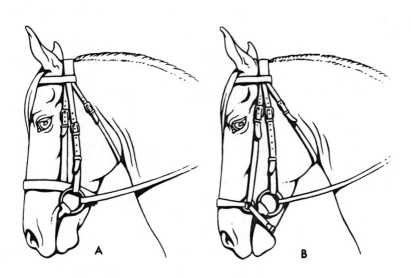

English cavesson nose band (A). A Hanoverian (dropped) nose band (B).

One ought also to be more critical of the various types of nose band indiscriminately used to prevent the horse from opening his mouth. They always hinder the desirable relaxation of the jaws, if they do not prevent it entirely as when they are buckled too tightly. Of course, as they prevent the horse from opening his mouth wide and baring his teeth when the rider is rough, they preserve appearances. However, ever since observing that no race-horse in good form gallops with his mouth wide open even at the height of tension, I have come to the conclusion that no properly balanced, freely moving horse needs a nose band for the purpose of keeping his mouth closed. I now ride all my horses in a snaffle, totally dispensing with the nose band; as for my very advanced horses, they move perfectly in a curb without even a bridoon; this is guiding them by the lower jaw encircled by the mouthpiece and the curb chain; needless to say, it requires considerable attention and sensitive fingers, but I have found that my horses carry themselves very well when thus bitted, with a moist, relaxed mouth and closed lips. I started riding with the curb only as an experiment and have had the same happy results a thousand times. It has taught me to feel better than ever the synchronised reactions of the muscles of the jaws, poll and neck and to discipline my hands so that I can instantly feel when I am asking too much, and so yield before the horse has had time to open his mouth. This has convinced me that it is senseless to use a nose band in the early stages of training with a snaffle, which is intended, after all, to teach the horse to salivate; the stiffness of jaws induced by the nose band extends to the entire system. For artistic displays, the use of a nose band is a matter of taste, but for hacking, competitions and showing, convention must be respected and a nose band must be worn; in any case, it does help to conceal tactless use of the hands.

Nevertheless, nose bands do serve a useful purpose in certain circumstances; they support the lower jaw, thus protecting the mandibular bones and joints and the muscles of mastication against the sometimes violent effect of the reins in show-jumping, hunting, cross-country or when the horse stumbles or falls; the dropped nose band is then preferable because of the better support it gives to the lower jaw underneath the bit. In the early years of my veterinary practice, cases of broken jaws and sprains of the mandibular joint were frequent, whereas nowadays, thanks to the dropped nose band, one never comes across such cases. Though it should not be used while giving the horse his elementary training, it is a very useful piece of equipment for sport. In cross-country events, when a horse has to arch his loins powerfully, in order to cover as much ground as possible with every stride of the gallop, and when a firm tension of reins helps him to do so, the support given by the nose band to the lower jaw is an advantage. It protects the muscles of the jaws and the neck against fatigue, assists the efforts of the muscles of the back and loins and helps the horse to maintain his equilibrium. Providing that the rider has a correct feel for relaxed muscular tension, this little piece of leather plays an important part in promoting performance and balance.

4 The Horseman's Tools

One should not think of the aids as mechanical contrivances, like levers and pulleys, by means of which the rider can transmit his force to the horse in order to produce or prevent movement. Aids are certain actions of the rider, by means of which he communicates with his horse and explains what he wants him to do. The aids must stimulate the horse's mental processes. Until he starts to be trained, he uses these mental processes solely for satisfying his own vital needs; but once we decide that the time has come to utilise his strength for our own purposes, we must develop his intelligence so that he learns to understand and obey our commands. We produce certain effects on his skin and mouth which he has to learn to interpret correctly. To start with, we teach him to control voluntarily the instinctive movements of his limbs; eventually, he must be taught to subjugate his desires to our own will.

Towards these ends, a clear vocabulary accessible to the horse's intelligence must be built up systematically, the words of which are the aids. One should not expect the horse to understand in a few lessons the complex language explained in manuals of equitation; the aids suitable for an advanced dressage horse are a combination of indications that a young horse would not understand.

Every rider would realise how much patience is required to educate a horse if he tried, at some time, to coach a group of ten- to fourteen-year old boys. It needs the patience of a saint to abstain from shouting and cursing before one learns that some children find it very difficult to control their limbs and use them effectively.

But, before we can hope to teach a horse to understand the aids, we must first teach ourselves to use them. If we do not learn to synchronise our actions with the natural movements of the horse, these actions cannot rightly be called aids. If the aids are used at the wrong moment—out of phase with the natural movement—they are just forceful actions which we resort to in order to destroy opposition to our demands, a resistance usually provoked by our own unreasonable demands. Such actions are based on the principle that Might is Right and ignore the fact that, the horse being the mightier, the issue of any conflict is usually settled in his favour. If we use the aids without understanding and feel of the movement, we annoy and perplex the horse with, to him, completely incomprehensible and irritating sensations which he will, eventually, resist or become indifferent to.

And before we can influence the movement by acting opportunely and with precision, we must learn to feel it.

Furthermore, we must learn to become conscious of our posture and of the movements of our limbs and also of the effects which our actions produce. It needs considerable mental application to avoid countermanding with one hand the commands given by the other, or hustling the horse with the legs while holding him back with the reins. No force applied to the body of the horse must ever be opposed by another; opposing forces must act alternately in a harmonious manner.

The intensity of the pressures which we apply to the body of the horse or on his tongue and the bars of his mouth by means of the aids must vary with the degree of training. The crude but unambiguous signs suitable for teaching a young horse to understand our commands and the discreet indications which an educated horse promptly comprehends bear little resemblance to each other. One does not call oneself a rider until one has learnt to use one's tools—or aids—with young and callow horses as well as completely schooled ones. Therefore, the rider ought never to be taught that there is only one correct way to use the aids. But learning to ride on riding school dolts, whose senses have been deadened by constantly thumping legs, leads to a total misconception of the aids, especially when the only teaching dispensed by the riding master are loud commands to "Drive on" and "Sit deep". The beginner is thus given the impression that he must exert himself with arms, seat and legs and that his exhausting efforts must mechanically produce the desired result, as if the horse were a cart that needed pushing and pulling or slowing down by applying a brake. The "sparking plugs" are in the horse's brain and will only function predictably if we apply our aids with intelligence. We can know, for example, that the pressure of our legs has produced a spark in the horse's brain, if he makes some movement with his ears and we must then take the appropriate measures to get him to react more or less quickly in the right manner. We can, at first, deliberately watch the horse's ears but, as we become more experienced, we will unconsciously register the play of the ears which indicates attentiveness. With a young horse, we must always give him time to interpret the signals. It is most interesting to note the delay between reception of the message and the response, and we must always be extremely careful not to cross the lines of communication. Each time, we carefully observe how long it takes for the "return message" to be sent out from the horse's brain and provide the right response; we learn to speed up the horse's reaction, thus developing his strength and his quickness of comprehension, until the responses become instantaneous. After years of mental application and self-criticism, we acquire the ability to feel and influence the movement almost unconsciously and to transform the horse's slow analysis of the message of the aids into a conditioned reflex. Yet, although the education of the rider in the use of the aids must be systematically planned, the effect of every individual rider on various horses can never be identical because there are a number of factors to take into account, such as rapidity of reactions, conformation and physical strength.

Usually the aids are classified as impulsive or restraining, but we should also distinguish the aids which utilise indirectly the friction of the ground, in order to speed up or slow down the forward movement, from those by means of which we influence the horse's posture, the tension of his muscles, his suppleness and balance. In practice, the distinction is not clearly marked; sometimes one kind prevails, sometimes the other, but we must know what effects the aids should produce and understand the influence of balance and fluent submissiveness on performance. We must know how to indicate either a change of speed or an alteration of posture and balance and also get the horse to understand what we mean, so that finally we have him under complete control.

A superficially educated rider will have been taught that impulsion is promoted by the legs, whip, spurs and seat and that it is moderated by the hands, arms and back. The matter, however, is more complex and this is what I will try to explain in the following pages.

LEGS

"Anyone who can push the horse forward with his legs can ride" is a commonplace much used by riding instructors. Its misinterpretation and man's propensity for violence has caused many a rider to wear himself out and even to strain severely the "rider's muscle" to get horses to go forward. Such exertion is futile, notorious and a total waste of energy. How can anyone sitting astride a horse push him forward by strength of legs? Besides which, if violent effort were required to set in motion as heavy a body as that of a horse, equally enormous strength would be needed to slow or stop the motion. If one enjoys physical training for the sake of developing powerful muscles, weight-lifting is a more satisfying activity than riding. "Anyone can ride once he has mastered the art of getting a horse to go forward" is a more apt expression, but still one which does not impart the right image.

I will try to convince sceptical readers that effective use of the legs is a knack rather than a matter of strenuous effort, by listing the various ways in which it influences the movement of the horse.

1 Legs simply cause the horse to move forward.
2 They regulate the forward movement.
3 They promote the swing of the hindlegs.
4 They determine the length of the stride.
5 They dictate the beat.
6 They influence the horse's posture; by influencing the tension of the back and neck, the actions of the rider's legs contribute toward the arching of the neck.
7 They prolong the flexion of the haunches to produce collection.

One cannot explain in so many words exactly what the rider does with his legs to produce different effects. The art of riding is black magic, is what my riding master, the famous Felix Buerkner, used to say. However, if one wants to discover the secret of the magic, one must start by learning one's A-B-C. Nevertheless, it is easy to realise that one does not use the legs in the same manner to produce a piaffe as to urge a horse forward to clear a big parallel obstacle.

The horse must be educated to understand the messages of the legs and taught to keep his mind attentive to the sensations they produce so that he eventually reacts as if their impulses were in his own flesh and blood; finally his obedience must become unconscious, unquestioning, like a reflex. At this stage, the leg aids become such slight indications as to be invisible to a spectator. Towards this end, the rider must use intelligence not strength. This requires tremendous concentration, consistency and frequent and regular practise.

The skill of riding cannot be learnt in a set number of lessons. It is a harmony of all the movements of the rider and the horse, consisting of various elements and each element must be learnt separately before they can be combined into one whole. The skill of using the legs, the seat, the hands, must be developed by study and separate attention to the feel and effect of the activity of each part. A rider must develop his deftness as conscientiously as a pianist, who continues to practise finger exercises for improving his nimbleness; similarly, a blacksmith cannot produce wrought-iron work of artistic quality with the filing and hammering technique of a farrier. The art of using the legs must be learnt in solitude, alone with one's thoughts and the horse. Shouted commands such as "Use the legs", "Drive on" are suitable noises for teaching week-end riders using riding school dolts who have both become so used to the automatic thumps of the legs that they occasionally need shaking out of their lethargy. In reality, the actions of the legs are complex and variable. They cannot be described accurately, because so much depends on the educated response of the horse and the promptness of reaction of the rider.

Should the legs be used alternately or simultaneously? I will not express a categorical opinion because the best masters disagree, as they do also on the value of pressures of the foot on the stirrup, regarded by some as the supreme leg aid of all. However, I can put both points of view and then let the reader experiment; this will at least prevent him from getting bored with riding. All experts without exception, however, agree that it is only with the lower leg, the parts below the knee, and not with the thighs or knees, that one must "talk".

The weight aid is subordinate and effective only in conjunction with the leg aid. Consequently, the lower leg must be perfectly free, so that it can perform its rightful function. By gripping with the calves to pull himself down in the saddle, the rider deprives himself of the use of the legs for controlling the movements of the horse. The legs must be relaxed but under the control of the rider's central nervous system; and not only should they be always ready to act, but also always ready to desist from acting, just like the foot of the motorist on the accelerator, which releases its pressure sufficiently to keep the car engine turning at a constant speed without wasteful consumption of fuel. A horse can respond to varying pressures as precisely as the engine of a car, providing of course that he has been educated to remain constantly attentive to the signals of the legs.

The alternating impulses of the leg make sense if one watches a saddled horse from the rear, with the stirrups let down. As the horse walks away, watch the oscillations of the stirrups and notice that each stirrup strikes the horse's barrel at the moment when the hindlimb on the same side moves in support. This happens also at the trot, the piaffe and the passage. Now, if the relaxed legs are allowed to weigh the stirrups down, the lower part of the leg will move with the stirrups and so the rider knows which hindleg is swinging forward and which one is in support. The movement can be studied at the beginning by glancing at the horse's shoulders at the walk; as the right shoulder starts swinging forward, the left hind is about to start its forward swing. Next, one learns to feel the movement with the eyes closed. Finally, one learns to accentuate the alternating contacts of the lower legs with the horse's sides and to stimulate the movements at the appropriate moment.

On the other hand, if the leg acts while the horse's hindfoot is pushing against the ground to thrust the mass forward, the aid makes no sense; the horse must either ignore it or respond to this hustling by hurrying.

Using the leg pressures alternately, one can either produce a more energetic forward swing of each hindleg in turn, or increase and prolong the flexion of the hock during the phase of support, thus producing a collecting effect. The difference depends on the duration of the pressure of each leg of the rider and the intensity of the pressure, all this being largely a matter of feel. A rider who has discovered the skill of influencing each hindleg exerts himself less and can produce collection with much reduced rein effects; the cardinal sin would be to act with the reins in the direction of one hindleg at the moment when it starts extending to propel the mass forward. Beat also is prescribed by alternating leg pressures: short, sharp contacts cause the horse's feet to detach themselves from the ground more briskly; conversely, a pressure prolonged after the moment of impact of the hindfoot prevents the force impact being converted immediately to propulsion, each hindleg supporting the weight of the mass on flexed joints for a moment before thrusting it upward and forward. This is how rider and horse dance to music.

The distinct feel of the movements of the hindlimbs turns lateral movements into child's play. On the contrary, if a rider lacks this feel, he tortures himself, squeezes or thumps with his legs, shifts his weight in the saddle, pulls the horse's head and neck sideways, thus destroying impulsion and rhythm, so that the horse pushes himself sideways with a hindlimb and cannot go forward without difficulty. On the other hand, the lateral movements are so easy and elegant if, in order to move obliquely forward and right, the rider only slightly displaces his left leg backwards and presses it against the horse's left side while the left hind is swinging forward; during this phase of its movement, the left hind is easily brought forward in front of the right and the lateral movement will flow forward in a smooth and natural manner. After a few steps, the rider stops the oblique progression by using his right leg during the moment of forward swing of the right hind and then, with touches of equal intensity of each of his legs in turn drives the horse forward on a straight course, before again going sideways by reversing his actions. One starts with six, then four strides, then two and eventually one only, in each direction, and finally one develops such an accurate feel of straightness that one can get a horse who normally straddles with the hindlegs to move on a narrow track.

The legs can be used alternately in piaffe and passage with a horse that moves easily in self-carriage with a very light tension of reins; he can be taught that alternate leg pressures mean collection while a simultaneous pressure of both legs means "forward". The transitions from walk to piaffe, from piaffe to passage, from passage to trot and back to passage can then be performed with extreme precision. However, if a horse that lacks impulsion has been trained to respond only to alternating leg aids, in passage and piaffe he will sway his croup from side to side, will advance reluctantly if at all and will be impossible to drive smoothly from passage to trot.

It is not just for dressage, but for riding in general that one ought to develop the feel of the movements of the hindlimbs. To indicate the canter, for example, if the rider gives the aid of his right leg at the precise moment when the right hind is about to swing forward, the horse can start the canter immediately with the right lead. On the other hand, if the rider's right leg acts as the right hind pushes against the ground, the horse cannot obey immediately or has to rush; if, to prevent the latter occurrence, the rider restrains the horse with the reins, the canter starts with the wrong lead. Sometimes, when passing through a corner of the manege, the outside hind tends to lag; a timely tap of the rider's outside leg or spur must then stimulate it to make the longer swing required of the outside limb on curves, so that the horse canters straight when he comes out of the corner. Even at the rising trot, a rider who has learnt to feel the movements of the hindlimbs can use alternating leg aids appropriately. If he rises with the outside diagonal (rising as inside hind and outside fore swing forward), his inside leg will press on the horse while he is rising, and his outside leg while he is sitting.

At the halt, a quiet touch of the leg on one side of the horse must cause the hindleg on that side to step forward if it is left behind and not supporting the weight of the croup as it should.

I can think of other examples, but only the rider can teach himself to feel how and when to act with each leg to influence beat and stride; short sharp touches at the moment when a hindfoot is about to swing forward will promote a more vigorous swing of the hindlimbs; more prolonged pressures of each lower leg in turn, combined with half-parades, during the first phase of support of each hindleg, will lengthen the shock absorbing flexion of the hindjoints.

Finally, with an example from bad circus riding, let me illustrate the principle that leg aids must harmonise with the movement of the horse's hindlegs.

The Spanish walk—an unnatural walk, in which the horse extends each foreleg, lifting it up high from the elbow joint—can be taught by tapping the horse on the shoulder with the whip, unloading the shoulder of the weight of the body and using the spur on the opposite side; eventually, the horse learns to extend each foreleg in response to the touch of the spur on the opposite side. If one watches the hindlegs, the jerkiness of their movements clearly shows the confusing effect on the horse's nervous system of leg aids which are not synchronised with the natural movement. The worried horse, instead of lightening the forehand by flexing his haunches, hollows his back and shuffles with stiff hindlegs or must move at an amble. This, of course, is the sort of circus act which is against nature and gives circus dressage a bad name.

Many excellent riders, however, use simultaneous and equal pressures of both legs to produce forward movement, a technique which is just as difficult to perfect as the one previously described. The mistake of most novice riders is to use excessive strength; it is the unnecessary effort which prevents the rider from feeling the horse's willingness to obey, so that the rider continues to press with his legs after the horse has already obeyed by moving forward or increasing speed. Worse still is the habit of tapping with both legs simultaneously. This is a very difficult habit to correct, particularly when the rider tries to prescribe the beat in this manner. It deadens the horse's sensitivity and eventually leads to total disregard of the legs. The frustrated rider then resorts to the whip, but uses its just as irrationally, until eventually loud blows of the whip resound through the manege at regular intervals, startling all the other horses but making little impression on the intended victim. This is the way to produce the famous riding school dolt . . . and yet some instructors absurdly maintain that a sluggish horse is the ideal instrument for teaching riders to use their legs!

From the very beginning of training, the horse must be taught to respond to light touches of the legs. And the first thing that the rider must learn, if he wants to achieve this object, is the feel of passive legs which maintain contact with the horse's sides by hanging loosely from the hip joint. Only passive hands can feel every movement of the horse's neck, head and mouth; similarly, passive legs must feel the movement of the trunk as it wobbles from side to side towards the supporting hindleg, and the movements of respiration of the chest. According to circumstances, to the movement required, to the stage of education of the horse, leg contact can vary from firm to light, but must never become a grip, pressure or squeeze of sufficient intensity to destroy all sensation of communication with the horse's nervous system. Lower legs must be consciously disciplined, and when they abandon their passive sensitivity in order to produce a reaction, the rider must control their action and instantly feel a response. Thus, the lower legs sustain pressure until the desired reaction is produced and then instantly return to a passive state of vigilance. The extent to which the rider's lower legs envelop the horse's body is of little importance; it is a matter of one's personal idea of elegance. Some riders are quite happy if only the top 10 cm of their boots remain in contact with the horse's sides while others like to feel the whole of the lower leg, down to the ankle, on the horse. Feel is all that matters; and that is another thing that a riding master cannot impart.

To educate the young horse to obey the command to walk—which should never be given until he has learnt to stand still—the rider presses gently with his lower legs while advancing his hands to loosen the reins completely. If the horse flicks his ears backward slightly and then makes one forward step, the rider must immediately relax the pressure of lower legs and knees. This is the only way to get the horse to associate cause and effect and if the rider does not appreciate the importance of this yielding action of the legs, or is too slow to give the reward, it shows that he himself does not understand the sense of his actions. The relaxation of the leg pressure must be consciously carried out to make a very clear impression on the horse and the procedure is used with all young horses or remounts in the early stages of training: as soon as they have relaxed, stop hurrying and start moving at a regular rhythm. Then one can start teaching them to obey the legs with increasing promptitude by frequently repeating transitions. During motion, the rider's legs must remain totally passive, in relaxed contact with the horse's sides for as long as the horse maintains the regular swing of his limbs; if he becomes lazy, the same light pressure is repeated.

From the beginning of training the horse to obey the legs, we must require him to continue working at the speed set by the initial pressure, even after the pressure relaxes and the legs become passive until he feels another indication, from the legs asking for more energetic forward movement, or from the hands or position of the rider indicating a reduction of speed or a halt.

The speed is then regulated by the legs or the hands, intervening only if the gait loses its regularity. The ability to maintain a steady, relaxed contact of the legs with the horse's sides and of the hands with the mouth, which never disturbs the regular swing of the legs, makes considerable demands on the rider's sensitivity and powers of concentration. During elementary training, respect for the principle of hands without legs, legs without hands, and no intervention from either providing that the gait remains active and regular, makes advanced dressage schooling easy. It is impossible to sit on a horse with unruffled dignity while concentrating on balance in the difficult movements of a test, if one has to exert oneself all the time and worry constantly about impulsion.

It would be too much to expect a young horse to respond promptly to a gentle pressure of the legs. Instead of resorting immediately to ferocious squeezing or to a thump, which is what most beginners do, one repeats the same gentle pressure and a well-bred and sensitive horse will then almost invariably respond by moving forward. If nothing happens the whip must be used with sufficient determination to make more than one stroke unnecessary; it is an aid respected by all unspoilt horses. Quite soon, the horse will understand that the slightest pressure of the legs forebodes a stroke of the whip unless he moves forward immediately from a halt, or more energetically if he is already in motion. Complete self-control and consistency are required by the rider, not only to make sure that he does not contradict the command of the legs by stopping the movement with his hands, but also to reward the horse for his obedience by relaxing the pressure of the legs.

A simultaneous pressure of both legs can have only one meaning; it is a command to go forward. As he progresses in his schooling, the horse learns to interpret the degrees of pressure as indications to move forward from a rein-back or a halt into walk, working trot or medium trot. It is an aid which makes an impression on the mind of the horse and we know that the message has been received if we see his ears flicking backwards. In contrast, the alternating pressures of the legs influence the movement of the hindlegs through the "reflex-arc" (connections within the spinal cord), so that the horse does not have to analyse the sensations registered by the nerves of the skin. Simultaneous pressure of both legs cannot therefore have any collecting effect. The natural elevation of the forehand then depends on energetic forward movement, and the shortening of the steps and collection are obtained by parades of various intensity. It needs great skill to act with the hands without impairing impulsion, so that every rider will have to contend with some resistances with all horses before a perfect mutual understanding is established. The parades will have to be done as precisely as a change of gear with a car and the one thing that must be avoided at all costs is using the reins like a hand brake; this has an irritating effect on a horse and provokes him to pull all the harder. Changes of speed are achieved by short, energetic parades which must shorten each step without slowing the beat. These are actions which a freely moving horse will not resist. The best way of polishing the technique is the frequent repetition of transitions from trot to walk without tolerating the least impurity of gait.

Which form of leg action is to be preferred is a question to which I do not propose to give an answer. Anybody with ambition to become a good rider will want to develop the feel of both techniques and does not require advice. The secret of success is the perfect relaxation of all the leg muscles which allows the legs to hang as freely as the stirrup leathers; the rider can then command the movements of the hindlimbs almost without thinking, using alternate pressures for elevation and collection, and simultaneous pressures to produce energetic forward movement and to demand transitions from one gait to a faster one.

The stirrup aid is the last finishing touch, the ultimate refinement of the leg aid; a mere hint of an aid, which becomes sufficient when total unity and equilibrium of horse and rider have been achieved. It is such a discreet driving action that it makes riding look like sorcery.

In reality, there are two ways of using the stirrups as an aid.

Firstly, a crude but powerful effect can be produced if the rider loads one stirrup more than the other by getting it to support an increased share of the weight of the rider's body. Some riders even lean sideways or displace their seat to sit on one side of the saddle to such an extent that to keep the line of gravity close to the centre of the base of support (the horse), they must bend to the opposite side from the waist. To counterbalance this external load, the horse is obliged by his instinct to move away from the loaded side. He can thus be compelled, for example, to canter from the trot before he is sufficiently schooled to respond to the conventional aids; his instinct forces him to do so in orer to protect his limbs against injury. Gradually, this very crude unilateral weight aid is reduced to a forward pressure of the inside seat bone combined with increased pressure on the corresponding stirrup, so that the horse starts the canter straight. Finally, the canter can be indicated simply by a movement of the foot from the ankle with a fractional increase of weight on the stirrup, and the seat aid becomes superfluous. Some people argue that the use of the weight in lateral movements is inelegant and unnecessary, but it can be refined as I have just explained and need not be visible.

The second use of the stirrup as an aid is based on the effect of backward or forward displacement of the weight. This also utilises the horse's instinct and has therefore an irresistible effect on the balance of the horse, regardless of his level of schooling. One can try it first at the walk on a loose rein. Using the stirrup, one extends the knees, pushes the seat back towards the cantle and then sits upright; the horse's steps become longer and slower. Then, by depressing the stirrups with the toes one slides the seat towards the pommel; the horse quickens his steps and increases the speed. By sitting on the rear part of the saddle, one produces increased flexion of the joints of the hindlegs with slower, more elevated action; conversely, sitting close to the pommel unloads the hindlegs, favours forward propulsion and a quickening of the steps.

The art of influencing equilibrium in this manner is extremely useful in all the gaits. Obviously the effect of the weight must not be cancelled by inappropriate actions of the hands.

The elegant use of the stirrups evolves from the above seat aid which can be utilised as soon as the horse is balanced and obedient, in order to forewarn him of the actions of the legs for an increase of speed, or of the hands for a slowing down. The pressure of the legs is then combined with a forward pressure of the seat, and the parades with a backward pressure of the seat, assisted, in the first instance by a downward pressure on the stirrups by the toes and, in the second, by a lightening of stirrup pressure as the heels are depressed. Eventually, the horse's sensitivity to the various degrees of tension of the stirrup leathers, produced by means of slight movements of the feet from the ankle joints, will have become such that the seat need no longer be used. More energetic extension is indicated by a downward pressure of the feet on the stirrup; parades are performed by stretching the calf muscles to lighten the weight on the stirrups while simultaneously the rider draws himself up from the waist. Again, tactful hands are needed to prevent any confusion. With sensitive, energetic horses, one can also loosen the contact of the knees with the saddle; the only points of friction between horse and rider will then be the relaxed buttocks, the top of the boots and the weight of the foot on the stirrups. The pacifying effect of this feeling of freedom on a strong horse who is inclined to get excited is astonishing; he starts carrying his rider with the sort of care which one needs for balancing an urn full of water on one's head.

The usefulness of unilateral stirrup pressure in lateral movements, on the other hand, is not a matter of total agreement between experts. It does seem unnecessary because the horse is contained between the pressures of a forward driving leg on one side of his body and a sideways driving leg on the other and these effects are much more potent than that of the stirrup pressure.

Stirrup weighing is an aid that can be used with horses as perfectly balanced as High-School horses must be, but they are dancers. Show-jumpers, eventing horses and race-horses are athletes. Balance and style are important for them also but, in their case, the rider's legs can give only one command: *"Forward"*. The show-jumper must bound forward as soon as his rider orders him to but not before. He must not be allowed to get excited, tear round the course and rush at obstacles. Each obstacle must be approached calmly, with the horse in control, and when the rider is not urging him on, the horse must canter quietly and regularly. The rider must remain composed between obstacles, attentive to balance, and drive with legs and seat only in the last strides before take-off.

However, show-jumpers, like dressage horses, must learn to interpret the various degrees of energy which the rider imparts to his leg aids; the legs are always used simultaneously and equally firmly, but solely for the purpose of increasing the speed. For security, the rider must rely on his sense of balance, that is his seat, a rather firm contact of the lower part of the thighs with the saddle and the support of the stirrups. Though the lower legs must not grip the horse's sides, they must remain passively in contact up to the moment of asking the horse to collect himself for the jump; in the approach, the horse must feel all the determination of the rider through the energetic pressures of the legs. Show-jumping riders must, therefore, discipline their legs as strictly as dressage riders if they want their horses to remain obedient to the driving aids.

Instead of spending most of the time jumping various obstacles, a novice rider who wants to dedicate himself to jumping must first learn the art of lengthening and shortening the gallop leaps merely by controlling his legs, either driving with repeated firm pressure or passively keeping contact with the horse's sides; for the purpose of acquiring the skill of regulating the activity of his legs, he should try to intervene as little as possible with his hands during these exercises; this will also teach him the use of the seat for the changes of speed. When it comes to jumping, he will already know how to activate the horse in the approach and how to remain passive from the moment of take-off until the horse's hindfeet have landed on the other side of the obstacle, then to drive on again; between two elements of a double, he must always drive with energy. Otherwise, how soon the legs must start driving in the approach to individual obstacles is a matter of experience because no two horses are alike. But a show-jumper who does not wait for his rider's orders and takes command of the situation cannot be properly controlled and cannot be trusted.

As for style, one should be less concerned about the rider's position than about the horses's obedience to the aids, his balance, intelligence and submission. To have a clear round against the clock, one must have a horse that can be driven, whose galloping strides can be regulated easily and who lets the rider plan the approach to each obstacle.

One of the best ways of teaching oneself to use the legs with discrimination is to induce a horse to descend into a deep ditch with steep banks, an intimidating sort of obstacle for inexperienced horses. The smallest step forward, even only a tentative move to jump the water at the bottom of the ditch, must be immediately rewarded by relaxation of leg pressure; if the horse hesitates again, leg pressure is renewed. Relentless squeezing or angry use of the legs or spurs would only provoke more misgivings and resistance.

The comparative merits of alternating and simultaneous leg pressures need not be discussed any further, providing that the principles are understood and respected: that is, all horses must be educated to distinguish between various degrees of firmness and must learn to obey promptly. A horse that obeys the legs reluctantly or that does not obey them at all is like a car with a dirty or completely clogged up carburettor; a horse that rushes and fights the bit is like a car with a jammed accelerator but, unlike a car, his engine cannot be put out of gear and using the reins like a brake is useless.

A horse must have become lazy before one can start to make him work; but when the horse is lazy, he must be driven forward and be made to obey the driving aids. For the novice rider, these statements must seem paradoxical and so let me explain myself.

Many of us will remember the frightening experience of sitting on a school bench for the first time. It is the same sort of apprehension that the young horse must be given time to overcome at the beginning of his training. He will only start moving freely and rhythmically when he becomes unconcerned by the presence of a rider on his back. If the rider sits as a relaxed passenger, he causes little discomfort, so that in a short time the horse feels free to move with long and easy strides. It is just as if he were saying: "I won't resist, providing that I am not annoyed." That is the sort of laziness one should want at the beginning and it's only when the horse has become almost oblivious to the presence of the rider that one can start to teach him carefully to obey the driving aids. Then, he must allow himself to be driven by the legs, which means that he should not move before he feels the commanding pressure of the legs but that he must obey commands promptly. Once he has secured this obedience, the rider must assume again the role of a relaxed passenger and let the horse proceed with long and easy strides.

There is no contradiction, as we are talking now about the early stages of training and the first lessons in comprehension. At a much later stage of training, one would expect the horse to remain constantly attentive to the rider and to continue working with energy until he feels the reins sliding through the rider's fingers as far as the buckle. This means that the lesson is finished. The horse is again allowed to drop his head and neck and to move lazily.

There are still many riders who have been taught to keep a strong knee grip at all times. This is a legacy from the cavalry. For centuries, horses were used to carry armies into battle. The strong grip gave the rider the solidity needed to use the sword or the lance or to prevent him from being thrown off by his opponent. Besides which, troopers were trained for two or three years at most and had to manage as best they could with the sort of horses provided by the army. The essential thing was to stay on. Spurs were for urging the reluctant horses forward; the curb for stopping. Instruction was in the form of drilling and every trooper was expected to have his horse at the legs and the hands all the time. Of course, any other kind of instruction would have been wasted on the average trooper and the average horse. I will never forget the favourite maxim of my first cavalry instructor: "A rider who has sufficient strength to drive a horse forward, always has sufficient strength to hold him back. All that one needs is more strength in the legs than the arms, and a horse will then go forward." I owe a debt of gratitude to that man, because the statement was so absurd that it started me thinking. It still took years of failure, reflection and experimenting to come to the conclusion that the art of riding consists of doing as little as possible —no more than enough—and has nothing to do with strength.

I may, nonetheless, be guilty of some injustice. Some spoilt, apathetic and dense horses need all the strength one can muster to drive them up to the bit. It did not occur to me at the time that my riding instructor might have been contending with such a brute; his outburst might have been a mere sally, which I, in my callowness, understood as a general principle.

The stereotyped instruction dispensed by the army was an unavoidable evil of mass education. Despite this, there always arose from the ranks a few men with the intelligence and inspiration to transform mere riding into the art of horsemanship. Many riders who have become internationally famous came from the cavalry. They were not necessarily exceptionally talented, but they must certainly have been intelligent, thoughtful, assiduous and instinctively good psychologists. Those are the qualities that enabled them to emerge from the level of "Push and Pull" riding. Instead of using brute physical strength, they took the trouble to understand the horse's mentality and develop his intelligence. It is in the same spirit that we must study the effects of the aids.

Using the legs or heels to punish a horse or, worse still, to vent one's anger, is despicable. How can one expect a horse to relax if, every time he feels the legs loosening their pressure, he expects a bruising blow on the ribs. Nevertheless, horses regularly treated in this manner eventually develop a total disregard for the hammering they are subjected to, become resigned to their destiny and turn into apathetic dolts. The army cannot be held responsible for this sort of brutality.

SPURS

Spurs are the prolongation of the lower leg, enabling it to be used with more authority or more precision. But before he buckles on his spurs, the rider must consider his reasons. Does he want to punish, to produce impulsion, to obtain collection and better engagement of the hindlegs? For the first two purposes, spurs are crude instruments for training young horses. They may augment the authority of the legs but equally good results can be obtained without. For collection and for determining a slower, more clearly marked beat, they have a more precise effect than the legs alone but they need to be used with discernment. Alternating short touches of each spur at the position of the girth, combined with half-parades, help to elicit the half-steps which are eventually transformed into the elevated steps of the High-School. Thus the horse can be schooled to understand that the pressure of the lower legs indicates a lengthening of the stride, while the touch of each spur in turn means a shortening of the steps and elevation of the forehand. It may seem paradoxical to use spurs for slowing down the speed but, in reality, they are of signal help when teaching the horse to perform transitions from trot to passage and passage to trot; alternate touches of spurs will mean passage; simultaneous pressure of both legs indicate trot.

To learn to use the spurs with the light touch which is appropriate in this case, one should wear trousers and shoes instead of breeches and boots so that one's Achilles tendon is protected by no more than the thickness of a sock. This will effectively discourage one from using more strength than necessary. However, the spurs should be sharp. Blunt ones and those with a knob or a small wheel do not produce a sufficiently precise effect and tend to irritate the horse, while sharp rowels easily become instruments of torture.

We must remember that the neat touch of the spur causes the horse to detach a hindfoot from the ground more briskly, to make him mark time more distinctly in the collected movements. It is illogical therefore to touch with both spurs at the same time; this would have a senseless, agitating effect. On the other hand, if the reason for wearing spurs is to get the horse to respond more promptly to the driving aids, one must use a firm pressure instead of a quick touch. Let us take the example of a young horse learning to respond to the aid for the canter. The rider uses a simultaneous pressure of both legs (inside leg in front of the girth, outside leg behind the girth); he starts with a pressure of the upper part of the boots, may have to extend this to a pressure with the whole length of the lower legs and, if the horse still does not get the message, pressure of both spurs is applied together with a stroke of the whip. Providing that these indications are given each time in the same manner and that the lesson is repeated at frequent intervals, the horse will soon start the canter when he feels the pressure of the top of the boots so forestalling the use of the spurs and the whip. However, for the purpose of obtaining quicker obedience to the legs, one should use the spurs as little as possible and eventually do without them. With all the aids, the ultimate object is as discreet a use as possible.

HANDS

From time immemorial, ever since man sitting astride the horse has had to control speed from the saddle, a bit and reins have been employed as an extension of the hands. This has allowed the hands to manipulate the forehand by taking advantage of the sensitivity of the tongue and the bars of the mouth. The pressure of the bit is uncomfortable. Most horses are sufficiently intelligent to understand that the quickest way to avoid the discomfort is to stop moving as soon as possible. Providing that the rider is just as prompt to release the pressure the moment the horse obeys, the very slightest of indications is enough to produce the required result. The beauty of the system is its simplicity. Yet there have always been riders unable to grasp the idea or to discipline their reactions and who have had to contend, for the duration of their riding experience, with resistance put up by every horse that they have tried to manage. One cannot stress sufficiently the importance of using the reins in a well-timed and fitting manner from the very beginning of training and throughout all the subsequent stages of schooling and utilisation of the horse.

The most intriguing thing, however, is that the purely physical effect of the sensations felt by the horse in his mouth can be transformed by careful training into a psychological influence and that, although at the beginning the rider has to move his hands actively, eventually he can produce the effect desired with passive hands and even dispense with reins altogether; the bit in the horse's mouth serving then the function of reminding the horse that he must remain attentive to the other aids. Before the second world war, in Berlin, a Spanish officer gave a dressage display of extraordinary beauty, during the whole course of which he rode the horse entirely with the aids of seat and legs only.

The evolution of the restraining influences of the rider on the horse's movement, through the stages of simply tugging, then of merely closing the fingers more firmly on the reins without having to move the hands, and finally being able to stop by means of an imperceptible movement of extension of the back, is just a matter of developing patiently the obedience of the horse through a fairly long process of education. Nevertheless, this requires on the part of the rider an enormous measure of self-discipline. If he cannot prevent himself from pulling, his arm muscles will be severely strained and he will produce horses with totally insensitive mouths; he must learn to control his hands as scrupulously as his legs, which means that he must use them with the least force necessary, with quickness to yield so that the slightest sign of obedience is immediately rewarded, even if he has to repeat his actions several times, either in the same manner or more firmly, to achieve the complete result he intends.

The best way to teach a beginner the correct use of the reins is to mount him on a calm and docile green horse that has not been schooled to respond too promptly to the aids. A manege horse or a dressage horse would tempt a novice rider to use the reins to produce the head carriage which he has admired; this is the last thing that we can allow him to do. On a fairly callow but placid animal that inspires confidence, the novice rider can be allowed to ride out-of-doors at walk, trot or canter with completely slack reins. Allowing him to tauten the reins when he gets worried about the speed quickly develops the habit of hanging on. He can be allowed to shorten the reins only in order to come to a halt. Obviously, the rider must be accompanied by his teacher who must inspire him with the necessary determination and show him how to take a short hold on the reins, sit up, resist the movement with his back and stop the horse, even if, in so doing, he causes the horse to throw up his head. The essential thing is to produce total immobility after the smallest possible number of strides of trot or canter. He must then immediately drop the reins and, if the horse jogs, repeat the same actions. The usual fault of all beginners is to grip fiercely with the knee. This causes them to lean forward, to let their legs slide behind the vertical, to lose their balance and to hang on to the reins, thus inducing the horse to resist the bit by running away.

Once this lesson is learnt, the rider must be taught to change from walk to trot, trot to canter, canter to trot and trot to walk. This will teach him not only to understand that the restraining aids need to be used with various degrees of energy but also to use his legs to determine forward movement as soon as he has succeeded in passing from the faster gait to the slower one. He will know whether he has yielded sufficiently and soon enough if the horse moves freely forward without jogging as soon as he changes into a slower gait; and if the horse does jog, the rider must be made to understand that it is because he is still restricting the movement with the reins. This manner of executing downward transitions is crude but the aim is to give a beginner the confidence to ride any horse at the walk, trot or canter, secure in the knowledge that he can stop when he wants to. It upsets horses much less than the hesitant and futile toying with badly understood rein effects to which beginners are prone; it teaches riders that any action of the hands is wrong unless it produces exactly the result expected. As surprisingly little force is needed, it also helps them to understand that the aids are simply actions of the rider that the horse must understand. Once this lesson is learnt, it takes little time to teach beginners a more refined technique.

Teaching the rider the feel of a fitting tension of reins is the next step. As we cannot expect any horse to maintain a perfectly steady head carriage when he is ridden by a beginner who cannot possibly be expected to have steady hands, we must teach our novice to accompany every movement of the horse's head with a constant and mild tension of reins, a tension just sufficient to prevent the reins from flapping. He should not be told to give and take, nor be allowed to let one rein become tauter or slacker than the other. With the only difference that the reins are now so adjusted that the rider can distinctly feel the movements of the horse's head, the same exercises are performed as before. It is the horse's action that will inform both the teacher and the pupil that the tension of the reins is suitable or excessive; if it becomes stronger than it need be, the horse will either move faster or more slowly. One of the most difficult things for a beginner to learn is the feel of a tension of reins that allows the horse total freedom of movement of his head and neck and yet is sufficiently positive to prevent any loss of contact with the mouth and any slackness of reins.

At this stage, most riders will notice that nearly all horses want to stretch the left rein more than the right and sometimes try to lean heavily on the left rein. It is better not to explain the reason, because we want the rider to continue concentrating on maintaining exactly the same light tension of both reins; but to enable him to do so the horse must maintain an active, free, forward movement. After a few lessons, the rider will be surprised to find that the horse's head and neck remain steady at the trot. This is because, by making sure that he keeps the same light tension of reins, passively letting his hands move exactly to the same extent as the neck, he has left the horse in peace and has not produced the slightest discomfort. The horse will remain on the bit, even if the parades are unnecessarily energetic, providing that obedience is always immediately rewarded by a sufficient relaxation of the tension of the reins.

Needless to say, the forearms and back of the hands must be perfectly in line with the reins, which, therefore, must be held short enough to permit this. If they are allowed to get too long, the hands will press down, thus preventing the elbow from acting as a supple hinge. A beginner ought not to be told, however, to keep his hands at the level of his waist with the wrists rounded, as one does with a perfectly poised High-School horse; this also would produce stiffness. Frequently, he should deliberately let the reins slide through his fingers and adjust them again to a suitable length; frequently also, he should hold them together in one hand and then the other, being careful to avoid any difference of tension which would cause the horse to alter the speed. A rider who unknowingly lets the reins get too long by letting them slide from under his thumbs, will never get out of the habit of pulling; while one who, almost unconsciously, establishes a fitting length again as soon as he feels the reins slip, will acquire feeling hands in a short time.

The best exercise for developing the feel of a light tension of reins is the "milking of reins", stroking them as if they were a teat of a cow's udder. The reins are held together, between thumb and finger of one hand, palm turned up; the other hand is then placed well forward, under the reins, which it also takes between thumb and forefinger and gently strokes back. The movement is repeated with each hand in turn, first slowly, then quickly, the reins never being allowed to get slack, the horse never feeling any difference in tension which would cause him to change the position of his head and neck. This is the best way of teaching the rider the feel of a passive tension of reins and of the relaxed pressure of the thumbs on the forefingers which prevents the reins from constantly slipping.

With a horse sufficiently relaxed and active who keeps his neck straight and steady, the rider who has developed the feel of a passive tension of reins can start concentrating on feeling the movements of the lower jaw. For this purpose, any kind of nose band and especially a dropped one is undesirable; it always gives a support to the lower jaw which prevents the rider from feeling the stiffening of the mandibular muscles when the horse resists. Hands acutely sensitive to the relaxed activity of the mouth can be produced only by riding the horse in a plain jointed snaffle with loose wire rings, without a nose band of any sort.

To acquire this extreme sensitivity to the activity of the mouth, the rider will, from the beginning, have to be intensely attentive; eventually, the skin and blood of his fingers must become imbued with the finest sense of touch. The so-called chewing of the bit is a very slight opening and closing of the jaws, and also a slight lateral movement of the lower jaw. Before he can allow himself to induce the mobility of the mouth, the rider must teach himself to feel it and to accept it passively. Enormous attention will be required before one can hope to acquire instinctive reactions. One must start by riding on circles. When one wants to circle right, one must advance the left hand by about 2 cm and passively maintain the same tension on the right rein as on the left, without actively drawing the right hand back. The horse must then flex laterally at the poll only, not in front of the withers, and start circling right. To change the direction of the circle, the right hand must now advance, but the left hand must not be retracted; the horse must relax the muscles of the right side of his neck, slightly turn his head left and smoothly start circling left. The rider is now learning to turn by yielding with the outside hand instead of pulling with the inside one and thus he avoids shortening the neck. Unless he is extremely careful not to pull, he will find the steps becoming irregular and the horse will start tossing the bit. There is nothing worse than losing patience and, instead of waiting for the horse to reach out for the bit as the outside hand advances, trying to force him to do so by pulling on the inside rein. This starts the habit of sawing with the hands, which causes the horse to shorten his neck, to overbend and drop the bit, and lose the regularity of the beat.

As he rides the loops of a serpentine, the rider notices that nearly all horses stretch the left rein more than the right and frequently try to lean on the left rein. They avoid the tension of the right rein and contact with the right side of the bit, thus slowing the movement in the turns or turning more rapidly than the rider expects. This peculiarity is possibly related to the habit most horses have of grinding food with the molars by moving the lower jaw from right to left, then letting the mouth open at the moment the left jaw protrudes on the left side at the end of the grinding motion. Whether or not this is the reason, the result is that the left part of the jointed snaffle rests directly on the bars of the left side of the lower jaw and the right part on the tongue, giving the rider a firmer feel of the left rein. Bruising of the left bar, significantly, is the most usual injury, the right bar being protected against the painful effects of a tactless hand by the tongue: a particularly hard right hand induces the habit of pushing the tongue out on the right side.

It is not until the rider has achieved a perfect feel of the movement of the jaw, and the very sensitive tension of the reins has encouraged the horse to chew the bit and salivate, that he can start learning to use his hands to promote, when necessary, the relaxation of the jaws. Until then, little attention need be paid to the driving aids, but once the rider starts using his hands to promote the relaxation of the mouth and poll, he must know how to act discerningly with his legs to prevent any loss of regularity of the movements of the hindlegs.

The end result should now be sufficiently clear. We want the horse to support the bit with his lower jaw with a very slight activity of the mouth but without parting the lips; the lower jaw must stop making any grinding motions. The carefully adjusted curb bit must rest on the tongue. At this stage, the rider's hands should be completely still, handling the bit through the intermediary of the reins as if it were made of the finest porcelain. When his hand advances by a small amount, to allow lateral rotation of the head at the poll, the lower jaw of the horse must remain straight. He must remember that the inflexion of the neck must never exceed the inflexion of the vertebral column as a whole and that, although the hands have a part to play in obtaining collection, they must not try to produce an unnatural, forced opening of the mouth.

The immobility of the hands is just the consequence of general relaxed tension of muscles of a horse moving in self-carriage. A rider who has not first taught himself to follow every movement of the head and neck passively, will stiffen and lose all sensitivity if he tries to keep his hands still. An obvious sign of stiffening, easily spotted by the instructor, is the whip of the rider tapping to the rhythm of the movement or sawing the outer seam of the rider's breeches.

Resorting to numerous ingenious bits and auxilliary reins in the hope of developing relaxed jaw muscles is a serious mistake. Some of these devices can be usefully employed for teaching a novice rider to get the feel of a relaxed seat and may have to be used when one has to cope somehow with a badly-schooled horse in a jumping competition, but their regular use will prevent one from ever becoming a horseman, in the true sense of the word, because they destroy all possibility of feeling the movements of the horse's mouth. And so when the rider has learnt to feel the mouth with passive hands, the rough-and-ready sort of parades described above are transformed and the displacement of hands can be limited to the small extent of the possible degree of elasticity of the jaw muscles. Yet, while maintaining a light tension of reins, the rider must remain effective and, therefore, the horse chosen for this lesson must have an established steadiness of head and neck and regular gaits; it would be utterly wrong to tell the rider to keep the head still by fixing his hands.

Assuming the above condition as fulfilled, the pupil must now learn to resist and yield, instead of tugging and yielding. To develop this feel, he should hold both hands against the mane and yield with one hand and the other alternately, merely by tilting the hand in such a manner that the little finger moves closer to the mouth by, at most, 2 or 3 cm. Thus the hands can remain steady, allowing the rider to feel how the horse avoids the discomfort of increased pressure from the bit on one bar of the lower jaw (which is the result of the decreased tension of the rein on the opposite side) by slightly turning his head. The rider will also be able to feel immediately any false flexion, whereby contact between the bit and the lower jaw is lost on one side. It is beautifully easy to manoeuvre with a horse that is genuinely "on the bit", just by yielding a little with one hand, thus passively getting the horse to yield himself to the inactively resisting opposite hand. Many very good riders inconspicuously guide the horse at times, on serpentines or straight lines with the same hand while just maintaining contact with the other, and then pass the control over to the previously passive hand.

Equal elasticity of the muscles of both sides of the jaws implies, of course, equal strength and suppleness of both hindlegs and elastic activity of all the muscles of the body. We know how difficult it is to obtain straightness—which amounts to equal elasticity of the muscles on both sides of the vertebral column—and we also know that the traditional manege exercises (circles, serpentines and work on two tracks), are nothing more than gymnastics for achieving this object. However, these gymnastics serve their purpose better if the rider understands that a horse that does not hold his jaws straight can never be straight. Obviously, it is most important to develop the sensitivity of the hands needed for feeling the movements of the jaws. For the purpose of developing this sensitivity, the practice of holding the reins frequently with thumbs and forefingers only, or just with the little fingers, is excellent. It automatically places the hands in a vertical plane and promotes the necessary suppleness of the other fingers.

When he has acquired an acute feel of the movements of the jaws, and not before, the rider can start to teach the horse to carry the bit straight. The same manege exercises continue to be used, combined of course with determined forward riding on the straight to preserve the horse's tendency to stretch the reins; in the changes of direction, however, the rider uses a slight rotation of the upper body rather than a movement of the hands. As soon as he feels the lower jaw protruding left, the left rein becoming tauter than the right, he sits against the left rein by bracing the left side of the small of the back. Thus the horse is made to punish himself against the bit whenever he tries to resist its pressure, while the unilateral bracing of the pelvis causes the left hind to engage towards the line of gravity instead of moving aside. The horse is then made to perform a few steps of lateral movement. If this procedure is followed perseveringly every time the rider feels a resistance against the left rein, the horse's attempts to cross the jaws will become few and far between and more tentative. Eventually, the unilateral bracing of the pelvis will become sufficient to forestall a resistance. When the horse has learnt to stretch both reins evenly, to keep his jaw straight and his mouth relaxed with the lips closed, a nose band can be used and, if this causes no deterioration to the softness of the mouth, the rider can happily assume that straightness is established.

One should never try to teach a rider to fix the hands and act with the seat only until he has developed independent hands. If one tried to get him to do so too early, he would acquire stiff arms, wrists and fingers. But once independence of the hands is achieved, he must learn to influence the equilibrium of the horse principally through his seat. The arms must then be kept close to the body, so that the cloth of the upper part of the sleeves touches that of the body of the jacket. The arms will then hang vertically in a relaxed manner from the shoulders, the forearms will be carried almost horizontally, the wrists and fingers relaxed. Thus the hands become a more or less fixed extension of the body and the parades will eventually be performed merely by straightening the back; this is not the same thing as bracing the pelvis, which is extending the hip joints. Of course, this is assuming that the horse has become extremely responsive to the balancing influence of the seat; until then, the hands may still have to intervene, but one should remember that the short muscles of the jaws can stretch to only a very limited extent. When the horse reacts submissively to the slightest straightening of the back, the hands stop playing any independent part in the preservation of equilibrium.

I hope that I have succeeded in explaining the part played by the mouth in fluent submissiveness. No strength of arms or fingers is ever called for. We have to use the horse's mouth to control speed and to produce collection but if we try to act only with our hands to produce relaxation of the jaws, fluent submissiveness cannot extend to the whole system. It is wrong to use restraint or fiddling actions with the reins for the purpose of inducing a relaxation of the mouth or an arching of the neck. It is because the bars of the mouth are sensitive that horses so obstinately object to forceful constraint. On the other hand, when the short jaw muscles are treated considerately, the powerful muscles of poll and neck relax also and become stronger and more elastic. The masseter muscles and the tongue should be thought of as delicate springs, as the pointer of a sensitive balance, or as a mechanical coupling with a restricted but precise action. The skill of using this fragile system to maintain poise in the collected gaits is undeniably an art and is what makes hands worthy of using the curb bit.

BETWEEN HAND AND LEG

If a sculptor used his tools with force, he would never turn out a recognisable form. Similarly, it is a futile use of strength to drive with the legs against resisting hands. It exhausts the rider and disheartens the horse, and is an absurd opposition of forces. Yet to do so is a common mistake. So few riders have the patience and knowledge to develop the horse's understanding of the aids or the will-power to educate themselves, and they think that they can produce satisfactory results by squeezing hard enough with the legs while pulling or restricting with the hands. How on earth can they hope to obtain collection, with elastic muscular tension, by holding the horse between the aids in such a laborious fashion?

After all, driving a horse is as simple, at least in principle, as driving a motor car: one never presses on the accelerator and the braking pedals at the same time. If horses, like engines, emitted smoke when they were driven with the hand brake on, many riders would either realise that something was wrong or would have to ride with a gas mask.

When the legs are being used to create impulsion, the hands must allow the impulsion to flow and while the hands are being used to check the speed, the legs must remain passive. There is no other way of teaching the horse to understand the aids, to remain obedient and to learn to balance himself by using his own strength. Frequent changes of speed must teach him to obey both the driving and the restraining aids and to support his centre of gravity equally with all four limbs without hanging onto the rider. Again, the rider must discipline himself. If he prevents the forward movement by driving while restraining, by thus holding the horse between the aids, he himself teaches the horse to balance himself by hanging onto the reins; as soon as he "strokes the neck" rhythm and co-ordination are destroyed. A horse held between hands and legs cannot help resisting, so that the rider has to use all the strength of his legs, seat and arms to maintain an appearance of fluent forward movement. But it is an appearance that does not deceive a knowledgeable spectator, because though the beat may be regular, it is not sufficiently brisk. It is the rhythm of a soulless machine. A genuine artist rides with relaxed knees and hips and can control an unrestricted horse with the strength of the little fingers. His horse will give the impression of moving of his own accord, as smoothly as if he were dancing or soaring through the air, thus allowing his rider to sit easily. The real meaning of "between the aids" is freedom from restriction, obedience to the lightest indications of legs or hands, but an obedience that derives from enjoyment of the gymnastics of dressage.

It is the seat that allows the accordance of the aids. Depending on the stage of training, the speed or the purpose of utilisation of the horse, the rider sits as upright as a church candle or with more or less forward inclination of his body, but he must always be sufficiently supple to co-ordinate his seat and his aids with the natural movement. The buttocks either cling to the saddle or, if they are kept clear of the saddle, press forward in the direction of pull of the muscles of the horse's back. It is the suppleness of the rider's loins that allow the hands to accompany the forward movement. This constant release of impulsion is especially noticeable in a race when jockeys fight for the lead in the last furlong. They appear to be pushing their horses forward with reins of steel in each leap of the gallop. In racing parlance, this is called "scrubbing" and, although the action is less obvious in the other gaits, the principle is the same: the hands, pressing in the direction of the horse's mouth, must allow the forward movement during the phase of propulsion of a hindlimb. Because the rider must never oppose the horse's force, parades must never be executed during this phase of the movement. Whenever there is opposition, the force of the horse's momentum will always prevail, with the result that the rider hangs on. But at the moment when a hindlimb bends at the joints to absorb the shock of impact, it cannot resist, so this is the moment during which the parades are executed. This is not a matter of making deliberate hand or arm movements. To produce a parade, the rider who has supple loins which allow the seat to accompany the movement sits up, against the movement, against the bit, during the split second of shock-absorbing flexion of the joints of the hindleg, and instantaneously again lets his seat and hand go with the movement, as soon as the hindleg begins to propel. The best gait for developing the feel is the canter or gallop. Providing that the horse is responsive to the driving aids and that the rider knows how to go with the movement with his seat, the speed will remain constant while the tension of reins remains constant; if the hands advance more as the result of the increased driving action of the buttocks, the horse will extend the gallop; conversely, if the rider sits up a little against the reins, the horse will shorten his leaps. A responsive horse can thus be ridden with the aid of the seat alone. The reins merely indicate the changes of posture which determine the scope of the stride.

A deep seat and a sense of movement are, of course, essential. A rider with stiff arms and wrists, loins and legs affects the horse as unpleasantly as a badly secured, inert load. On the contrary, the seat of a supple rider fuses with the movement of the back of the horse.

The varying pressures of the lower legs determine the bracing of the bow behind the saddle; the reins accept and direct the impulsive force of the hindquarters and either limit the output or allow it to flow forward freely. The rider's waist is the coupling between hands and legs, which not only joins the parts, but also balances their influences and ensures the smooth interaction of the aids.

When the day comes when we feel that we control the bow in front of the saddle and the bow behind the saddle as a completely integrated whole, with curves that can be determined in the sagittal or transverse plane; when we can consciously co-ordinate the effects of these two bows in order to produce precisely the movement we desire; we will think back on all the time it has taken us to understand how all the seemingly independent parts and hinges of the horse's body can be joined in the shape of two bows functioning as one. Between the aids, we will have at last created a united horse.

I think it would be more helpful to our pupils if we referred to the checking actions of the reins as a tenth of a parade, a quarter-parade as well as a half-parade or a full parade. It might assist them in comprehending the relation of the rein aids to the gait and in understanding that up to four or even ten single, attentively executed parades, co-ordinated with each step, may be necessary to achieve the total result desired. They would learn to link the rein aids to the movements of the hindlimbs and learn to appreciate that only horses advanced in their schooling can be expected to respond promptly to half- or full parades. Young horses must be restrained by a succession of carefully graduated checks and this is also how novice riders must be taught to control the speed. But we must also impress upon our students that every fraction of a parade must produce some result, in the form either of a change of gait or a change of posture, that is a shortening of the steps or a more collected posture. If one or the other of these results is not obtained, the rider will find himself hanging on. And the pupil must be taught to use the driving aids also with discretion. He must learn to change the speed by shortening or lengthening the stride while maintaining the same beat and also to produce a livelier beat and thereby a more energetic swing of the limbs in order to develop either the middle trot or the extended trot. Eventually, one must learn to use the legs to shorten each step more and more and finally produce the elevation of steps of the High-School. Again, just as he has learnt to combine the actions of hands and back to modulate the parades, the rider must learn to combine the driving effects of legs and seat and hands; the stride is lengthened, and the beat is quickened if the hands yield while the legs drive; on the other hand, the driving actions combined with parades will have a collecting effect. There are numerous combinations of aids, but the rider must know what he wants to achieve and his horse must understand him: the horse is not a machine.

One can never mould a horse into a beautiful form if either the driving or the restraining aids are not in phase with the natural movements of the limbs. Fiddling with the reins and tapping with the legs is useless. It is by using his trunk muscles discerningly that the rider merges with the horse's body and acquires the ability to flex and extend the vertebral column of the horse and give a final polish to his deportment. The art of shaping the body of the horse is based on fulfilment of fundamental conditions and a thorough comprehension of the co-ordination of aids; it is a difficult art and not merely a technique which will produce results within a predictable period of time. During the whole process of development, one must avoid souring the horse's disposition, sapping his strength and alienating his good will.

As for the essential conditions, they are:

1 Obedience to the driving aids, that is impulsion.
2 Fluent submissiveness to the parades.
3 Responsiveness to the inflexion and directing influences of the legs.

If the above conditions are met, the final shape depends on the degree of collection and elevation that the rider is capable of producing. This is a matter of talent. One must first learn to shorten the steps, then to produce "half-length" steps and finally piaffe-like steps while maintaining forward movement and elastic muscular tension, even when the length of the individual steps does not exceed half the length of a hoof. Insisting on movement absolutely on one spot always spoils the feel and is detrimental to the purity of the movement. Again, the rider must learn to control his own muscular activity, know how to sit up straight without becoming rigid and be able to feel the action of the hindlegs with his eyes closed. He must understand how to perform parades by contracting the back muscles to act with the reins and how to sit against one rein, instead of pulling, whenever he feels that the horse is not engaging a hindleg and is stiffening it, thereby excessively propelling the body forward. The base of support must be shortened by limiting the propulsive effect of the hindlegs, by getting the hindfeet to alight under the mass, by elevating the forehand without impairing the play of the hind joints. The rider's first concern is with the development of strength and elasticity of the muscles of the horse's loins, though the muscles of the neck must also be strong to give the neck the necessary firmness and suppleness without impairing the elasticity of the muscles of the poll. Nevertheless, in perfect self-carriage, the horse will arch his neck of his own accord, and the more elevated, the more collected the steps of walk and trot, or the leaps of the canter become, the more willingly the horse assumes a collected posture. In this work, the rider will find it helpful to sit a little further back and it is therefore an advantage for High-School work to have a saddle that is deepest in the rear third of its length. The bow of the loins behind the saddle is closer to the seat and thus easier to influence. The hindfeet then alight just beneath the common centre of gravity of horse and rider, in a better position to support it. It is the opposite of what one does with a young horse, whose loins and hindquarters must be unloaded as much as possible, because the first thing which we want of the young horse is free forward movement and determined propulsion. It is enlightening to study the engravings of Ridinger illustrating the seat of the High-School rider in the 18th century. If one tries to imitate this position on a supple, submissive and highly poised horse, the backward inclination of the body with the legs stretched forward feels less ridiculous. It is possible that the riders of the classical period, as they are depicted by Ridinger, understood more about the art of riding than we do nowadays.

The lateral movements with inflexion are of the greatest help in obtaining collection because they deprive the horse of the ability to shirk the flexion of the joints either by propelling himself forward with stiff hocks or refusing to go forward. At the canter, however, the brief moment during which the aids can be used effectively to produce collection happens just before the phase of suspension, when the head and neck are up; it is precisely at that moment that we press ourselves strongly against the saddle by sitting particularly deeply and heavily. This has an automatic collecting and elevating effect.

I repeat, once more, that we must resist any temptation to try to improve the deportment of the horse by toying with the bit. The collected outline must be the inevitable consequence of total collection, that is, storing of energy. Outline and collection are entirely co-related. It is only during fleeting moments of slackening of attentiveness, which might cause the horse to neglect his posture, that the rider must act promptly and strictly to prevent an argument which can easily lead to stubborn resistance. We must guard ourselves even more against the temptation of trying to fashion just one part of the horse's body, the neck for example. Manipulations or constraint for the purpose of giving an arched form to the neck distort the whole image and break the continuity of the outline.

There are no special, mysterious aids for producing an elegant posture. The horse must first learn to obey all the aids and to move in a natural form before we can concentrate on producing the conventional outline of the highly collected horse. The intensity of the effects which we can produce varies so much that it takes years of concentrated attention to all our actions before we become so integrated with the horse's body and reactions that we can influence them unconsciously. However, if we can achieve this state, the aids become instinctive; all our personal impulses emanate from the horse. We then need no longer think of head, legs, seat and hands; we will have become completely fused into the mind and body of the horse.

5 Elementary Biomechanics

The active agents of locomotion are the muscles. Muscles are attached to two or more bones which they cause to rotate around one or two joints. The skeletal muscles are commonly called voluntary muscles because it is assumed that they can be controlled by the higher centres of the nervous system, but this assumption is not absolutely true. Many movements are automatic reactions to stimulation of nerves transmitting sensations from receptor cells in the skin, ears, eyes and muscles to the central nervous system and more or less immediate return impulses from the central nervous system to various muscles along other nerves. These automatic reactions, called reflexes, are constantly adjusting the tension of groups of muscles (either prime movers, antagonists, fixators or assistants) to produce, control and co-ordinate the movements of the various parts of the body, and to prevent loss of balance.

The organisation of the bones and muscles of the horse's skeleton make him more a perfect example of the relation of form to function. Evolutionary changes of the bony framework have produced a system ideally suited to carry weight and transport it at speed. Evidence of these changes has been provided by the discovery of the fossils of ancestors of the modern horse showing how the bones of the feet have been reduced in number gradually from five to one, until each limb became one bony pillar with only vestigial remains of other bones (the splint bones and the ulna).

This gradual regression of the bones of the limbs must have been accompanied by muscular adaptation and a change in the pattern of movement. The muscles must have altered their arrangement and their structure. The arrangement will be examined further on. The changes in structure concern the direction of pull, and the number and length of the muscular fibres. Some muscles consist of parallel bundles of long fibres, tapering at their extremities and prolonged by long, slender tendons which insert into the periosteum of the bones involved. Because of the length of their fibres, they can lengthen and shorten to a very considerable extent and are responsible for

Muscles of the horse's head and neck. *(a)* Masseter: the pair close the mouth; one acting alone carries the lower jaw toward the side of the contracting muscle. *(b)* Sternocephalicus: acting together, flex head and neck; acting singly, inflex head and neck. *(c)* Sterno-hyodeus and omo-hyodeus retract the tongue. *(d)* Splenius: acting together, elevate head and neck; acting singly, inflex head and neck to the side of the acting muscle. *(e)* Brachiocephalus: when head and neck fixed, draws foreleg forward; if foot is fixed, extends head and neck if muscles act together, or incline them to one side if one is acting separately.

The skeleton of the horse.

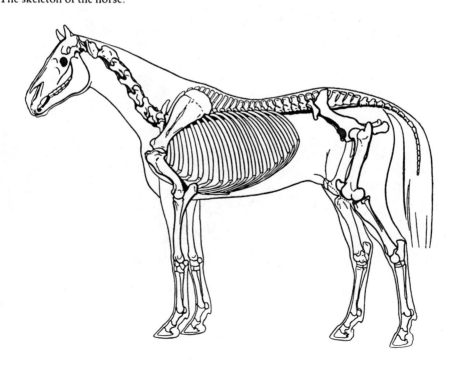

Imaginary line representing the "bow in front of the hand" and "the bow behind the hand".

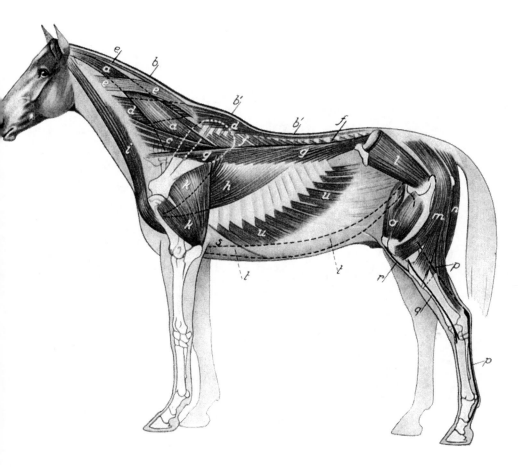

Muscles of the horse's neck, trunk and hindquarters. Some superficial muscles have been intentionally truncated to show underlying ones:

(a) braces of the head;
(b) and *(b')* nuchal ligament;
(c) rhomboideus cervicalis;
(d) complexus;
(e) splenius;
(f) spinalis and semi-spinalis;
(g) longissimus dorsi;
(h) latissimus dorsi;
(i) brachiocephalicus;
(k) triceps;
(l) gluteus medius;
(m) and *(n)* lateral hamstrings;
(o) quadriceps femoris;
(p) and *(q)* almost entirely tendinous peroneus tercius and superficial flexor of the
       digit;
(r) straight patellar ligament;
(s) deep posterior pectoral muscle;
(t) rectus abdominus;
(u) external oblique abdominus.

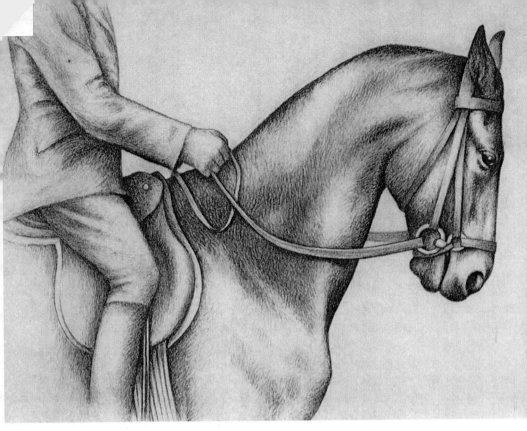

Wrong flexion: *(above)* behind the bit; *(below)* boring on the bit.

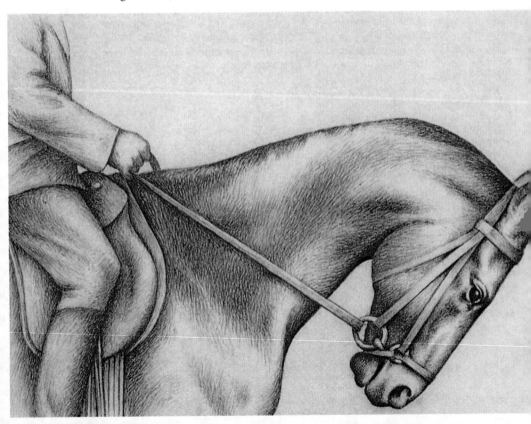

movement. They are so designed that they can contract and relax rapidly. Waste products (carbon dioxide, lactic acid, and so on) rapidly accumulate amongst their fibres if they have to maintain tension; fluid exudes into the connective tissue and the resulting pressure on the nerve endings produces stiffness and pain. Conversely, rhythmical alternation of relaxation and contraction promotes good circulation in the veins and lymph vessels and rapid excretion of those waste products.

On the other hand, postural muscles contract and relax slowly and can maintain tension with less expenditure of energy. They are re-inforced to a greater or lesser extent by fibres or tendinous connective tissue, either at their extremities or forming sheets or cords running through the whole length of the muscle, connecting the tendons at both ends. Some muscles are indeed almost entirely tendinous, functioning like ligaments. They brace joints when a limb (or all limbs) has to resist gravity, either during motion or in the standing position. The tough, inelastic tendinous tissue relieves the contractile muscular tissue of the effort of supporting the weight. The muscular fibres are short and end within the muscle belly with a more or less pennate arrangement, running obliquely to the longitudinal axis of the muscle. This may mean that their direction of pull is slightly out of line with that of the whole muscle, but greater force can be exerted by the presence of many short fibres. The strength of a muscle is in relation to the number of working parts (fibres) entering into its composition.

Muscles which contract and relax rapidly, the quick twitch muscles, are whiter than muscles which contract and relax slowly, the slow twitch or "red muscles". The proportion of "red" or "white muscle" varies between individuals, and this determines whether a horse is built for staying or for sprinting; the same differences are found between one type of human athlete and another. This depends to a very large extent, not only on conformation and hereditary influences, but also on the activity of the endocrine glands, that is on temperament. There are very few completely versatile sportsmen and optimum performance depends on self-knowledge and training. Weight-lifting, for example, is the wrong sort of exercise for the sprinter.

Similarly, we must be able to recognise whether a horse's hindquarters are designed for speed or elevation, for sprinting or long distance or jumping. The flat racer does not need the bulky

Strap (fleshy) muscle *(left)*; bipennate muscle *(centre)* reinforced by tendon down the middle; unipennate muscle *(right)* reinforced by tendon along one side.

thighs of the High-School horse and the dressage horse falls somewhere in between. Inability to recognise natural aptitudes is the cause of frustrating battles. Beyond a certain stage of development, horses must be trained for the special purpose to which they are suited. Trying to improve performance in several directions results in all round deterioration.

The muscles which move the limbs are generally called flexors and extensors. Either the flexor or the extensor muscles are alternately prime movers or antagonists. Muscles can pull, but cannot push. Before they do work again they must be elongated. The termination of the action of any muscle is followed by a more or less sudden diminution of tension, thus allowing whatever forces are acting against the muscle to elongate it. Thus every muscle when it acts as a prime mover (or agonist) has an antagonist able to restore it to its "resting length". Often this elongation will be accomplished by the opposing antagonistic muscle, but it may be brought about by gravity or other forces.

In some conditions, however, muscles whose primary function is to flex or extend joints, must also behave like elastic braces and shock absorbers. For example, when a horse lands from a jump, the whole weight of the body falls on one forelimb. For a short moment of time, both the flexor and extensor muscle groups hold their tension to prevent excessive movement of the joints of the foot, but they must immediately resume their normal pattern of action to produce movement.

Although exercise develops the strength and bulk of muscles, this is only providing that they function in the manner for which their structure is fitting. If muscles which are primarily muscles designed for movement have to maintain continuous tension, they become inflamed. Blood and lymph circulation in their substance is impaired, and the muscle fibres cannot absorb the nutrients and oxygen which are necessary to their development in bulk and elasticity.

This understanding of the functional anatomy of muscles is elementary knowledge which all teachers of horsemanship and trainers of any type of horse must possess. It helps them to diagnose causes of resistance or a lapse in performance.

CARRYING THE RIDER

How does the horse learn to carry the rider? We shall address ourselves to this question, but first must look at the structure of the horse's back.

The vertebral column of the horse can be compared to a loaded girder suspended on two pillars; the long neck and heavy head form a counterweight in front of the forelegs to the weight of the ribs and internal organs. The column is made up of small, irregularly shaped bones, the vertebrae. Between each vertebra, there is a cushion of fibro-cartilage, an intervertebral disc. Movement between the vertebrae is extremely limited; the arrangement does allow some rotation and bending to occur, especially in the neck, but elsewhere this is checked by the articular facets of the vertebrae, by the intervertebral discs, by dorsal and ventral ligaments and by muscles which run the length of the column.

The horse has 7 cervical, 18 thoracic, 6 lumbar, 5 sacral and 20 coccygeal vertebrae. The sacral vertebrae are completely fused and form one bone, the sacrum, which articulates with the ilia of the pelvis (the hip bones). This joint is very tight, the bones being held together by numerous ligaments, but a very small amount of movement does occur, which serves to prevent fracture under the sudden application of force. The sacrum and pelvis receive the thrust of the hindlimbs and transmit it to the vertebral column and forelimbs.

Each one of the vertebrae articulates with a pair of ribs. The first ten ribs are directly joined to the sternum and serve mainly as an attachment for the muscles which bind the trunk to the forelimbs, and so there is very little possibility of movement in this region, but the remaining ribs are not directly connected to the sternum and thus allow for expansion and contraction of the lungs and a small degree of mobility of the vertebral column.

All the vertebrae have projections called processes. The upright ones are the spinous processes, the horizontal ones, the transverse processes. (The lumbar vertebrae have also got mamillary processes, between the transverse and spinous processes.) They gradually change in direction and length along the body: the lumbar processes and those of the last two thoracic vertebrae point headward, the ribs and the spinous processes of the first fifteen thoracic vertebrae point rearward. The sixteenth thoracic vertebra has a vertical spine and is called the anticlinal vertebra. The weakest part of the back, where most of the movement occurs, is in the region of this vertebra which represents the junction of the lumbo-sacral segment with the thoracic segment.

The tips of all the spinous processes are bound together by a band of fibrous tissue which is prolonged by the "nuchal ligament", extending from the first thoracic vertebra to the head and suspending the vertebral column from above. Normally, the thoracolumbar column of the horse has a ventrally concave bow which is maintained by a ventral ligament. This ventral bowing can be cxaggerated (made more concave) by contraction of the abdominal muscles and when the hindlimbs and forelimbs come closer together.

While the muscles of the limbs can be classified as flexors or extensors of the joints, this description is not very accurate in the case of the back muscles. Their main function is to render the vertebral column sufficiently rigid, preventing wasteful movements when speed is required. The most medial muscle is the multifidus. It consists of a series of bundles which lie on the sides of the spinous processes from the sacrum to the neck; each bundle passes over several vertebrae, the fibres originating on transverse and mamillary processes to become inserted on to more cranial spinous processes. In front of the last thoracic vertebrae, the muscle is called semi-spinalis dorsi.

More lateral muscles make up the sacrospinalis muscle. Its fibres originate on the crest of the ilium and the dorsal surface of the sacrum. They run cranially and laterally and are inserted on to the transverse processes of the lumbar vertebrae. In the thoracic region, the muscle divides into two branches, a more medial longissimus dorsi and a more lateral costalis dorsi; both branches are inserted onto the ribs and receive fibres from the semi-spinalis dorsi. The sacrospinalis serves to brace the front part of the body on the hindlimbs; the semi-spinalis is able to transfer the weight of the hinder part on to the forelegs. Thus the girder can be braced mainly on the front or mainly on the hindlegs, or on both.

On the underside of the trunk, the abdominal muscles have broad tendinous insertions which meet at the "white line". This is a fibrous mass extending from the sternum to the pubis which supports the weight of the internal organs.

The deeper fibres of the back muscles on either side of the vertebral column have long tendons and are obviously not designed for sustained tension. However, since all the above described muscles are closely bound together by fasciae (sheets of fibrous connective tissue), contraction of any individual group extends to all the associated groups. If the weight of the rider inflicts discomfort to one part, the activity of all the muscles of the back is affected, and as the muscles of the back connect the muscles of the hindlimbs to the muscles of the forelimbs, smoothness and efficiency of movement depend on the relaxed activity of the back muscles.

When a young horse feels the weight of the rider, he first braces the bow of the thoracolumbar column by contracting the abdominal muscles, but as he loses his fear and wearies of this effort, he allows those muscles to slacken and the weight of the trunk to hang on the ligaments.

Untrained or badly trained horses alternately stiffen and slacken the back, and some horses continue to do this all their life. They never learn to use their backs elastically, and stiffen as soon as they are asked to work, and so they remain incapable of achieving any sort of athletic performance. This is what makes their gait unsteady and irregular. At times, the rider feels that he is sitting on a board, at other times, in a hammock. When fatigue of the back muscles causes them to sag, the limbs straddle, the hindlimbs trail, the shoulders stiffen under their excessive load. The trunk drops between the scapula, the tendinous floor of the abdomen receiving all the weight. In this posture, the horse can still support the weight of the rider, but when the overstretched abdominal muscles begin to ache, the horse again tenses them rigidly. He arches his back, shortens his steps and moves jerkily. It then becomes impossible for the rider to sit easily to the trot or to keep his balance without gripping.

Conversely, a rider who relies on forceful gripping to safeguard balance will never be able to feel, preserve and promote the essential elasticity of the back muscles of the horse. Neither will he be able to feel and influence the movements of the hindlimbs or ever achieve unity between himself and the horse.

Since the back muscles and abdominal muscles are not designed to sustain continuous tension, which then are the muscles which can brace the vertebral column, so that it can support the weight of the rider without impairing the elasticity of those muscles?

This is the task of certain muscles of the neck and of the nuchal ligament. From the spinous processes of the third thoracic vertebra to the occiput, the nuchal ligament forms a strong elastic brace. Attached to it there is a sheet of ligamentous fibres inserted on to the cervical vertebrae. The neck muscles are situated on either side of this sheet. They fill up the large gap between the nuchal ligament and the cervical vertebrae. There are numerous neck muscles, with different points of origin and insertion, but I will only mention the most significant ones, since they can all be grouped according to their joint action. One group connects the thoracic and cervical vertebrae to the occiput and supports the head. The muscles of the second group connect the thoracic vertebrae and the scapula to the cervical vertebrae and support the neck.

The most deeply situated neck muscle for the support of the head is the complexus. It is a pennate muscle, strongly reinforced by tendinous tissue, and therefore capable of sustaining prolonged tension. The superficial and largest muscle of the same group is the splenius, an extensive, flat, triangular muscle, originating on the third, fourth and fifth thoracic spines and the scapula, and inserting on to the occipital bone and the mastoid process. This is a purely fleshy muscle. Acting together, the splenius muscles of both sides elevate the head and neck; acting singly, the muscle on one side inflexes the neck laterally.

The spinous processes of the thoracic vertebrae increase in length to the third and fourth and then gradually decrease. They form at the withers a lever arm which is pulled forward by the nuchal ligament and the neck muscles when the neck is lowered by the pull of gravity. The pull is transmitted to all the vertebrae of the thoracolumbar column by the ligament which prolongs the nuchal ligament and by the semi-spinalis dorsi and multifidus muscles. The direction of the pull is forward and the tension of the ligament and muscles preserves the natural bowing of the vertebral column.

On a young horse, the rider must sit as close to the pommel as possible to facilitate the task of the neck muscles. We have here an example of a first order lever, the fulcrum being situated between the load and the power: the rider represents the load; the head and neck form the lever arm, and the fulcrum is situated at the highest point of the withers. The shorter the load arm, the longer the lever arm, the more efficient is the leverage. The rider must not only press his buttocks towards the pommel, but he must also incline forward from the waist to encourage the horse to allow the weight of head and neck to stretch the yet insufficiently developed neck muscles. Nevertheless, there are exceptions to all rules, and we certainly do not want any horse to move with his nose to the ground as if he were searching for truffles. A horse with a very long neck or a heavy crest has an unfair advantage over the rider and can develop the habit of leaning on the bit and hands. At a later stage of training, one would experience considerable difficulty in obtaining the lightening of the forehand. In this case, even at the beginning of training, we should not hesitate to sit well back. Furthermore, even though we may allow a young horse to utilise the weight of his head and neck to counterpoise the weight of the rider, we cannot allow him either to drag his hindlimbs or to hurry. The regular beat must be maintained.

Thus at the beginning of training, it is gravity, the weight of the head, that tenses the neck muscles. The distance between the poll and the withers, representing the length of the lever arm of the balance, must be as great as possible. Eventually the neck muscles will gain in volume and strength; their elastic tension will brace the thoracolumbar column and allow a relative elevation of the neck. Since the neck muscles are inserted on to the occiput, the nose will drop to the vertical from the poll. If instead the rider actively held the neck up, thus depriving the horse of the advantage of the length of his neck, the neck muscles would have to shorten. This active elevation is not only ugly; it also weakens the muscles of the neck and back. The ventral cervical muscles, flexors of the head and neck, must never be involved in the arching of the neck because their contraction causes the horse to get behind the bit. And so, when the hands advance, the neck must straighten as a result of the elastic rebound of the ligamentum nuchae and of the cervical muscles on either side of the vertebral column. Relieved of the effort of supporting the weight of the rider, the muscles of the back and loin can then perform the task for which they are designed, which is the transmission of the propulsive effect of the action of the hindlimbs to the forelimbs.

We must not exaggerate however, for if the horse is allowed for too long to use his head and neck as a counterweight, he will continue to balance himself too much on the forelimbs. This may be admissible in the early stages of training, but it is not a principle, as some advocates of the forward seat would have us believe. Sooner or later, the load will have to be distributed more equally between the hindlimbs and forelimbs, so that the rider can obtain better control of the speed. The horse will eventually have to learn to collect himself by shortening his base of support. Instead of unloading the thoracolumbar region, gradually we will have to load it by sitting further back.

Hence the choice between the upright, loading seat, or the forward, light seat, is based on a different rationale. The light or forward seat, in which posture the rider is balanced mainly on the stirrups, is used to allow the horse to use his loins and hindquarters principally for the purpose of developing forward driving power; but the horse must learn to move in horizontal balance even at a fast gallop; therefore the light seat must always remain "a seat", that is a crouch, with the buttocks as close to the saddle as possible so that the rider remains able to promote the engagement of the hindlimbs.

While horses with a long back and relatively weak back muscles quickly learn to utilise the weight of the head and neck to stretch the back muscles—and in fact tend to lower the neck too much and to lean on the bit, especially if they have a long neck with a broad base of attachment to the chest—it is very difficult to induce a horse with a short back to relax the back muscles by lowering the neck. A horse with a roach back associated with a short or weak neck will never become a good saddle-horse.

These well-known facts are easy to explain. A short back can carry heavy loads for long periods of time, since short muscles are better able than long ones to hold a shortened tension. To get a horse with a short back and neck to relax the tightened muscles of the topline necessitates great skill. Conversely, the horse with a long and relatively weak back quickly learns to avoid unnecessary effort by counterpoising the weight of the rider with the weight of the neck. Generally, the long-backed horse is easier to train and, provided that the training is rational and that the rider has a good seat, the longissimus dorsi soon becomes bulkier and the back consequently better able to carry the weight. On the other hand, a short, heavily muscled back should become flatter as a result of training.

Despite the fact that the lowering of the neck must be passive and purely the effect of gravity, the tension felt by the dorsal neck muscles becomes painful after a while. If a young horse starts tossing his head after thirty minutes of working trot in a long outline, this should not be considered to be a sign of resistance; it is a symptom of fatigue. It would be unfair to punish the horse by using running reins or restricting the movements severely in any way. The rider ought to dismount and let the horse rest for five or more minutes until his neck muscles stop aching.

The shape of the neck of the trained horse reveals more about the quality of the training than any other part of the body. Horsemen often say that the muscles must move from the underline of the neck to the topline, but this, of course, is nonsense. However, when a horse works efficiently, the muscles of the topline of the neck are supporting a heavy load, and all muscles that are frequently required to work grow in bulk and strength; as a result of this work, the neck of the well-trained horse becomes broader, and the triangular space between the cervical vertebrae and the mane, so clearly visible before training, fills up. Conversely, since the flexor muscles of the neck must remain inactive, they atrophy like all muscles which are not regularly exercised, and the jugular groove will become more clearly defined.

The outline of the vertebral column itself must also change as a result of good training. As the muscles of the neck which carry the weight become stronger, they pull up the last cervical and first thoracic vertebrae. The neck, which is "s" shaped before training, must become regularly arched and the hollow in front of the withers must gradually disappear as training progresses. And since those muscles must have stretched while also becoming bulkier, the whole neck will appear to have become longer. It is the "lengthening contraction" of the powerful neck muscles resisting the pull of gravity that eventually ensures the firm connection of the base of the neck with the withers which is essential for dressage.

Holding the neck up with hands or check reins weakens and shortens those neck muscles, while rational training strengthens them and all the other associated muscles which hold the rib cage and the base of the neck on the forelimbs. An enlightened observer can therefore appreciate good horsemanship merely by noticing the change in the shape of the neck.

The jowl is the space between the vertical part of the mandible (lower jaw bone) and the cervical vertebrae or rather the muscles of this region. If the parotid glands which are situated in this space are over-developed, or if the space is inordinately small, flexion of the poll compresses the glands, causes pain and outward bulging of the parotids. This is not a very common defect of conformation. Although a heavy jowl may be a cause of difficulty in obtaining the flexion of the poll when the neck is elevated, it should not interfere with the tension of the neck muscles or make any difference to the tension of the reins. Usually by the time the horse is ready to work in collection, the muscles will have relaxed and the area will have fined down. But when riders fix their hands to enforce a vertical position of the nose, they not only prevent movement of the head and neck, but also prevent engagement of the hindlegs and cause compression of the parotid glands. In this case, compression of the parotid glands is due to the unrelenting pressure of the bit on the bars of the mouth or on the tongue. The horse attempts to avoid the discomfort either by poking his nose, thus shortening the muscles of the topline of the neck, or by contracting the mandibular muscles to hold the mouth open or to lock the jaws. These resistances are never shown when a rider has good hands. The mandibular muscles and the hyoid muscles (muscles attached at one end to the tongue) are related to the muscles of the neck, thorax and shoulders. The sterno-mandibularis is a long, slender muscle which extends along the ventral and lateral aspects of the trachea from the sternum to the angle of the jaw. Like the masseter muscle it is inserted on to the posterior border of the ramus of the mandible. Thus it connects the jaw to the neck and the breast. The sternohyoid and omohyoid are the muscular ties between the tongue at one end, and the sternum and scapula at the other end. If only one muscle in this group remains contracted in a shortened state, the stiffness is communicated to the poll, the neck and shoulders. Conversely, pain or even some discomfort in the region of the back are reflected by tightening of the muscles of tongue and jaw, as well as by restriction of the forward engagement of the hindlegs. Relaxation of all those muscles, free forward movement and elastic tension of the muscles of the topline are completely related. The neck of the horse must be firmly stabilised by the firmness of the muscles which attach it to the withers and it is their tone which prevents oscillations in the vertical or the horizontal planes. For the horse to be straight, the neck must be straight, but it is always wrong to enforce straightness by constraining reins and hands. Freedom of shoulder movement is essential, and it depends entirely on absence of severely restraining influences of hands and reins which provoke faulty tension of the neck muscles.

The splenius being an entirely fleshy muscle is a muscle for movement. It is inserted onto the occipital bone, the mastoid process and the wing of the atlas by means of strong tendons which blend with the tendon of the brachiocephalicus. This latter muscle extends along the side of the neck, from its insertion on to the bones of the skull and on to the atlas, to its distal attachment to the humerus. When the head and neck are fixed, it draws the forelimb forward. The common origin of splenius and brachiocephalicus indicate a reciprocal action. The tension of the lengthened splenius, when the neck is elevated and flexed at the poll, puts tension on the brachiocephalicus, producing a more expansive gesture of the forelimb. This, of course, can only happen if the splenius is in a condition of lengthened tension; if on the contrary the splenius is held in a shortened state (shortening tension), the horse throws up his head and is difficult to control. This produces the ewe-neck, poking of the nose and downward compression of the base of the neck and of the thorax between the scapulae.

The common origin of splenius and brachiocephalicus explains why the neck carriage determines the movement of the forelimb. A shortened neck, impacted between the shoulders restricts the play of the shoulder joint and shortens the steps. A horse can land safely when jumping only on condition that he can extend a foreleg well forward, and this is possible only if he has complete freedom of neck. The outline of the neck of a properly trained horse also depends on the lengthening tension of those two muscles. Furthermore, the scope of the steps, the balance and safety of the horse depend on perfect synchronisation of their action. The rider must be able to feel this co-ordination when he is mounted as well as noticing the correct arching of the neck when he observes the moving horse from the ground.

Skilful training strengthens the neck muscles, but quite exceptionally good hands are needed to school a horse with a long but slender
neck. The "swan neck" is rightly considered to be the most difficult
and dangerous of all faulty neck carriages. If the training of this type
of horse is hurried, too much weight is transferred to the hindlegs,
and eventually the horse gets in the habit of overbending and being
constantly behind the bit. The neck is elevated and flexed at the poll,
but the flexion is produced by contraction of the ventral muscles of
the neck instead of by force of gravity. An overbent horse is always
unreliable; he may be behind the bit at times, and lean on the hands at
other moments, but he never stretches the reins properly and
overbends to escape control. Imparting correct muscular tone to an
overbent neck is frustrating work even for a good rider, but it is not
totally beyond the ability of the very good horseman.

ACTIVITY OF THE BACK

We will now deal with the longissimus dorsi, one of the most
important of the trunk muscles. It is the longest and largest muscle of
the body. It has a very complex structure. The posterior part is
greatly developed and is covered by the lumbo-dorsal fascia, a sheet
of fibrous tissue which blends with the ligaments of the ilium and
sacrum. In its forward course, the muscle receives fasciculi from the
lumbar and thoracic vertebral spines; the fibres insert on the lumbar
transverse and articular processes, the thoracic transverse processes,
the spinous and transverse processes of the last four cervical
vertebrae and the lateral surfaces of the ribs. It must be noted that it is
only for convenience of description that the attachment of muscular
fibres are described as origin or insertion. The direction of pull of a
muscle depends on which end is fixed. If the fixed end is at the rear,
when a hindleg is supporting the body weight, contraction of the
longissimus dorsi lightens the forehand. Conversely, if the fixed end
is at the front—and also whenever the muscle remains tightly
shortened—the back is pulled down and stiffened, giving the rider
the feel of being astride a rigid board.

At the walk and the trot, the contractions of the muscular fibres of
longissimus dorsi occur alternately, first on one side of the vertebral
column, then on the other, at the moment when the corresponding
hindleg is propelling the body forward. Simultaneously, the gluteus
muscle attached to the longissimus dorsi, also contracts to extend the

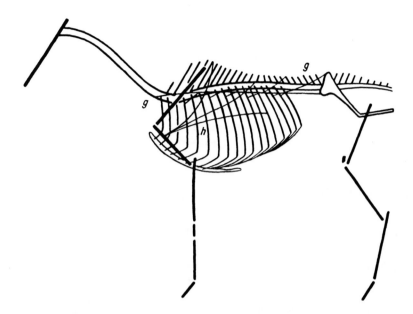

Longissimus *(g)* and latissimus dorsi *(h)*.

hip joint. Both muscles must then be lengthened to allow the hindleg to swing forward. At the gallop, contractions and relaxations occur simultaneously on both sides of the vertebral column, and the lengthening and shortening of the muscles are greater, which is why frequent periods of galloping are the best way of loosening a stiff back or of strengthening a weak one. At the trot, the muscles can be seen and felt to bulge and flatten alternately on each side of the midline. As the muscle of the right side contracts and swells just behind the saddle, the muscle of the left side relaxes and becomes flatter. Maximum shortening and swelling occurs at the moment when the hindleg of the same side is supporting the body weight, and maximum elongation when it swings forward. This is what the rider has to teach himself to feel; one half of the seat will feel lifted as if it were on a ridge during the moment when the hindleg is in support, while the other half will drop into a furrow. At the halt, he must concentrate to feel whether both hindlegs are supporting the weight equally, or whether one hindleg is less loaded, or even completely unloaded. It requires much practise and concentration to feel whether the horse is standing perfectly squarely.

The free swinging of the hindlimbs, impulsion, liveliness of the gait and lightening of the forehand depend on the strength, activity and elasticity of the longissimus dorsi. A springy, ground covering trot, an extended trot to which the rider can sit easily, shows proper, elastic tension of the back muscles. A jerky extended trot that tosses the rider is not an incurable peculiarity of the horse, but merely a symptom of tightly contracted, insufficiently active back muscles.

As the lumbo-dorsal fascia is a mutual attachment for the longissimus dorsi and the gluteus medius, back and croup muscles must work in harmony. The hindlegs cannot swing freely if the back muscles are insufficiently active and, conversely, the back muscles cannot work properly if the rider prevents the freedom of movement of the hindlimbs.

The latissimus dorsi is another large muscle intimately related to the longissimus. It is a wide triangular muscle that covers the longissimus and originates from the lumbo-dorsal fascia, extending from the lumbar and thoracic spines, as far forward as the highest point of the withers. It ends in a flat tendon, inserted onto the medial aspect of the humerus. Stiffness of the longissimus inevitably affects the elasticity of the latissimus and consequently prevents the free forward swing of the forelimb. Thus freedom of action of the shoulder also depends on the activity of the back muscles. And as some of the fibres of the longissimus dorsi are inserted onto the ribs, its stiffening restricts the respiratory movements of the rib cage. A tense horse holds his breath and audible blowing shows that he is loosening up. It is a pleasing sound for the experienced trainer, but the rider who schools his own horse should be able to feel the movement of the rib cage.

The tail carriage also is symptomatic of the state of the back. The dock should be carried horizontally, so that the tail hangs in an elegantly arched manner and can be seen from the rear to swing in rhythm with the movements of the hindlimbs. A limp upright set of the dock indicates slack back muscles; a tightly held down tail is a sign of overall stiffening. Congenital malformation of the vertebral column shows up not only as unilateral hardness in the mouth and stiffness of neck and back, but also in the set of the tail to one side. A flamboyant tail carriage coupled with a stiff-legged gait is a healthy sign of exuberance and excitement when a young horse is fresh because of long confinement to a box.

One of the main causes of improper tension of the back muscles, is the rider with a rigidly straight back. There can be nothing more painful and fatiguing for the horse than the sitting trot without stirrups when the rider is forced to maintain a smart military posture, with an exaggeratedly straight back; this exercise used to be described picturesquely in the German (and French) cavalry as "pepper pounding". With a young horse, when he sits to the trot, the rider ought to sit on the buttocks, leaning forward from the waist (not the hip joint), so that the pelvis can be tilted very slightly backward and move in the direction of the movement, towards the pommel of the saddle. However, with all young horses, the beginning of every lesson must be either at the rising trot or at the canter with the buttocks clear of the saddle. The full seat should not be used before the back muscles have relaxed and the horse invites the rider to sit.

It must never be forgotten that the back muscles are muscles for movement, and that their elasticity must not be impaired by the effort of carrying the weight of a rider who clamps the saddle with the strength of his legs. Because of its relationship to the forelimbs through the latissimus dorsi, and to the hindlegs through the gluteus medius, the longissimus muscle is totally involved in the movements of all the limbs. Strong, elastic back muscles are developed by free forward movement. Again, free forward movement cannot exist without elastic tension and rapidly alternating shortening and lengthening of the back muscles.

The programme of training the young horse must aim principally at developing the strength and elasticity of the back muscles and for this purpose, the gallop is much more favourable than the trot. Frequent periods of cantering in the manege, long gallops out-of-doors, galloping up gently sloping ground are all excellent practices. In the course of training, one must continually observe the state of the horse's back. Eventually the muscles should be seen to bulge on either side of the spines of the vertebral column and their activity should be clearly visible.

THE HINDQUARTERS

The architecture of the horse shows that the hindlimb plays the main part in pushing the body forward and that the forelimb, carrying more than half the weight of the body, is principally a shock absorber. The forelimb is not jointed to the vertebral column and the whole transmission of weight is accomplished by muscles. The muscle mainly concerned is the serratus ventralis. This is a large fan-shaped muscle, consisting of a cervical and a thoracic part. The serratus cervicis attaches the scapula to the last four or five cervical vertebrae, and the serratus thoracis binds the scapula to the lateral surfaces of the first eight ribs. The two muscles form an elastic support, which suspends the trunk between the two scapulae.

The hindlimb, on the other hand, has a bony joint with the vertebral columns, the head of the femur fitting into a deep cup on the pelvis.

A saddle-horse must be comfortable to ride and therefore the hindlimb must not only propel the body forward, it must also act as a shock absorber by bending at the hip, stifle and hock at the moment when it has to support the weight. This phase of the movement is called "flexion of the haunches" and is the one which puts the greatest stress on the muscles of the hindquarters. Obtaining flexion of the haunches without impairing impulsion is the greatest difficulty of dressage. It requires abnormal effort which the horse is quite

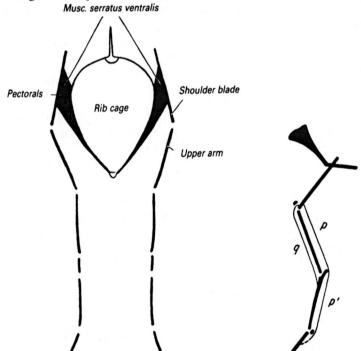

Muscles *(left)* holding rib cage to foreleg: serratus ventralis, thoracic part and pectorals; *(right)* reciprocal stay apparatus of the hindleg: *(q)* peroneus tercius; *(p)* tendinous superficial flexor muscle of digit; *(p')* superficial flexor tendon.

naturally loath to make. He is equipped to be able to flex the hock while the limb supports the weight of the body, because although the muscles producing movement consist of fleshy tissue with few tendinous reinforcements, there are also in the hindlimbs a number of almost entirely tendinous muscles that function like ligaments. Nevertheless, the flexion of the hock delays or slows down propulsion, which means that much more muscular effort is required to drive the hindleg back and the effort is proportionate to the degree of flexion of the hock. The rider who tried hopping or skipping without straightening his knees would easily appreciate the difficulty; in the human also, straightening of the knee joint takes the tension off the muscles of the front of the thighs. It is perfectly natural that the horse should try to support the weight of the rider by straightening his hocks.

One should try to observe as many horses as possible being worked in hand in preparation for the piaffe and see how some of them cheat. To avoid flexing the hocks and stifles, they bring their hindfeet too far forward and the fetlock does all the work. In a genuine piaffe, the stifle remains flexed and all the joints of the supporting leg must yield like resilient coiled springs.

Before one can train a horse for High-School work, one must have studied the mechanics of the hindlimb in considerable depth and trained one's powers of observation.

Muscles, as we know, can perform two functions; they can act as braces, holding the parts of the body in place, or they can move the limbs to produce locomotion. In certain conditions, however, the muscles of the hindlimbs whose natural function is the production of movement—a dynamic function—have to act as shock absorbers—a static function.

The joints of the hindlimbs are angulated, which allows them to flex under compression and immediately return to their normal shape, thus acting like springs and levers to impart motion and to prevent concussion. For the purpose of locomotion, this is obviously an admirable arrangement, but for the purpose of supporting weight, the angulation of the limb would be a disadvantage, were it not for the presence of the stay apparatus of the stifle and hock, or reciprocal system.

The stifle and hock joints are tied together at the front by the peroneus tertius (also known as the tendo femoro-metatarsus) and at the back by the superficial digital flexor in such a manner that one joint cannot flex or extend unless the other one does the same. In fact, both muscles consist entirely of a strong tendon and have practically no more elasticity than ligaments. In the standing position, the patella (held to the tibia by ligaments) hooks on top of a ridge of the femur and is held in this position by the tendon of the quadriceps femoris. The latter muscle is a purely fleshy one, not designed to maintain sustained tension, despite its very considerable size. But in the standing position, when the patella is locked, it can relax because the stability of the joint is maintained by the reciprocal action of the tendinous peroneus tercius and superficial digital flexor. This stay apparatus of the hindlimbs is far more effective than the bulkiest of muscles could be; it converts the hindlimb into a rigid column capable of bracing the weight of the body in the standing position without expenditure of effort. The hip joint, on the other hand, is not so equipped with tendinous muscles; it is braced by fleshy muscles which soon fatigue in the standing position. This is why a standing horse frequently shifts his weight from one hindleg on to the other.

As for the muscles of locomotion, they form four groups:

1 The gluteal muscles of the croup.
2 The flexors of the loin, the ilio-psoas group.
3 The group of extensor muscles, forming the hamstring.
4 The extensors of the knee, quadriceps femoris, which sometimes act as braces for the patella.

Despite their structure, these muscles must act as muscles for movement or muscles for holding, according to the phase of the movement of the limb.

The gluteal muscles are tied to the pelvis and sacrum at their upper extremity, and are inserted into knobs on the femur, known as trochanters. Two of these trochanters are below and in front of the hip joint; the largest knob is a projection of the femur behind the hip joint. Therefore, some of the croup muscles are flexors and the others are extensors. As the flexors do not have to act against the resistance of the ground, they need not be as strong as the extensors. For their part, the extensors have to fulfil two functions:

1 They produce forward movement by contracting *isotonically*,
   that is shortening without increase of tension.
2 They must act as braces, exerting a force which is called
   isometric, and does not initiate movement. In other words, their
   function is alternately dynamic and static.

The largest of the gluteal muscles, the gluteus medius, is intimately involved with the longissimus dorsi, because both muscles have common attachments to the lumbo-dorsal fascia. This means that, whether to produce movement or to brace the weight of the body on the hindlimb, they must act in harmony. If the back muscles are inactive, either because they are rigidly contracted or because they are slack, the pull of the gluteal muscles can neither lighten the forehand nor produce smooth, effective movement: the movement is jerky, constricted and irregular.

The flexor muscles of the loin (ilio-psoas) tie the ventral surface of the lumbar vertebrae and of the ilium to the trochanter minor on the medial anterior aspect of the femur. Together with the gluteus superficialis, they pull the hindlimb forward and are thus flexors of the hip joint. In the canter and gallop, assisted by the abdominal muscles, they also flex the loin. In the horse, the up and down flexion of the back is very limited but nonetheless amplifies the movements of the hindlegs. But these muscles can also exert a pull in the wrong direction, thus stiffening the back (and in human beings contributing to the stiff hollowing of the back).

The hamstrings (biceps femoris, semitendinosus and semimembranosus) fill out the space behind the stifle. They arise from the sacrum and the ischia and have various points of insertion: on the distal end of the femur, on the proximal part of the tibia and on the patella. The biceps femoris and the semitendinosus at their lower end form a tendinous band inserted on the tuber calcis (point of the hock). Their action is rather complex. By virtue of their attachment to the gluteus medius, they extend all the joints of the limb to propel the body forward. Alternately they flex the stifle and the hock. But besides this dynamic function, they also fulfil a static one. Their tension effecting a pull on the patella stabilises the knee in the standing position and, in the flexion of the haunches, protects the stifle and hock joints against excessive flexion. This isometric tension increases their tone and allows the subsequent extension of the joints to be smoother and more powerful.

At the front of the thigh, the quadriceps femoris is an extensor of the stifle and a flexor of the hip. It has four heads, one of which, the rectus, arises from the ilium, above and in front of the hip joint; the other three arise on the lateral or the medial surfaces of the femur. All four are attached to the patella, which is also tied down to the front of the tibia by ligaments. Thus, isotonically, the quadriceps femoris co-operates with the hamstrings to extend the joints of the hips and propel the body forward; a dynamic function. Isometrically, it assists the static function of the hamstrings, tightening the patella on the femur to limit the flexion of the haunches.

The saddle-horse must be comfortable, and therefore all the muscles of the hindquarters must be used not only to propel the mass in a forward direction but also to cushion the rider against the shock of locomotion and for this purpose the joints of the hindlimb must flex, yield to the force of gravity during the phase of the movement when the limb supports the weight. All the extensor muscles are involved in this static function, assisted by the tendinous, inelastic muscles of the stay apparatus. As has already been explained, the effectiveness of the reciprocal system depends on the locking of the patella on the expanded distal end of the femur. In the standing position, this locking of the patella allows the hindlimb to become a rigid column upon which the back can be braced without much muscular effort. In the flexion of the haunches, on the other hand, tension builds up in the muscles. Stifle and hock must flex under the force of gravity, acting as shock absorbing springs, and the patella is lifted off its ridge by the pull of the quadriceps femoris. Yet the limb must remain sufficiently stable to support the weight of the body, so the displacement of the patella is resisted by the lateral ligaments, by the tendinous muscles of the reciprocal apparatus and, in addition by the tension building up in the quadriceps femoris, the hamstrings and the gastrocnemius muscle (extending from the distal end of the femur to the point of the hock). During this phase of the movement, the extensor muscles act like strong elastic braces, developing an isometric tension, requiring much more energy than the rapid alternation of contraction and relaxation when moving the limb into flexion and extension for the production of movement.

Now the extensor or flexor muscles of the hindlimb are preponderantly fleshy; they have very little tendinous reinforcement and are therefore not ideally designed for sustaining tension. It is not surprising that a horse resists the flexion of the haunches, and for this function the muscles must be carefully developed by progressive training.

In all the gaits, the movement of each hindlimb consists of four phases: forward swing, impact, support and propulsion.

One must first learn to observe the movement of the hindlimbs of a horse at liberty:

1 The limb is advanced, hock and stifle flexed.
2 The foot impacts, the hip joint is flexed, hock and stifle are not completely extended.
3 All the joints yield while the limb supports the weight.
4 All the joints straighten to propel the mass forward. This is the natural movement, which we must so carefully preserve during the early training of the horse. Throughout this period of training, head and neck carriage and tension of reins are relatively unimportant. If one worries too much about them then, it is always to the detriment of free, natural forward movement. And as free forward movement is naturally rhythmical, all that the rider has to think about is a regular beat.

What happens to the movement of the hindlimb if the rider restricts it? We know that the moment of maximum expenditure of energy is the phase of support when the joints of the hindlimb yield to the force of gravity to reduce concussion. Eventually, the rider wants to prolong this phase, so that he can feel it better and impart more spring and vigour to the movement. But the horse, on the other hand, understandably wants to shorten the period of support and frequently resists the flexion of the hock, muscular effort being much reduced if the stifle can be locked in extension during the phase of support. Towards this end, he must shorten his strides. He can either lift the hindfoot too early, shortening the phase of propulsion and will then either idle, or hurry with shortened steps; or he can shorten the phase of forward swing, put the foot down too soon, immediately converting impact into propulsion, with the result that the croup is lifted up. Forward movement is then purely the result of momentum and forward loss of balance. On the other hand, a good, smooth, ground covering gait is produced by a sufficient yielding of the joints of the stifle and hock of the hindlimb in support, giving the other limb sufficient time to swing forward.

What are the usual causes of the deterioration of the horse's natural forward movement? Sometimes, it is temperament or freshness but much more frequently it is the rider holding back with the reins, with particularly disastrous results if a double bridle is used. The restraining aids must not restrict the forward swing of the limb, they must however enable the rider to control propulsion. The parades, or rather the half-parades, are rhythmical actions of the hands which must coincide with the moment of shock-absorbing flexion of the supporting hindlimb, thus prolonging the supporting phase and delaying the extension of the joints. They must be done in such a way that only one hindlimb is affected, and the hands must yield as soon as that hindlimb starts to extend. During the period of propulsion, the horse is stronger than the rider and will resist any restraint by the reins, but if the flexion of the haunches is prolonged, the phase of propulsion is automatically shortened. The horse submitting to the parades will give the rider the impression of having grown higher in front. As the muscles of the hindquarters must not be submitted to painful strain, it is essential that the half-parades be rhythmical, timely and preceded and followed by a cautious relaxation of tension of the reins. Synchronisation of the half-parades with the bending phase of the hindlimb in support comes naturally to a rider with a feeling seat. Obviously, the relaxation of rein tension does not mean a complete loss of tension; contact between the mouth and the hand must remain constant. On the other hand, prolonged resistance by the hands always provokes the horse into stiffening the supporting legs; according to temperament, the result is either excessive momentum if the horse opposes the pressure of the bit by trying to push it away, or insufficient forward movement if he tries to avoid the pressure by throwing up his head and neck and bracing himself against momentum with the forelegs.

The movement will also be irregular if the joints of the hindlimbs are overstressed by a rider with insensitively fixed hands, or one who rides with reins too long and has to pull on them to maintain contact. To relieve the strain on his hocks, the horse resists the bit and this mental opposition to the restraining aids shows up in the movements of the hindlimbs. A horse constantly on guard cannot swing his limbs in an easy, rhythmical manner.

The highest possible degree of flexion of the haunches is seen in the movements of the High-School piaffe and passage. In these movements, the stifle and hock of the supporting leg must remain flexed, storing energy, as long as possible, the croup swinging from side to side (in the horizontal plane) on the sacro-iliac joint. The thrust is not produced by a gradual extension of the joints, but by the sudden elastic rebound of the highly compressed shock absorbers. Although the horse appears to be higher in front, in fact he is lowering his croup. The movement, which must be in diagonals like the trot, is correct when the stifle and hock bend deeply and extend powerfully and simultaneously, with the result that for a while at the passage all four feet are off the ground. The rider must be able to sit perfectly vertically, glued to the saddle without effort. A horse's muscular strength and his submissiveness need to be developed to a very high degree to produce a flexion of the haunches that lasts as long as the period of extension and results in a highly elevated movement. But even in the working trot, there is always a period of suspension, sometimes so short that it cannot be discerned by the eye of the observer. Nevertheless, a trot without any suspension, with the hooves trailing on the ground, is the sign of a ruined horse. It is lameness in all four feet.

In the canter also, the period of shock absorption must be noticeable, each leap being a spring off well-flexed haunches. If the hind joints are straightened at impact, the gait becomes either a flat and hurried gallop, or a choppy movement with dragging hindfeet. To be effective, the half-parades must be executed at the precise moment when the inside hindfoot impacts. If the rider pulls when this hindlimb extends, the horse's reaction will be the very opposite of the one intended and much more violent than in the trot. Spirited horses fight the bit more obstinately, force the rider's hands and take charge.

The equestrian vocabulary is not as clear as it should be; for example, the expression "engagement of the hindlegs" is often misunderstood. Although it is true that the foot of the swinging hindleg must impact under or nearly under the centre of gravity, balance requires that the supporting hindleg flexes during the flight of the opposite one. This gives the forelimb time to reach forward by taking the weight off the forehand. If the stifle extends too early, the effect is to lift the croup upward, throwing the mass onto the forehand and delaying the flight of the forelimb. Consequently, either an over-reach results, or the hindfoot must alight beside the trace of the corresponding forefoot. The result of collecting a horse by driving the hindfeet far forward under the body by means of the legs or the spurs, while holding the head in, produces a rigid arching of the back and puts the horse in a position of a resistance just as effective as the opposite position, with the hindlegs extended behind the body. An over-engaged horse will rear rather than rein-back. Over-engagement is not collection. The same fault can be produced when the rider hauls at the reins to make a horse step backward. The rein-back is not correct if the supporting hindleg does not flex.

The principle of free forward movement applies to all the stages of schooling, but every horse is an individual, with an individual gait.

We cannot hope to alter the gait radically, any more than we can hope to mould all horses into the same shape. The rider must acquire the feel of the appropriate speed in each gait for each horse and must learn to improve the gait with the lightest possible tension of reins or even without tension. At the beginning of training, it is propelling power that must be developed and the gait must be free, easy and rhythmical. The gallop is the most suitable gait, particularly uphill. It strengthens the quarters while avoiding the tendency of the rider to hang on. One should not start the gymnastic flexing of the haunches or try to slow the speed by means of parades on taut reins before the hindquarters are sufficiently strong and the horse is capable of walking, trotting and galloping in natural balance, that is, without seeking the support of the reins and without overloading the forehand.

THE FORELIMBS

The muscles and tendons of the forelimbs must be examined with an appreciation of their function. Neck, back and hindlimb muscles are seldom stretched beyond their capacity and damage to the muscles of these parts is rarely due to strain, because horses can protect them as soon as fatigue begins to be felt. Injuries to the hindlimbs are nearly always confined to the joints and are usually the result of defective conformation. Except with horses that race in harness, strains of muscles, tendons and ligaments of the hindlimb are infrequent. Although the forelimbs do play an active part in propulsion, this is insignificant compared to their passive role which is to reduce concussion, especially when the horse lands from a jump. When choosing a horse for sport, the first thing one must look for is a good forehand. The other parts can be exercised and shaped without fear of injury but the forehand, although its muscles must also be developed by exercise, will always suffer strains of tendons and ligaments if it is basically weaker than the rest of the body. Horses most likely to sustain injury are precisely those who have especially good natural movement. As all statistics show, lameness in the forelimbs is much more frequent than lameness behind. The conformation of the forehand is described in all textbooks, so I propose here to discuss only the muscular and tendinous structures.

In the standing position, whereas each hindlimb in turn supports the weight of the body, allowing the other to rest, the forelimbs are furnished with a stay apparatus that allows them to carry the weight of the front of the body without any muscular effort at all. This stay apparatus, as we will see, is also involved in the movements of the limbs.

In the standing position, the flexor tendons of the foot are tightly stretched. The deep digital flexor tendon is tied to the lower row of the carpal bones of the "knee" and to the top of the cannon bone by a check ligament and the superficial digital flexor tendon has a check ligament tying it to the radius above the knee. The check ligaments make the tendons function as ligaments by cutting off the muscular attachment above and they thus prevent the fetlock settling under the weight of the body without need for muscular energy. The stay apparatus of the foot includes also the suspensory ligament and the ligaments of the sesamoids which form a sort of sling across the back of the fetlock. The remaining joints of the forelimbs are fixed in an extended position by the tendon of the biceps muscle; this long tendinous insertion runs through the muscle and divides at its lower extremity into two portions. The short one is inserted into the radial tuberosity; the long one blends with the fascia of the forearm. Thus both the elbow and knee are maintained in extension by this tendinous reinforcement of the biceps; while at the back of the limb, the tension of the biceps is opposed by the tension of the slender but almost entirely tendinous superficial and deep digital flexor muscles. Thus in the standing position, no muscular energy is required to support the weight of the forehand on the forelimbs.

During motion, the elbow joint is stabilised by a ring of strong muscles which oppose the pull of the biceps, so that the scapula and humerous move as an almost rigid frame. Furthermore, the neck is also involved in the movements of the forelimb. A bundle of muscles penetrated by tendinous insertions, the triceps brachii, arises from the posterior border of the scapula and inserts on the point of the elbow (olecranon), extending the elbow joint; while arising from the anterior border of the scapula, serratus ventralis cevicis inserts on the transverse processes of the 7th, 6th, 5th and 4th cervical vertebrae. These same vertebrae are also tied to the first rib by the scalenus. Thus the lowering of the neck simultaneously draws the upper end of the scapula up and forward and extends the elbow. When these muscles are particularly well developed, the forelimbs have a tendency to slope backward. In the show-jumper, this is not a bad point. Scalenus and serratus ventralis cervici are almost entirely fleshy showing that their principal function is dynamic. They co-operate with the pectoral muscles in producing the movement of the shoulder-arm system.

Thus the strong stay apparatus of the forehand is admirably designed to enable the horse to remain standing without fatigue for long periods of time. However, it is also involved in movement and it is its strong tendinous structure which is responsible for the preponderance of strains of tendons in the forelimbs. The culprits are the check ligaments of the digital flexor tendons. When the downward acceleration of the mass forces the fetlock joint into dorsiflexion, the digital flexor muscles contract to resist this force and protect the joint. Were it not for the check ligaments, fatigue of the digital flexors would soon cause such pain that the horse would have to stop, or even lie down like an exhausted dog, and if he were compelled to continue galloping, he would no doubt strain or rupture his muscles like a human athlete or a greyhound. In the horse, however, the check ligaments make it possible for him to continue galloping while relaxing the fatigued digital flexor muscles. Tendons, as we know, have very little elasticity and they cannot withstand prolonged straining. Eventually, some or all of their fibres will rupture. As the superficial flexor tendon has never been found damaged above its attachment to its check ligament, it is obvious that it is the slackness, and not the contraction of the fatigued digital flexor muscles which is the cause of strains of tendons in the forelimbs. The strain on the suspensory ligament and the superficial digital flexor tendon occurs at the moment when the fetlock joint extends (dorsiflexion) to absorb the shock of impact, while the deep digital flexor tendon is stressed at the moment when the whole limb extends to propel the body forward. Injury to the deep flexor tendon is rare in the galloping race-horse, but not uncommon in the draught horse under heavy load, particularly when starting to pull. Stumbling in his case is the cause of check ligament strain and the tendon itself is often torn above the check ligament. The draught horse also, in contrast with the saddle-horse, is exposed to strain of the muscles and tendons of the hindlimbs.

A good hunter must show good development of forearm muscles and must have plenty of "bone" below the knee. Strong tendons spare muscles and, conversely, strong muscles that do not fatigue too quickly protect tendons. Nevertheless, despite the most favourable conformation, a horse can be galloped into the ground and suffer strain or rupture of the fibres of the suspensory ligament and the superficial digital flexor tendon: that is, a breakdown.

The stay apparatus of the shoulder-elbow joint, on the other hand, rarely suffers from strain. The braces of these joints, being almost entirely muscular, cannot possibly be over-extended like the inert tendons and ligaments of the check apparatus of the foot.

It is in jumping and galloping over hilly terrain that the muscles of the forelimb are most severely taxed. In jumping, insufficient power behind can be compensated for by increasing the speed of the approach; speed, in any case, is always required to negotiate wide obstacles. For high jumping, however, strong forelimb muscles are very important. On landing from a jump, the mass of the body falls on the forelimbs which must absorb the shock of concussion, balance the mass and project it up again. The structure of the forelimb does not appear to be designed for an effort of such magnitude. Nevertheless, a concussion dampening mechanism does exist, which permits smooth conversion of the kinetic energy of the downward movement of the centre of gravity into potential energy. The downward displacement of the centre of gravity is not checked abruptly, provided that the horse develops a good landing technique. It is like catching a ball; the force of the moving ball will "sting" the hand unless the energy of the moving ball is absorbed by yielding of the arm around one or more joints. The linear motion of the ball is converted to rotating motion, and the energy stored by the yielding of the arm is available for the return of the ball. We have a similar example when a man lands from a high jump; the extensor muscles of the thighs yield as the knees bend, thus storing energy while dampening concussion and this energy is available for returning to a standing position. The horse, however, does not return to a standing position and forward movement in his case is the essential element of the protective landing mechanism. Landing technique has to be learnt and perfected. An inexperienced horse receives the weight of the body on a fully extended forelimb, giving himself and the rider a disagreeable jolt as the forward movement is interrupted for a fraction of a second before the horse collects himself to continue galloping. This defective landing technique jars the forelimbs which would be more frequently injured were it not for the elastic muscular union of the shoulders with the trunk. Nonetheless, the grunting produced by a horse when he lands clumsily clearly proves that he does not enjoy the experience.

A horse who has been taught to jump in good style lands smoothly. The first impacting forefoot will not be extended forward as the body accelerates downward but will be already moving backward when it touches the ground. In fact, it just glances on the ground and the weight of the body is received by the second landing forefoot, which yields at the fetlock joint, sometimes so much so that the fetlock sinks down to the ground. At that moment, the first foreleg is already swinging forward and the hindfeet are coming into support. The supporting foreleg lifts the mass and starts the first stride of the new gallop and a very fast moving horse may even start the new gallop with the leading foreleg before the hindfeet have had time to hit the ground. This shows the importance of the springing power of the forelimbs and of the necessity of quick resumption of the galloping movement. The speed of resumption of forward movement depends entirely on the strength of the muscles of the forehand and indeed all the muscles which tie the forelimb to the neck, the rib cage and the back are involved. The neck muscles insert on the upper part of the scapula; the back and thoracic muscles, on its lower extremity and on the upper arm. They all act like elastic springs which must dampen concussion and immediately lift and propel the load forward. To fulfil this function, they need not only to be strong, but also to have complete freedom of movement.

Nowadays, nobody denies that the horse must be able to reach forward and down with his neck in order to land safely after a jump. (We are talking here of a movement of the neck and not of head and neck carriage.) The forward movement of the neck carries the centre of gravity forward beyond the point of impact of the first forefoot to touch the ground, allowing the mass to roll over this foot, and protecting the whole limb against the full force of the downward accelerating body. The forward and downward pull of the neck is communicated to the serratus ventralis cervicis, which ties the upper border of the scapula to the last cervical vertebrae and the tension built up in this muscle increases its tone, storing energy for the spring of the forelimb. This tension of the neck muscles is transmitted to the muscles of the back (longissimus and latissimus dorsi) which arch the loins, thus allowing the hindfeet to engage well forward. Shortly before the hindfeet impact, the neck is lifted up with the effect of bringing upward and backward the fixed point of action of the brachiocephalicus muscle and lifting the forelimb so that it can reach forward again. The role of the neck in helping the horse to regain his balance is especially obvious in puissance jumping of the wall. In some cases, the horse will almost touch the ground with his nose, obliging the rider to make a deep forward plunge or to let the reins slide through his fingers. The consequence of hanging onto the reins at that moment is at least a loss of impulsion; more frequently, it is a fall of horse and rider.

The movement of the forelimb can also be divided into four phases: swing, impact, support and thrust, but from the point of view of the rider, all that matters is the scope and springiness of the movement. He must understand what can cause a sound horse to move with a short and choppy action. The relation of the neck carriage to the activity of the back muscles and the swing of the hindlegs has already been explained and this complex and extensive interaction means that the action of the forelimb cannot possibly be improved by any special gymnastic schooling movements. It improves automatically when the horse starts to use his back and hindlegs more effectively, thus lightening the forehand. If the forward swing of the hindlimbs is impaired, the weight of the body has to be supported by the forelimbs; the result is a shuffling gait, with forefeet sticking to the ground and a swaying of the body from one foreleg onto the other. If the longissimus dorsi stiffens, so does the latissimus dorsi, impairing the free swinging of the shoulder–arm system. The scope of the movement of the forelimb depends also on the head and neck carriage because of the insertions of the brachiocephalicus on the skull at one extremity and the arm at the other. At the gallop, a neck stretching well forward will produce long, bounding strides, while active elevation of the neck produces a high stepping action, covering little ground. When the neck is shortened, as a result of star-gazing or of overbending, the points of attachment of the brachiocephalicus are brought closer together, thus slackening the tension of this muscle and shortening the steps also. On the other hand, relative elevation, which is the result of good schooling, tauten the brachiocephalicus and the result is a springy, smooth and ground covering action.

Yet, although we cannot directly improve the action of the forehand by manege schooling, we must not neglect the development of the muscles of the forelimbs.

Engagement of the hindlegs for the purpose of lightening the forehand is a principle that can be misunderstood and which at some time has been so misinterpreted that riders would lean back as much as possible when jumping in order to unload the forelimbs, some believing, more absurdly still, that horses should land with hindfeet first after a jump. This was mixing up cause and effect. The forehand cannot be lightened and protected against injury by overloading the hindquarters.

On the contrary, the muscles of the forelimb, of the shoulder, arm and forearm, and the digital flexor tendons must be strengthened by being exercised. Their strength and elasticity can be improved by combining frequent jumping of obstacles with schooling on the flat in the manege and many famous show-jumpers have been trained in this manner. But this training over jumps is usually practised with the wrong ends in view.

In contrast with the muscles of the hindquarters, the muscles of the forehand can never be healthily stressed by gymnastic schooling on the flat and therefore cannot be strengthened by such work for their important role as shock absorbers in jumping. Tendon and ligament strains are bound to occur when the muscles of the forelimb are too weak to perform this function. The object of all training must be the development of strong elastic muscles and the forehand must be considered as much as the hindquarters. And the most suitable gait for strengthening the forehand is, again, the gallop. Not short cantering periods of two minutes or so in the manege, but long, steady gallops outside, at the so-called canter of the race-horse in training.

Comparatively little skill is required to get even very young horses to gallop steadily, once they have found out that galloping is not a rare and exciting experience, but routine work which they must perform regularly to the point of fatigue. Within limits, providing that blood vessels do not become congested, the production of lactic acid in muscles promotes bulk and elasticity. Over-exertion certainly produces an accumulation of lactic acid, fatigue and inflammation but over-exertion is rarely, if ever, risked by long periods of calm galloping. It is usually the consequence of excessive speed or of galloping on heavy going. A rider who knows his horse soon learns to feel the onset of fatigue. Young horses that have been rationally exercised with long periods of galloping do not get excited when their jumping training starts. Whenever possible, they should be exercised also over uneven terrain and frequently made to jump up short steep inclines. This is excellent gymnastic work for both forehand and hindquarters.

THE ABDOMINAL MUSCLES AND BREATHING

The principle role of the abdominal muscles is to support the internal organs, but they also serve forward movement to some extent. The external oblique and the internal oblique abdominal muscles support the contents of the thorax and the abdomen like a sling suspended from the loins and the pelvis. The rectus abdominus assisted by the tough tendinous "white line" forming the floor of the abdomen also helps to support the internal organs, but, additionally it functions as a brace maintaining the arching of the vertebral column. The aponeurosis of the external oblique and the internal oblique are interwoven and their fusion forms the outer sheath of the rectus abdominis which blends at the white line with that of the opposite side. In the gallop, the rectus abdominus assists in drawing forward the pubis and thus helps the arching of the loin and the forward swing of the hindlimbs, adding spring to the leaps of the gallop. The rectus abdominus is a "multipennate muscle" consisting of numerous short fibres ending in many small tendons joining within the muscle belly. It is therefore a very powerful muscle. The fibres of the external oblique arise from the last ribs and the lumbo-dorsal fascia; they run downward and backward to insert on the white line. The aponeurotic insertion is continued by a broad fascia, the abdominal tunic, which extends into the fold of the flank and blends with the femoral fascia covering the muscles on the medial surface of the thigh. This is how it is also involved in the movement of the hindlimb.

We need not concern ourselves here with the principal function of the abdominal muscles, which is to support the internal organs. As for their involvement in movement, it is not as important as one might think. A strong tension of these muscles which extend from the sternum to the pubis would subject the intestinal tract to a very uncomfortable pressure and would also interfere with breathing, since some of their fibres are inserted on the floating ribs. If the horse had to brace his abdominal muscles to arch the loins and hold the hindlimbs under the body in the collected movements, he would not be able to breathe. Nevertheless, they do contribute to the movements of the gallop, contracting powerfully during the phase of suspension, when the hindlimbs swing forward. At that moment, of course, they do not have to work against resistance. By drawing the pubis and sternum closer together, they arch the back as well as the loins and the rider feels the horse's back pressing against his seat. The fact that the external oblique, connecting the ribs to the medial aspect of the stifle, contracts rhythmically at the gallop and not at the other gaits can be verified by listening to the breathing. At the walk and the trot, the breathing rhythm is independent of the rhythm of the gait but at the gallop the horse breathes in as the hindlimbs swing forward and breathes out when they extend. Horses rarely develop the same breathing techniques as the human runner and the ability to breathe in during two or three galloping leaps and breathe out during one or two leaps is developed by a few individuals with exceptionally capacious lungs and particularly steady nerves. Even in their case, it is the result of very careful training.

When horses worked on the farm, it was a well-established principle that pregnant mares should not be ridden but rather worked in harness as the gallop was believed to put too much strain on the abdominal muscles. On the other hand, it was also well known that no amount of work in harness could tauten a belly which had sagged after a long rest at grass or as a result of pregnancy, while if young mares were given rational galloping exercise after foaling, they regained their figure within a period of six months. Galloping is the best gymnastic exercise for toning up the abdominal muscles.

The external oblique abdominal muscle, as has already been explained, arises from the ribs. It is covered by the cutaneus muscle, a thin muscular layer intimately adherent to the skin. Posteriorly, it forms a fold, which, covered by the skin, forms the fold of the flanks and ends on the fascia above the stifle. Stimulation of the cutaneus muscle by one leg or spur will cause it to contract, flex the hip joint and draw the hindlimb forward. The reaction is of a reflex nature; hence engagement of the hindlimbs and collection should be inevitable and completely automatic. Unfortunately, this is not the case. Though a young horse always reacts somehow to the actions of the legs or the spurs, he will not necessarily move away, and he may just twitch his skin as if getting rid of an insect. Many horses will also swish their tail or advance a hindleg to loosen the skin when they feel the prick of the spur. In reality, all horses must be educated to understand that they must always respond to the touch of the lower leg of the rider by lifting, flexing and advancing a hindleg. They must learn that they will not be allowed to avoid the pressure of the lower leg by drawing away from it, nor to resist it by pushing against it. Obedience must become an educated reflex which the rider can utilise to stimulate the engagement of each hindleg

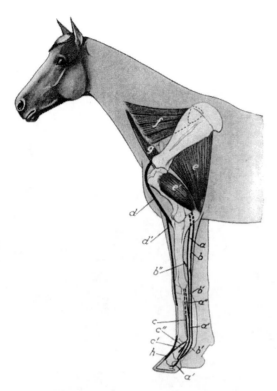

Muscles of the horse's shoulder girdle and stay apparatus of the foreleg *(above)* and muscles and tendons of the foreleg *(below)*:

(a) deep flexor muscle of the digit: *(a')* its tendon and *(a")* its check ligament;

(b) superficial flexor muscle of the digit: *(b')* its tendon and *(b")* its check ligament;

(c) suspensory ligament of fetlock, superior branch: *(c')* inferior branch and *(c")* lateral branch to extensor tendon of digit;

(d) biceps and *(d')* its long tendon, braces of shoulder and knee;

(e) and *(e')* the two parts of the triceps, braces of the elbow;

(f) cervical part of serratus ventralis;

(g) scalenus, staying neck on the rib cage;

(h) extensor tendon of the digit.

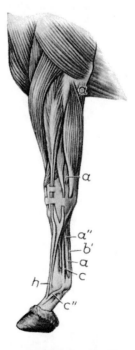

David Broome on Sunsalve. Note engagement of the hindlimbs, the horse collecting himself in front of a broad obstacle.

P. d'Inzeo on The Rock. Here the horse is engaging his hindlimbs and collecting himself before a high obstacle.

Good landing technique *(left)* permits fluent resumption of forward movement; the rider will return smoothly into the saddle without compromising the horse's equilibrium. *(Below)* Poor landing technique: smooth resumption of forward movement is impaired and there is severe stress on the forelegs.

alternately. A small area of the skin, just behind the girth, can be made so sensitive to the slightest pressure of the lower leg that it is often called the "neuralgic spot". With a horse that has been educated to respond quickly to the pressure of the leg at this particular point, a flick of the lungeing whip on the neuralgic spot will cause a more energetic flexing of the joints of the hindleg and detaching of the foot from the ground.

A rider who has not learnt to feel the lateral oscillations of the horse's rib cage should take his feet out of the stirrups and allow his legs to hang freely from the hips. He will then perceive that each calf in turn is hit at the rhythm of the gait by the chest of the horse. Upon feeling a brief touch of the rider's calf at that moment, which coincides with the end of a lateral oscillation, an obedient horse instinctively incurves the corresponding side of his chest. The end of the lateral oscillation corresponds also with the moment at which the ipsilateral hindfoot impacts with the ground and if, at that instant, the rider prolongs the contact of his calf, he will stimulate the reflex which induces all the joints of the supporting hindlimb to flex, provided again that the horse is relaxed and obedient. This is the beginning of the flexion of the haunches. Some riders make these leg pressures very obvious, but it is preferable that they be so discreet that they cannot be seen.

Thus it is that the relaxed activity of his legs enables the well-balanced rider to feel the movements of the horse's trunk and hindlimbs, but these movements can also be sensed by his seat-bones and in his waist. When the right hind of the horse, for example is swinging forward—or when it is resting more or less slackly at the halt—the right side of the back will be lower than the left, and the rider should feel that his right seat-bone is in a hole, and his left on a hump.

At the trot, before the horse has been gymnastically trained to use his back and hindlimb muscles elastically, the rider will feel a jolt on the side of the hindfoot that hits the ground, and then a lifting of his hip on this side at the moment when the hindlimb is in the phase of support. The jolt will no longer be felt when the horse has become sufficiently strong and submissive to protect the rider against the jars of the trot by flexing the hocks under load, but the lifting of each of his hips in turn will continue to be felt by a straight and supple rider. A rider with a good posture will also be able to feel immediately whether the horse has come to a square halt, and will stimulate the resting hindleg to extend if he feels that one side of the back is even slightly lower than the other.

Learning to feel and utilise these reflex movements of the horse will considerably help the rider to develop impulsion, collection and straightness. It is of course essential that he be straight and supple himself. A stiff, one-sided rider will not be able to feel whether the horse is moving straight and using both hindlimbs with equal force either to balance or to repel the load.

The abdominal muscles evidently participate in the overall movement when the horse is relaxed. Tightening the abdominal muscles is the cause of "wind-sucking", the noise made by stallions and geldings at the trot and sometimes also at the canter when they are not properly submissive. The stiffening of the abdominal muscles causes the sheath to make spasmodic movements, sucking in air. It is a symptom of resistance, and it indicates that the horse is either:

1 Lacking impulsion.
2 Hypertense in the extended movements.
3 Worried when he is learning a new movement.
4 Excited or frightened.

The gaits can never be considered correct when the sheath makes a noise because the noise is a symptom of hypertension.

Habitual sheath-noise which cannot be quietened by loosening exercise is a vice peculiar to horses that hollow their backs by tightening the sublumbar and abdominal muscles and stiffening the hindlegs. They never come on to the bit genuinely. A skilful rider, able to produce collection, can stop the noise by compelling the horse to flex and engage his hindlegs and let it start again by allowing him to become disunited. As wind-sucking is always a sign of insufficient swing of the hinglegs, the rider must concentrate his attention on the feel of the movement through his seat, so that he can anticipate and prevent a re-occurrence of the noise. Long periods of trotting to the accompaniment of this noise are a sure way of weakening the muscles of the back and the hindlimbs. In dressage tests, the noisy sheath must be noted as a sign of stiffness and irritability.

A Horseman's Diagnosis

A veterinary surgeon makes a clinical diagnosis by investigating the symptoms and causes of disease or lameness. In the course of his examination, he will note the conformation, muscular condition, carriage and behaviour of the horse. Finally, he will want to see him ridden. He must be able to make a horseman's diagnosis as well as a clinical one, and to assess the horse's form and his state of training.

Experienced horsemen will unerringly single out in a parade of horses shown in hand those subjects which have been properly trained and ridden. Their judgement is based not so much on conformation as on outward signs of good development of certain important groups of muscles. They do not need to see a horse ridden to determine, by the appearance of under-development of these muscles, what kind of resistance to expect and they can formulate immediately a plan of training which will correct the particular weaknesses and eliminate resistance. All riders should educate themselves to acquire this sort of perceptiveness. Before mounting an unknown horse, one should examine the animal carefully and be able to form some idea of the kind of ride to expect. On the other hand, it is by examining the muscular development of horses whose good and weak points are known and that one has ridden, that one acquires the experience needed to become a reliable judge. One must be able to distinguish between serious faults of conformation and weaknesses which can be compensated for by good muscular development. One must also learn not to stick doggedly to an inflexible plan of training and schooling for all horses. Every horse is an individual, for whom an individual programme of training must be devised. This is neither as complicated nor time consuming as it sounds. On the contrary, individual training enables progress to be achieved much more rapidly and eventually makes it much easier to assemble a good class of evenly matched horses. And one must never forget that exercise must play at least as important a part in the training as schooling. Having recognised the weak points, the trainer must devise the most suitable exercises for remedying them. He must also be able to determine whether certain resistances are inherent in the horse or are produced by the rider. If the resistances are due to weakness of certain muscles, they must be eliminated by appropriate gymnastic work and, at the beginning, the movements to practise must be those which are natural and easy for the horse and the rider. For example, the strength of the hindquarters can be developed by manege exercises in collection which promote the suppleness of the hind joints. However, such schooling exercises are beyond the skill of many riders, in which case it is preferable to arrive at the same result by frequent transitions to canter, long steady galloping out-of-doors almost to the point of fatigue, climbing uphill, all exercises which promote the propelling force of the hindlimbs, strengthening their extensor muscles, whose weakness is the cause of most resistance to the flexion of the haunches, and thus making subsequent manege schooling towards collection much easier.

Here is a list of points of weakness and of strength and of suitable exercises for developing the right muscles:

THE NECK

Signs of weakness
Visible outline of the vertebral processes; over-developed flexor muscles, slack extensor muscles; triangular depression at the base, in the space between the vertebral column and the topline; observed from the saddle, the neck's broadest part is at the level of the vertebral column.

Good points
The vertebral column is deeply embedded in muscle; the triangular depression at the base has filled up and the muscles bulge in front of the scapula. The flexor muscles of the underside of the neck have dwindled; the jowl is clean-cut and the jugular groove is well marked. Observed from above, the broadest part of the neck is the top part.

A properly shaped neck is the result of self-carriage and freedom of movement. It is wrong to try to improve it by any localised gymnastic exercise.

THE BACK

Signs of weakness
Flat, even sunken back muscles; processes of the vertebrae in the saddle and loin regions are prominent.

Good points
The longissimus dorsi fills up the region of the loins so that it is level at least with the tips of the spinous processes. A particularly well-muscled back shows a groove down its middle, as does also the back of a human athlete.

Appropriate exercises are all those which promote the relaxed activity of the back muscles; regular, energetic gaits, frequent transitions to canter from the walk and the trot, prolonged galloping, changes of speed at the gallop, alternately in forward seat and full seat, trotting over cavaletti, riding out-of-doors over undulating terrain and galloping uphill.

HINDQUARTERS

Signs of weakness
Seen in profile, the croup is flat; the quadriceps femoris, over the front of the thigh between the hip and the stifle is under-developed; the divisions between the hamstring muscles are blurred; the buttocks are flat. Seen from the rear: flat croup, flat thighs, thighs "split-up", weak, flat gaskins.

Good points
Rounded, domed croup, marked grooves between the muscles of the hamstrings, bulging buttocks, broad gaskins, bulky adductor muscles causing the thighs to rub and sweat profusely during movement; lateral bulging of the gastrocnemius. When choosing a horse for dressage, one should always examine him attentively from the rear; at the level of the stifle, the thighs should be as broad or broader than the hips.

Promoting the natural, propulsive function of the extensor muscles by vigorous forward movement is the best way of developing the strength needed for the flexion of the haunches and of diminishing resistance to collection. Therefore, besides manege exercises, one should practise frequent transitions to canter, riding over undulating terrain and climbing hills at the gallop.

FOREHAND

Signs of weakness
The outline of the scapula is visible, as is also its spine. When the

muscular braces of the neck and shoulder are weak the outline of the shoulder-elbow region is hollowed; the muscles are flat in the angle of the shoulder-joint and the forearm has a small circumference. There is a marked gap between the elbows and the ribs and the girth groove is ill-defined.

Good points
The scapula is concealed by bulky muscles; the base of the neck is broad. The extensor of the elbow (triceps) bulges between the scapula and the elbow. The lattissimus dorsi fills up the groove between the shoulder and the ribs, thus preventing the saddle from sliding forward. The muscles at the front of the forearm are prominent while at the back they form a straight vertical line from the elbow down. The stability of the forehand depends on a strong forearm and careful observation of its state of muscular development must never be neglected.

Wasting of the shoulder muscles is rarely the result of strain and much more often due to insufficient relaxation. As well-developed shoulder and forearm muscles will compensate for many defects of conformation, their strength must be increased by long hacking at the walk, prolonged periods of galloping, riding over undulating terrain and, especially, frequent jumping of small obstacles. Fluent movement at all gaits and especially over jumps is essential to avoid concussion, which is the most frequent cause of lameness. During training, fatigue of muscles is easily avoidable.

ABDOMINAL REGION

One cannot really talk about good or poor development of abdominal muscles. A horse must have a belly, in the sense that his flanks must be round and well filled out. Neither a gross belly with a hollow between ribs and hips, nor a herring gut or wasp waist are desirable, but one is often compelled to ride horses that fall short of perfection in this part of the body. The grass belly of young horses is nothing to worry about; very young horses, like small children, tend to have distended bellies, which soon retract, however, as general muscular condition improves. One thing that one should never do is try to reduce quickly the distended belly of a young animal by drastically cutting down on roughage.

As for the tucked-in abdomen and the herring-gutted appearance, it is not always easy to determine whether it is inherited conformation or the result of insufficient nourishment in youth and consequent insufficient intestinal capacity. Up to the age of six years, it remains possible to change this condition by feeding as much roughage as the animal will eat. But if the tucked-in abdomen goes with generally weak muscular development, the horse must be either sick or grossly undernourished. In this case, one must feed him well and handle him regularly, but he should not be ridden for some time. One should note also that this conformation is usually a sign of a nervous temperament.

Finally, let us remember that the outward appearance of any horse can never be a sufficient indication of its potential performance. Constitution, which is an inherited factor, is equally important. Having selected one or more individuals in a show on account of their conformation, one must always base one's final judgement on the ride. This is the only way of assessing correctly performance and stamina. A good judge will never decide on the final order before finding out which horse gives him the best ride. For a good rider, there is nothing more interesting than judging hunters. But if one accepts to act as a judge, one must have confidence in one's knowledge and practical experience; this confidence can come only to somebody who has gained the feel of many, many horses between his legs.

Although it needs great experience to assess a horse's potential and the sort of work required to make good his weaknesses and defects, and the time it may take to train him so that he can be ridden by anybody, it needs greater experience still and much far-sightedness to picture him in imagination as he will look when one has finished "modelling" him. I seem to remember that Felix Buerkner was the first to use this happy choice of a word for describing the art of the dressage trainer. Modelling a horse means that, on the basis of careful observation and with a clear view of realistic aims, one decides on the sort of work that will improve his carriage and movement, make him stronger, more fluent, more handsome and more intelligent. Only mature riders, the sort that have the patience to plant trees and watch their slow growth, will ever be able to produce this sort of horse.

A veterinary diagnosis based solely on a clinical investigation of symptoms without taking into account the way in which the horse has been ridden can be faulty. This fact, however, is of interest only to veterinary surgeons although it will not hurt the layman to hear it mentioned; but riders are notoriously sceptical and do not like criticism even when it comes from an expert. However, if a well-fed horse loses weight and becomes more ungainly in the course of his training and a careful clinical examination fails to reveal any organic disease, the vet should always ask to see him ridden or, better still, should ride him himself; after all, the result of training should always be improvement of condition and appearance.

A veterinary surgeon who cannot ride is liable to misinterpret the symptoms and history of a disorder particularly in the following cases:

a) Unthriftiness, loss of appetite and indigestion may be due to a sore back causing referred pain which is felt as a pain somewhere along the intestinal tract.

b) Unaccountable behaviour, especially excitability, is quite frequently and glibly attributed to the nervous disposition of the horse, whereas the cause is sometimes a painful back.

The shape of the back must be carefully observed. A back that slopes down gradually behind the withers is much less sensitive to pain than one in which the withers slant down sharply, forming almost a right angle with the lowest part of the back in the region of the girth. With this latter conformation, enforced elevation of the head and neck will cause severe back pain, for which the best cure is the gallop with maximum lowering and freedom of neck. An exaggeratedly high tail carriage, with the dock projecting vertically instead of horizontally, shows stiffness in some part of the loins; the horse objects to being collected and, when jumping, trails his hindlegs over the obstacle instead of tucking them under his body. A crooked tail carriage or a tail clamped down between the buttocks can be due to some malformation of the vertebrae which cannot be corrected but may be a visible sign of forcible collection and considerable mishandling. De-nerving the muscles of the tail to conceal malformation would be a scandalous fraud which no vet can countenance and if scars or wasting of the tail muscles are detected correction of a drooping or one-sided tail carriage is hopeless. If, however, the muscles at the root of the tail are equally developed, improvement of tail carriage is a matter of training; the clamped down and one-sided tail carriage indicates reluctance to move forward. The only way of finding out quickly whether these faults are pathological in origin or whether they can be cured is to get the horse to gallop fully extended; if he then carries his tail straight, the rider may be able to remedy the fault within a fairly short period of time if he can be persuaded to let the animal unwind by allowing him complete freedom of movement at all gaits.

c) Young horses that look like worn-out cab horses are suffering from overall wasting of muscles due either to pathological inco-ordination or to overwork.

d) Ignorant and over-demanding riders can be the cause of violent resistance in the horse (attacking handlers, bolting and so on), when the behaviour of the animal will usually be attributed to temperament, or emaciation and even to cardiac disorders.

e) A vet should always advise against the purchase of horses with wounds or scars of the head, which are usually around the eyes, if a perfectly genuine accident cannot be proved; in the throes of pain from colic or meningitis, the horse may have hit his head against the walls of his box, otherwise injuries to the head should cause one to suspect mental derangement, excitability or head-shyness. Sensible, alert horses never hit their head against solid objects.

f) Restraining reins will cause horses to go wide behind and to turn the toes out. I have known horses of perfect conformation developing this fault after only a few months of training. Perplexed by the rider's conflicting aids, they do not know where to put their hindfeet and the ungainly gait is developed as a valve to protect the hocks against the effect of the contraining reins. Whereas an energetic horse will then develop the habit of jogging, a placid one will choose the line of least resistance. By going wide behind and turning out the toes, avoiding engagement of the hindlegs, by sluggishly dragging his hindfeet and slowing their movement, he passively resists all the rider's efforts to get him on the bit.

g) Impure gaits (bridle-lameness) can become an inveterate manner of moving.

h) Straining of the suspensory ligament, exostosis and splints can be the result of uneven loading of the limbs and the excessive practice of badly ridden and wrongly understood lateral movements.

i) Strains of the suspensory ligament associated with the formation of splints at the back of the knee where the fibres of the suspensory ligament arise are an injury peculiar to dressage horses that are forced to produce collection before they are sufficiently relaxed. Inexpert attempts at producing piaffe and passage-like steps with horses that are not relaxed are a sure way of developing a progressive lameness of both forelimbs and, because the lameness is progressive, the rider does not notice the first signs and the vet is not consulted until the damage is past remedying. This type of lameness resembles lameness from strain of the deep digital flexor tendon, and as is the case with all foreleg lameness, lesion in one limb leads to lesion of the other.

j) Strains of the flexor tendons and the suspensory ligament are not invariably the result of fatigue and over-exertion, but can also be caused by a temporary loss of balance. For this reason, riders who lack feel for balance have no right to demand speed in any of the gaits, and must be particularly careful to avoid abrupt pulling up.

k) Improperly performed lateral movements, especially leg yielding, the favourite and indiscriminate practice of the novice rider, is bread-and-butter to the veterinary profession. The joints of the horse's limbs are constructed to serve mainly straight, forward movement and are protected against abnormal, excessive rotation by strong and almost totally inelastic ligaments. It is always dangerous and damaging to bones, joints and ligaments to force a stiff horse to side-step by using powerful aids.

The vet should also be able to base his prognosis—either a confident prediction of complete healing or, more frequently, the likelihood of a recurrence of injury—on his ability to judge a horse's natural balance and suppleness. A normally relaxed horse of good conformation uses his limbs more cleverly and has a much better chance of recovering and remaining sound in his limbs than a stiff horse whose conformation tends to put too much weight on the forelimbs.

It is also an advantage if the vet is able to assess the rider. A horse ridden by a rider with a feel for balance is more likely to remain sound after repair or injury, whereas another rider may lack the suppleness to maintain balance without stiffening and will cause the horse to stiffen and injure himself again, in which case the art of the vet cannot help. The worst offenders are riders who overwork young horses, over-exerting themselves as well as the young animal in their senseless use of strength to drive the horse up to the bit. They are responsible for the majority of cases of cardiac disorders, sprains, galls, splints and nervous indigestion that veterinarians are asked to treat. A favourable prognosis is difficult to make if the horse remains in the same hands.

Strain of the spermatic cord is not unusual in young stallions before they have learnt to relax. When it is unilateral, it can produce such a severe lameness in one hindlimb that the horse may refuse to move and a superficial examination can easily lead to a wrong diagnosis of thrombosis of the femoral artery, especially as the lameness can become acute after a period of galloping whilst the horse may have appeared sound before work.

The veterinary surgeon should have no difficulty in distingishing between the noise of true roaring or whistling and the noise of breathing impeded by constricting reins or obstruction of the respiratory passages by catarrh. The so-called noise frequently disappears with a rider with lighter hands who knows the feel of a horse genuinely on the bit.

On the other hand, some horses may flex at the poll without being genuinely on the bit. They avoid the pressure of the bit on the bars by holding it up with the tongue and in so doing may produce a noise that is difficult to distinguish from true roaring. A freely moving horse relaxes the muscles of the tongue. While true roaring is aggravated by forced respiration at a strong gallop, the false roaring of a horse that is not genuinely on the bit disappears when the horse is made to extend himself at a strong gallop.

Loud blowing through the nostrils at every leap of the gallop indicates a deficient breathing technique. It is often a sign of insufficient impulsion (desire to go forward) and freedom of movement, of an ungenerous temperament. Such horses have little stamina and after hunting or fast cross-country galloping they often suffer from circulatory disorders, congestion of blood in the pulmonary veins, loss of appetite and indigestion. The fit and relaxed horse should not blow at the working canter.

Tense horses, who never relax the back and thoracic muscles properly, get excited as soon as they are asked to perform, hold their breath at all paces, are predisposed to broken-wind and pulmonary emphysema.

Hardened pullers should be examined for signs of damage to the bars of the mouth; these may be bruised or sore, or an exostosis may be developing. Horses are remarkable; their first reaction to pain is to try and drive it off; therefore when the pressure of the bit becomes painful, they fight against the rider's hands. One should never resort to a stronger bit if signs of injury to the bars are detected.

Vets are frequently asked to examine the eyes of horses that shy, stumble or stubbornly refuse to jump. In most cases, they cannot find anything wrong, but it is difficult to tell the rider that the horse has lost respect for the aids. It is not very tactful, either, to pull to pieces a horse that the owner has just purchased. It will neither convince nor help the owner and certainly not increase his faith in the vet.

Injury is more often the consequence of fighting the rider's hands than of over-exertion and high performance, although too much and too little exercise, and lack of education can also be blamed in many cases. Freshness, excitement, excessive firmness of hypertense muscle produce inco-ordination and lead to trauma of one kind or another and frequent lameness. If their conformation and aptitudes justify the trouble, over-active, insubordinate horses should be starved and driven into submission by hard work over plough until they become sober. The same cure could well be advised also for experienced show-jumpers who suddenly get it into their heads that they can stop or run out. It is a mistake to think that an experienced show-jumper can become bored or tired of jumping. In his case, if it is not pain and lameness, the cause is freshness and the discovery that he is stronger than his rider. Punishment is then useless. It can safely be said that most riding horses get too little work. They would be much more reliable if they were frequently stressed to the point of fatigue. Horses must be obedient always and not only when it does not inconvenience them. Fatigue is the best remedy for freshness. Besides which, we would see fewer cases of contracted heels if the horses spent less time resting in their box.

A trusting relationship between owner and vet depends on whether the rider is sufficiently modest to accept advice and the vet prepared to prove the accuracy of his diagnosis. Sympathy and tactfulness will be required on both sides. If the vet's analysis of the problem is accurate, a good rider is the best physician. But it needs considerable psychological perspicacity to dare to voice one's thoughts. Depriving conceited riders of their self-esteem is not doing them good service.

Conclusion

As the study of the history of equitation shows, convincing the riding world that the best methods of training are the most natural ones has never been easy. Time after time, strong personalities with exceptional talent have made discoveries and dazzled contemporaries by their successes. Fillis utilised impulsion to get his horses to produce the most astonishing movements and mesmerise audiences already accustomed to the spectacle of extraordinary circus acts and artificial airs. Baucher and Plinzner were followed because what they taught seemed easy to imitate. The greatest of all innovators was no doubt Caprilli, the originator of the modern jumping seat and of schooling by the natural method. But although all of them were specialists, they claimed that their methods could be applied to all forms of equitation. We are returning to a general acceptance of the principles of classical equitation and we can let all those specialists rest in peace. In practice, there is only one way leading to one and the same end, even though one may prefer to follow it in one direction—dressage—or the other—jumping. The paths should not really diverge. The principles are the same: impulsion, harmony of movement, obedience.

To assert that there is only one classical art of riding may be true in a limited sense but we should not be supercilious. Who would think of claiming that only one manner of painting is beautiful or that, in the art of healing, there is only one treatment for all conditions? Nevertheless, for men of wholesome taste and sensibility art must be a recognisable image of nature. Beauty, power, harmony and wholesomeness are standards that humanity must continue to fight for in its search for perfection. We must learn to recognise and reject all that is unnatural and ugly and have the courage to denounce performances that contravene accepted principles.

For the novice rider, it is difficult to distinguish between the genuine and the sham. To start with, the difference between right and wrong may be small and, secondly, methods may appear so diverse that, without serious study, one becomes totally bewildered. We must remain broad-minded and never outrightly condemn any method before trying it out and assessing the results.

The art of riding is only partly based on biological, anatomical and physiological factors and the technique of the aids cannot be explained solely in terms of physical laws and mechanical principles. The rider's spirit counts for much. The temperament of each individual expresses itself in the training and performance of his horses.

The judging of dressage competitions, similarly, must be influenced to some extent by the different temperaments and preferences of the judges but, nevertheless, it must remain their duty to defend principles. Anybody who has a say in dressage must be the apostle of the truth. Their task is not an easy one since dressage has become competitive and they are supposed to select a winner. They must not discourage participation in the sport, because a broad participation is necessary to ensure its survival and the occasional artist will arise from the multitude. But let the judges not forget that we want to rejoice as much in a spectacle of beauty as in the excitement of watching the scoreboard.

Yet, when all is said and done, what matters most is the love of the horse and riding for pleasure is as worthy a motive as riding to win in competitions.

I did not write this book only because of my dedication as a veterinary surgeon to the welfare of the horse. It is a token of my love for the animal and of my gratitude for all the hours of pleasure that horses have given me. One of them even saved my life during a war. What can I give in return, except this book which may help riders to understand them better.

CPSIA information can be obtained at www.ICGtesting.com
Printed in the USA
LVOW06s1105221215

467490LV00010B/34/P